Donated to the
Heritage Library
March 3, 2004

By

Bill Robinson

WM. P. ROBINSON
~~1224 N. BAY RIDGE RD.~~
APPLETON, WI 54915

Best Wishes

THE SUN ROSE CLEAR

Lowell Peterson

**STORIES OF WWII
EDITED AND TOLD BY
LOWELL PETERSON**

WITH A SPECIAL FOREIGN CONTRIBUTION BY PIERRE DEHAY

Copyright © 2002 Peterson House

All rights reserved.
No part of this book may be
reproduced in any form without
permission of the author.

First Edition

ISBN Number: 0-9719128-0-7

Library of Congress Number: 2002107018

Published by
PETERSON HOUSE
2627 Beechwood Court
Appleton, WI 54911
SRoseClear@aol.com

Book cover and design by
GRAPHIC LIAISONS, LLC
Waupaca, WI 54981
graphicliaisons@excite.com

PRINTED IN THE UNITED STATES BY
WORZALLA
Stevens Point, WI 54481
www.worzalla.com

Lowell and Kermit Peterson
1945

Dedicated to my uncle:
Kermit H. Peterson,
Ensign, United States Navy,
Retired.
World War II
Veteran of the South Pacific.

An inspiration
to me
and to my family.

"…alert and healthy natures remember that the sun rose clear.
It is never too late to give up our prejudices."

Henry David Thoreau
Walden, Chapter I

*Needlepoint
by
Kitty Peterson
Freelance writer, New York City, NY.*

DEDICATION iii

CONTENTS

FOREWORD
   Robert F. Froehlke, Captain, United States Army Infantry, Retired ix

ACKNOWLEDGMENTS xiii

I
A CLEAR SKY WITH DISTANT CLOUDS

WORLD WAR II—INTRODUCTION As told by Lowell Peterson 3
THE ORIGINS OF WORLD WAR II As told by Lowell Peterson 6

II
CATACLYSM FROM THE RISING SUN

THE RADIO As told by Lowell Peterson 11
REMEMBER PEARL HARBOR As told by Mrs. Theodore Vonck Sr. 14
THE BARBER BROTHERS As told by Lowell Peterson 17
THE SULLIVAN ACT As told by Lowell Peterson 25
THE CAMEO BRACELET As told by Peggy Ebben 26

III
TYPHOON: RAIN OF STEEL

CORREGIDOR As told by Werner Jensen 31
THE TB TRAIN As told by John H. Steiner, M.D. 40
THE BATTLE OF THE PHILIPPINES As told by Numeriano Hollero, M.D. 41
EARLY PHASE OF THE PACIFIC WAR 1941-42 As told by Lowell Peterson 47
THE USS *HORNET* AT "IRON BOTTOM SOUND"
   As told by Leonard Duescher 50

IV
STORM CLOUDS IN ASIA

CHINESE-JAPANESE RELATIONS 1850-1945 As told by Lowell Peterson 63
CHINA SERVICE As told by Malcolm Rosholt 69

V
HEAVY STORMS

DUNKIRK As told by Lowell Peterson 75
THE ESCAPE As told by Pierre Dehay 77
DANGER IN THE NORTH ATLANTIC: THE NAVY ARMED GUARD
    As told by Lowell Peterson (*Name of interviewee withheld by request.*) 93

VI
TOWARD FIRST LIGHT

FROM D-DAY TO V-E DAY As told by Roland H. Vogt 99
HEDGEROW COUNTRY As told by Dr. Earl Spangler 112
THE BATTLE OF THE HURTGEN FOREST As told by Sid Miller 119
THE LONGEST YEAR As told by Bill Cook 133

VII
DARKNESS OVERHEAD

MONUMENTS: CHARLES GOTTSCHALK As told by Lowell Peterson 141
THE 367th FIGHTER GROUP As told by Arnold Abel 147
"SWEDE" As told by Lloyd "Swede" Nelson 152
PILGRIMAGE OF A COMBAT GLIDER PILOT
    As told by Harold "Bud" Menzel 156

VIII
WINTER SKY

THE TENTH MOUNTAIN DIVISION As told by Lavern Trinrud 171
483rd BOMB GROUP As told by Harlin G. "Noggin" Neuman 175
COMBAT FROM AFRICA TO ITALY AND FRANCE:
    MY STORY As told by Leo Lang 182

IX
DAYLIGHT OF HOPE

FROM DEPRESSION TO WAR As told by Lowell Peterson 193
FREEDOM OF WORSHIP As told by Lowell Peterson 196
SUNDAY DINNER As told by Lowell Peterson 200

X
COMES THE SUN
CALL ME DIXIE As told by Richard Broesch 205
THE UNLIKELY PATRIOT As told by Lowell Peterson 210

XI
HEAT OF THE DAY
IWO JIMA: OPERATION DETACHMENT As told by Lowell Peterson 215
A TATTERED OLD FLAG As told by Harold Short 218
MT. SURIBACHI As told by Thomas H. O'Brien 220
TOWARD KITANO POINT As told by Courtney L. Coffing 226

XII
THE LAST STORM
SUGAR LOAF HILL: THE BATTLE OF OKINAWA
    As told by Raymond Moe 231
THE AIR APACHES As told by Albert W. Gruer Jr. 239
THE GHOST OF ERNIE PYLE As told by Lowell Peterson 254
A MOTHER'S LOVE As told by Lowell Peterson 261

XIII
THE SUN ROSE CLEAR
THE THRESHER MAN As told by Lowell Peterson 267
THE BENEFICIAL EFFECTS OF WORLD WAR II
    As told by Earl Spangler, Ph. D. and Lowell Peterson 273
THE FINAL REVEILLE As told by Lowell Peterson 277

SOURCES 283

FOREWORD

Compared to other armed conflicts of the twentieth century, World War II was unique. In spite of the pacifism and isolationism that pervaded the period between World War I and World War II, there was no significant dissent when World War II began. Pearl Harbor took care of that. The conduct of the war was delegated by the public to the president, his generals, and his admirals. Protesters, pacifists, and anti-war activists realized they had no significant support. Hitler's egomaniacal ambitions and unprovoked atrocities of the Japanese made dissent unpopular and unthinkable. This was a war against evil. Conflict on the battlefield was preferable to an uneasy peace when the world was facing the threat of tyranny and dictatorship. In all wars, there are advocates who favor peace over the hardship of war. During World War II, this was not possible.

Dr. Peterson does an excellent job of describing World War II through the experiences of Wisconsin natives and others who participated in that war. As you read this book, you will sense both the singularity of pride that veterans have for service to their country in time of need and the emotional human feelings of the men who experienced the war firsthand.

I enlisted as a private in World War II, rose to the rank of captain in the infantry, and served with pride. My fellow veterans, this book will help you recall both the good and bad you encountered in that war, and will renew your pride in what you accomplished while serving your country.

I served as the Secretary of the Army during the Vietnam era, and I recall the vigorous dissent, and the lack of desire of many young people to serve their country. I also remember those who served with pride. All those who did and did not serve in World War II and subsequent wars of the twentieth century should read this book. You will recognize that there are times that service in the Armed Forces is necessary, and that those who have contributed are proud of having served, and are deserving of the respect of their fellow countrymen. I believe that this is important, because there will come a time in the future when this country will again face armed conflict and ask its young people to commit to duty, honor, and country by their service.*

Robert F. Froehlke, Capt., U.S. Army Infantry, Ret.
Secretary of the Army, May 1971-1973

* *The Foreword was written prior to the Afghanistan conflict.*

"In this century hundreds of thousands of G.I.s died to bring to the beginning of the 21st century the victory of democracy as the ascendent political system on the face of the earth. The G.I.s were willing to travel far away and give their lives, if necessary, to secure the rights and freedoms of others. Only a nation such as ours, based on a firm, moral foundation, could make such a request of its citizens."

Excerpt from:
The American G.I.
by Colin Powell
Time
June 14, 1999
Vol. 153 No. 23

"It is well that war is so terrible,
else we should grow too fond of it."

General Robert E. Lee

ACKNOWLEDGMENTS

First and foremost, I acknowledge the kindness and cooperation of the World War II veterans and their families, who welcomed me into their homes and provided me with materials, books, diaries, pictures, reminiscences, and conversation that became the basis of this publication. The memories, sometimes painful, were shared in a spirit of trust, with the hope that a better understanding of their ordeal might ensue. Immeasurable thanks are owed to these veterans and their comrades for what they experienced on our behalf. The WWII veterans who share their experiences today are the survivors. They were lucky. Those not so lucky became casualties on the battlefield. I acknowledge the dedication, heroism, and commitment of the living, the dead, and the wounded of this war.

I specifically acknowledge Dr. Earl Spangler, whose passion for history in general, and the history of World War II in particular, reignited the light of inquisitiveness in my heart that had been dim since my college years. His encouragement and critique, based on firsthand experience in the war, gave credibility to my effort. Likewise, Malcolm Rosholt, from his experience spanning the 1920s to the 1940s, provided me with an insightful knowledge of Asia and China. Dr. Spangler and Mr. Rosholt, I think, were pleased to find one more inquisitive student with a desire to learn, understand, and, more than anything else, pass on to future generations the memories from an era that they lived through—an era that defined the Twentieth Century.

I wish to thank my typists, Margie Martin and Kristy Johnson, who eagerly typed and retyped my manuscripts without hesitation and always with a smile. My wife, Mary, and my daughters, Kristin O'Callaghan and Linda Peterson-McKenzie, M.D., kindly made suggestions for improvement. My son, Jim Peterson, handled the legal issues and contracts. Carolyn Kott Washburne edited the manuscript, Marcia Lorenzen proofread and corrected it to its final form, and Camin Potts created the graphics and design.

I would like to thank Mr. Bob Cloud, editor of the *Waupaca Post* newspaper, as well as friends, patients, and associates who encouraged me to pursue the effort. Thanks also go to Al Gruer Jr., who, through our breakfast conversations, refueled my interest in the adventures of air combat and gave me many leads to pursue for the stories you are about to read.

—Lowell Peterson

The author at Ie Shima, Okinawa, 1965.

A CLEAR SKY WITH DISTANT CLOUDS

WORLD WAR II—INTRODUCTION
As told by
Lowell Peterson

As an impressionable child in the early 1940s, I was caught up in the drama and patriotism of the conflict known as World War II, and as a teenager I witnessed young people, not much older than myself, going off to fight a "police action" in Korea that almost evolved into World War III. When I entered college in the fall of 1954, a strange mix of eighteen-year-old kids and battle-hardened veterans from Korea shared classrooms and dormitories, similar to what occurred following World War II. Young men with wounds on their bodies and emotional scars on their minds reentered society through college, trying to regain a semblance of "normal" lives. My early adult life led to involvement in the Vietnam conflict. It was a war that almost destroyed the most powerful nation in the world, not only on the battlefield, but on the streets and campuses at home. In the early 1990s, the peace of the world was again threatened by the Gulf War. Conflicts in Yugoslavia, Chechnya, Afghanistan, Pakistan, Korea, the Mideast, and many other places continue to threaten stability and peace around the world.

During the early 1940s, World War II consumed every facet of energy of the United States. Sons and daughters left the comfort of home to serve in active combat or military support roles while others left rural areas to be employed by the military-industrial complex of the cities. War touched everyone.

Awareness of global geography expanded rapidly. Tobruk, Kassirene Pass, Messina, Anzio, Normandy, Ardennes, Bastogne, Remagen, and Omaha Beach became household words. Likewise, Midway, Tinian, Tarawa, Guadalcanal, Leyte Gulf, Bataan, Corregidor, Iwo Jima, Coral Sea, Ie Shima, and Okinawa became etched in the memories of a nation at war.

The hostilities of World War II ceased more than fifty-five years ago, concluding the greatest single catastrophic event in the history of mankind. Fifteen million American men would serve in the armed forces during this conflict and, in less than five years, the war would touch every populated continent, every island nation, every ocean and sea. The scope of the war's destruction in human and materialistic terms was enormous. The human toll of the war is beyond comprehension. No devastation since the bubonic plague epidemics of the fourteenth century had wrought such havoc on a populace.

Infrastructures of nations were destroyed, and the economic cost of the war rose to multi-billions of dollars. Historian Dr. Thomas Childers of the University of Pennsylvania described this devastation in his recorded lectures for *The Teaching Company*, titled *World War II: Military and Social History*, 1998. He noted the following figures: The national debt in the United States rose from $49 billion in 1941 to $259 billion in 1945. Fifty-five million people lost their lives as a direct result of World War II. The conflict directly led to 1,800,000 German military personnel killed, 1,000,000 missing, and 500,000 German civilian deaths. The British military lost 390,000, the French 810,000, and the United States 259,000. Japanese casualties were 1,800,000. Poland could not account for 4,500,000 people, of whom 4,000,000 were civilians. The Russians suffered the greatest loss, with 11,000,000 military dead and a total loss of 22,000,000 people, which was 10 percent of their population. Six million Jews lost their lives in the Holocaust. People just disappeared. The Allies suffered 8,809,000 wounded and the Axis Powers 8,175,000, of which 7,250,000 were German. The United States had 671,278 wounded casualties and the Soviet Union 5,000,000. At the end of the war, there were 12 million refugees. Childers concluded, "The war caused the greatest human sacrifice of any generation in history."

The jubilation that followed the Allied victories in the European and Pacific theaters soon gave way to postwar reality. It was a time to be thankful and a time to forget.

As a result, the men and women who served in this great war have been willing to honor their service and commitment in silent contentment for the greater part of two generations. Chronicles of the war were left to authors such as historian Stephen E. Ambrose in his books, *Citizen Soldiers* and *The Victors*. Movies such as *Midway*; *Torah, Torah, Torah*; *Patton*; *The Longest Day* and, more recently, Steven Spielberg's *A Band of Brothers* were reasonable depictions of what occurred.

A recent rekindling of interest in World War II has risen from the ashes of time. Why now? Why have Tom Brokaw's books, *The Greatest Generation*, and its sequel, *The Greatest Generation Speaks*, become instant bestsellers? Why has the graphic depiction of war in the movies *Saving Private Ryan*, *The Thin Red Line*, and *Pearl Harbor* awakened the conscience? This phenomenon needs careful and thoughtful examination.

Today, World War II veterans are in their 70s and 80s, retired, living their lives in various levels of comfort, health, and interest. They, unfortunately, are also decreasing in number by more than thirty thousand per month. Whole libraries of experience and information are dying, along with the veterans, and being lost forever. More than any other event, World War II defined their lives. It stole their youth.

In these waning years of their lives, these servicemen and women realize, and are willing to admit, what they silently knew all along, "Hey, we did something important! We counted. We made a difference. We persevered in the worst of conditions in a conflict that changed the course of history!" Sharing that experience with current and future generations, as terrifying and unpleasant as it might have been, is their legacy to mankind and the world. The United States and the Allies won World War II and America loves a winner! At the end of the millennium and at the end of the twentieth century, it is only natural for veterans and the nation to look back and review these accomplishments.

In the December, 1999 issue of the *345th Bombardment Group* newsletter, Vol. 17, Issue 4, historian Arthur Schlesinger Jr., observes that, "War remains hell, but a few wars have been driven by decent purposes and produced beneficial results. The generation that fought World War II was like most other generations in American history. It consisted of plain people, who, confronted by mortal threats to their country, accepted their duty and performed it laconically, modestly, self-effacingly, without show, without flourish. Their lives and deaths reassured new generations that they, too, might have the right stuff. World War II reminds us that ordinary people, … could have, when put to the test, capacious reserves of courage and steadfastness." Schlesinger concludes, "That search for deeper meanings may be why new generations are so eagerly engaged in the discovery of the second World War."

In the series of stories about World War II and the early 1940s to follow, I will attempt, through anecdotes, interviews, personal remembrances, first-person testimonials, and fictional expansions of actual events, to paint a picture of an era and a people that we should not forget. You may be able to relive a bit of the experience with me. This storytelling approach is simple but honest. This book is not meant to be an all-inclusive history text or a documentary of every battle, but rather a journey and emotional adventure through a difficult period of time in our nation's history.

Many of the personal testimonials and interviews were obtained in and around the community of Waupaca, Wisconsin. In every city, village, town, or crossroads rural community in this nation, there are dozens of interesting historical stories from World War II that could fill libraries. In a few short years, the opportunity to record these firsthand accounts will be lost forever. This book is my contribution to preserving the legacy.

THE ORIGINS OF WORLD WAR II
As told by
Lowell Peterson

The origins of World War II are difficult to define. It is naive to assume that the Battle of Britain in 1940, the sneak attack on Pearl Harbor in 1941, or the German invasion of Poland in 1939 initiated the hostilities. Dr. Thomas Childers, in the lectures referred to in the previous section of this book, noted that, "World War II may have been just an extension of World War I with a peaceful interlude of twenty years," or, as Winston Churchill put it, " ... that period of exhaustion which has been described as peace."

The Treaty of Versailles ending World War I, signed in the Hall of Mirrors, totally humiliated the German nation. The treaty terms imposed penalties in a vindictive, harsh, vengeful retaliation that stripped Germany of territory, such as Alsace, Lorraine, and the Rhineland, as well as demanding huge monetary reparations. Germany was economically drained. It was impossible for the German Republic to pay these reparations during the extreme inflationary period of the 1920s, capped off by the Great Depression of 1929 and the early 1930s. Germany's government destabilized as the emasculated nation, totally disarmed and its self respect and pride gone, was on the ropes.

Further, the German people mistrusted the postwar Weimar Republic government and its impotent leadership, laying the foundation for the rise of tyranny and the ascent to power of Adolf Hitler. Hitler provided an image for the German nation that it thought it needed at the time: a strong leader, a shrewd politician, and a spellbinding orator with a messianic charisma. Adolph Hitler stabilized the government of Germany, illegally rearmed the country, eliminated much of the poverty, created new jobs, and gave the people hope. Unfortunately, his expansionist nationalism and his deeply-rooted inner hate for Jews and Bolsheviks, as well as his association with extremist right-wing groups, would not only lead to World War II but also to the ultimate destruction of Germany and millions of people.

Hitler was able to boldly lie, bluff, and politically finesse his opponents without expectation of serious European opposition. As soon as Germany reoccupied and re-militarized the Rhineland, any hope of restraining Hitler's invasive expansionism had been forever lost.

Likewise, the expansion of the Japanese Empire, throughout China, Indochina, Malaysia, and the Pacific Islands, went unchecked by a weak Chinese, Russian, and British resistance, and an isolationist United States. When the government of Japan was turned over to the military leaders Tojo and Yamamoto in 1940, the die had been cast for military expansionism, culminating in the attack on the Hawaiian Islands in 1941. The goal of the attack on Pearl Harbor on December 7, 1941, was to neutralize the United States, the only military force in the world capable of stifling Japanese advances in Asia and the Pacific.

The United States would declare war on the empire of Japan on December 8, 1941, and Hitler would declare war on the United States shortly thereafter. The possible march to Armageddon had begun! In the stories that follow, we will examine the unfolding saga of World War II through the experiences of a few of those who experienced it.

CATACLYSM FROM THE RISING SUN

THE RADIO
As told by
Lowell Peterson

Today's generation cannot comprehend a world without television, the Internet, computers, satellite dish networks, or a world lacking access to multiple events around the world with the click of a remote control. In spite of all of these technological marvels, the radio has not been replaced. There are more than two radios for every man, woman, and child in this country. Transistors, chips, and circuit boards have made the radio compact and portable. It can go anywhere! In the 1930s and 1940s, the home console radio was an indispensable beacon to the ears of the nation.

The radio stands unobtrusively in a corner of the room, quietly alone, ready to come alive like a flower opening its petals to the morning sun after a cold dark night. This technologic innovation of the early twentieth century is vigilant to the unfolding history of the world, as electromagnetic waves bounce off the stratosphere to be received by this box full of wires, magnets, and vacuum tubes, thereby opening vistas for the common people everywhere. As the world of communication progressed from the printed word of the newspaper to the airwaves of the radio, the dissemination of news and, more importantly, knowledge was reduced from days and weeks to minutes and seconds.

In the 1920s to the 1940s, there were no local radio stations. Programs came only from the large cities. In Waupaca, Wisconsin, I listened to *Jolly Joe*, sponsored by Ovaltine in the morning from WLS in Chicago, and my mother tuned in to *Betty Crocker* at noon from WCCO in Minneapolis. Business, weather, and agriculture reports from Milwaukee, Wisconsin, stirred Dad's interest. The soap opera was born, thanks to sponsorship by laundry soap producers of Oxydol, Ivory Flakes, and Duz ("Duz does everything"). Situation dramas, such as *The Guiding Light, Just Plain Bill, Ma Perkins,* and *One Man's Family* created a fantasy world each afternoon. Syndicated family entertainment was broadcast each evening, with stars such as Jack Benny and Rochester, Milton Berle, George Burns and Gracie Allen, Bob Hope, and comedy from *Fibber Magee and Mollie,*

THE SUN ROSE CLEAR

and *Amos and Andy*. Mystery shows like *The Shadow*, *The Thin Man*, and *Inner Sanctum* frightened and entertained equally well.

The World Series and heavyweight title boxing matches were the only sporting events broadcast live. The music of Tommy and Jimmy Dorsey, Benny Goodman, Duke Ellington, Glenn Miller, Harry James, Bing Crosby, and Frank Sinatra provided listening and dancing reprieve from the stresses of a changing world. The most powerful radio broadcast event of all time, Orson Welles' imaginary *The War of the Worlds*, on October 30, 1938, created panic, insanity, and suicide across the country. The radio provided United States President, Franklin Delano Roosevelt, through *Fireside Chats*, an opportunity to reiterate his inaugural promise during the daunting days of the Great Depression that, "the only thing we have to fear is fear itself."

Family members shared the supper hour together. The food was hot, the fare was simple, and the radio was on. The six o'clock news reports from Walter Winchell, Lowell Thomas, H. V. Kaltenborn, Edward R. Murrow, or Gabriel Heater from Washington, D.C., New York, or London told the country of its hopes, its successes, and its failures. No one of that era can forget Gabriel's "entry" each night, with "There's bad news tonight," or my namesake, Lowell Thomas' sign-off, "So-long until tomorrow." In the late 1930s and the dawning of the 1940s, as the dark curtain of World War began to spread like a San Francisco fog across Europe and Asia, the radio became the sentinel and beacon to history in the making as Edward R. Murrow reported, "This is London calling … " The garage mechanic, the farmer, the grocer, the blacksmith, the teacher, the factory worker, and the housewife tuned in to the radio for reports of the world news. The fate of the nation and the hopes of a generation were dependent on the uncertainties of a world in conflict, faithfully reported daily from that electronic box in the corner.

On a gray, cold Sunday in December 1941, the status quo changed for all mankind forever, when the RCA, Philco, or Westinghouse radios announced to each household, in the quiet comfort of their homes, that on this morning, "Pearl Harbor in the Hawaiian Islands has been attacked by the Japanese. Casualties are heavy." The radio news was continuously monitored, as citizens of the United States held their breath. Every family awaited the nation's response.

On December 8, 1941, the front page of the Appleton, Wisconsin, *Post-Crescent* newspaper printed the entire content of President Franklin D. Roosevelt's speech to a Joint Session of Congress carried live on the radio earlier in the day. He said:

Yesterday, December 7, 1941, – a date which will live in infamy – the United States of America was suddenly and deliberately attacked by naval and air forces of the empire of Japan.

The United States was at peace with that nation and, at the solicitation of Japan, was still in conversation with its government and its emperor looking toward the maintenance of peace in the Pacific.

Indeed, one hour after Japanese air squadrons had commenced bombing in Oahu, the Japanese ambassador to the United States and his colleague delivered to the secretary of state a formal reply to a recent American message. While this reply stated that it seemed useless to continue the existing diplomatic negotiations, it contained no threat or hint of war or armed attack.

It will be recorded that the distance of Hawaii to Japan makes it obvious that the attack was deliberately planned many days or even weeks ago. During the intervening time, the Japanese government had deliberately sought to deceive the United States by false statements and expressions of hope for continued peace.

The attack yesterday on the Hawaiian islands has caused severe damage to American naval and military forces. Very many American lives have been lost and, in addition, American ships have been reported torpedoed on the high seas between San Francisco and Honolulu.

Yesterday the Japanese government also launched an attack against Malaya.

Last night Japanese forces attacked Hong Kong.

Last night Japanese forces attacked Guam.

Last night Japanese forces attacked the Philippine islands.

Last night Japanese attacked Wake Island.

This morning the Japanese attacked Midway Island.

Japan has, therefore, undertaken a surprise offensive extending throughout the Pacific area. The facts of yesterday speak for themselves. The people of the United States have already formed their opinions and well understand the implications to the very life and safety of our nation.

As commander-in-chief of the Army and Navy, I have directed that all measures be taken for our defense.

Always will we remember the character of the onslaught against us.

No matter how long it may take us to overcome this premeditated invasion, the American people in their righteous might will win through to absolute victory.

I believe I interpret the will of the Congress and of the people when I assert that we will not only defend ourselves to the uttermost, but will make very certain that this form of treachery shall never endanger us again.

Hostilities exist. There is no blinking at the fact that our people, our territory, and our interests are in grave danger.

With confidence in our armed forces—with the unbounding determination of our people - we will gain the inevitable triumph—so help us God.

I ask that the Congress declare that since the unprovoked and dastardly attack by Japan on Sunday, December seventh, a state of war has existed between the United States and the Japanese empire.

REMEMBER PEARL HARBOR
As told by
Mrs. Theodore Vonck Sr.

On the quiet Sunday morning of December 7, 1941, ninety-four U.S. Naval vessels were moored at the docks of Pearl Harbor. At 7:55 a.m., whistles piped from the boatswains on each ship, calling sailors to formation on deck, in preparation for raising the colors. At about the same time, without warning, 260 Japanese planes dove in waves attacking the anchored U.S. Navy ships, and the surrounding Army and Navy military facilities. The Japanese achieved complete surprise and by 9:45 a.m., the attack was over. In less than two hours, four battleships had been sunk in Pearl Harbor and four were damaged. Many more small ships also sank. Two thousand four hundred three Americans had died. One thousand one hundred seventy-eight others had been wounded. The Japanese lost twenty-five airplanes, five midget submarines, and less than one hundred men.

For thousands of troops in the Pacific Theater, the war had been thrust upon them without warning in the attack of December 7, 1941. For some it was to be the only day of war that they would experience.

"Hey Ted, come on, rise and shine! We have to get going!" shouted his buddy, Jim. "Breakfast is at 0800. We only have thirty minutes to get ready."

"Okay, Jim, I'll be ready," Ted answered. One thing about Hawaii is certain: the sun is going to wake you up every morning or the eighty-degree temperature in the barracks will bake you out of your bunk. "Turn the fan on, will ya? Let's get some air moving."

Jim replied, "Ted, the mess sergeant promised us fresh eggs this morning. He has been out scrounging on the native economy again. It sure will be a welcome change from those powdered eggs we've been getting."

"Ya, Jim, he's really a good cook. Too bad we give him such a hard time, but what else is there to complain about in this paradise except the food?"

Jim agreed, "We sure were lucky to get this assignment for our first military post. Can you imagine being stuck in Mississippi or Missouri compared to this?"

Ted called, "I'm ready for breakfast. Let me at the eggs and bacon! Come on guys, join up, let's get on over to the mess hall."

Jim paused, "Ted, I think I'll go over to the chapel for mass after breakfast," he said.

"Okay, Jim, I'll go to church with you. We probably need a little soul cleansing. The Padre seems like a real nice guy."

"Sounds great. Now for those eggs!"

As they walked to the mess, Jim asked, "What should we do this afternoon? How about getting an off-base pass and going down to Waikiki to swim, watch the surfers, and check out the girls?"

Suddenly he stopped. "Ted, what are those explosions down by the harbor? What's all the noise on Sunday morning?"

"Jim, there must be a big firepower demonstration exercise underway down by the shore!" Ted replied. "But what are those airplanes doing overhead?"

Planes were diving in low-level passes so close to Ted and his friends that they could see the pilot's face and the markings on the tail of the airplane. Both the face and the markings were Japanese! The planes started shooting! They appeared to be strafing communications towers and targets of opportunity. The group stood frozen in disbelief. A bullet hit the ground near Ted and he picked it up. It was so hot, he had to spit on it. He then spit on it a second time in anger and hate.

Jim screamed, "I've been hit, help me, help me!" Ted yelled, "Get him under the barracks out of sight and send someone for a medic."

As they carried Jim to the barracks, he began talking non-stop. "Ted, we told them, didn't we? We saw those Japanese fishing boats close to the island. We knew the Japs were up to something. We told headquarters and they did nothing about it. We told them, we told them! Ted, am I going to die?"

"No, no, no, Jim. You can't—we've got a lot of living to do," Ted said in comfort to his friend. "Jim, I'll be back. I've got to get a weapon." Then Ted turned to his lieutenant.

"Lieutenant, what do you want us to do?" he asked.

The lieutenant, having been rudely awakened by the attack, yelled to Ted and the others, "Troops, get into formation." The lieutenant probably didn't know what else to say under the circumstances. Bullets were flying everywhere, and everybody was scrambling for cover behind anything that looked solid. The lieutenant finally decided a more realistic plan would be to go to the armory to get weapons and ammunition. When the troops got there, they found everything was under lock and key. They finally did get their weapons and ammunition released, but most of the surprise attack was over.

The rest of the day was a blur of activity. Pure chaos! Ted noted, "I never did get my eggs." The activities of the whole island had been disrupted.

Looking out over Pearl Harbor, Ted could see ships burning and the smoke billowing up, obliterating the sun. "Tears came to my eyes as I stared in disbelief. I felt violated. Where would this all lead?"

>Ted Vonck's wife, Becky, also served her country during World War II, becoming a nurse cadet after nurses training. She stated, "I was assigned to the Percy Jones Hospital, which had been the Kellogg tuberculosis sanitarium in Battle Creek, Michigan, converted for military hospital use during the war. I nursed the returning veterans from various theaters of war who arrived directly from the front lines via field hospitals. The carnage that war had ravaged upon the young men of our nation was horrendous to behold. Limbs had been blown away, shrapnel wounds were too numerous to count, and there were gunshot wounds of every type and location. Because most of the wounds were infected, the troops were shipped to our hospital with maggots placed in the wounds to devour the dying flesh. Unfortunately, we couldn't save them all, and some that survived would have physical and mental disabilities for the rest of their life." The experience left a lasting impression on this young enthusiastic nurse.
>
>After the war, Becky married Ted, whom she met at a social outing to a bowling alley. Together, they raised seven children and were married for forty-eight years. Theodore (Ted) Vonck Sr. died in 1999 in Appleton, Wisconsin, after a lengthy series of serious illnesses dating back to 1984. He was eighty-four years old. Ted never shared very much of his war experiences, even with his family. Becky noted, however, that Ted was very proud of his military service and proud of the fact that he had survived the attack on Pearl Harbor. Becky rarely differed with Ted, who preferred not to talk about the war, but she felt, and still feels, that the horrors and tragedies of war that they both had seen and experienced should be shared with future generations to enhance their understanding of what war is like and the sacrifices that people, especially young people, made to preserve freedom.

(The author obtained information for this story in a recent interview with Mrs. Vonck. It is based on facts as her husband revealed them to her.)

THE BARBER BROTHERS
As told by
Lowell Peterson

At 2:30 a.m. on Sunday, December 21, 1941, two weeks following the December 7, 1941, Japanese surprise attack on Pearl Harbor, police delivered a telegram to Peter and Gertrude Barber, confirming that the battleship USS Oklahoma had been sunk during the attack and that the three Barber boys were missing in action and presumed dead. Malcolm, LeRoy, and Randolph Barber remain entombed in the USS Oklahoma in the waters of Pearl Harbor. This is their story, recreated by the author as imagined through the eyes of Randolph Barber, the youngest of the three brothers.

Randolph, Malcolm, and LeRoy Barber, December, 1941.

"I don't want to hear another word of this business."

"But Mama, you let LeRoy and Malcolm go. Why not me?"

"Randolph Barber, didn't you understand me?" Mother was using her sternest voice and, when she referred to me by my whole name, I knew she was digging in her heels and proclaiming her maximum maternal authority. It didn't look like I had much of a chance of convincing her. She was a soft-hearted lady and a good mother, but she could be stubborn. Then a miracle in disguise wearing bib overalls and a denim jacket walked in. Dad appeared.

"What's going on in here? What's all the arguing about? I could hear you two all the way out by the barn," he said.

Mother was embarrassed that her voice had been raised to a level that suggested anger rather than sternness and she hesitated to answer my dad. This was just long enough to give me an opening to blurt out the debating points that, until that moment, she thought had been put to rest.

"Dad, I want to enlist in the Navy. I'm eighteen years old. LeRoy and Malcolm are already in the Navy and you let them join. Their letters say that they love it and are learning so many new things and seeing a world they didn't know existed. They think I should join the Navy before the war in Europe heats up more and our country gets involved. Then I'd end up getting drafted into the Army."

Mother recovered quickly.

"Randy, first of all, Malcolm and LeRoy are older. Malcolm is 21 and LeRoy is 20. They're more mature. You're barely dry behind the ears! Secondly, I don't think America will let itself get involved in a war in Europe. There is no sentiment in this country for that happening. Hitler, the British, French, Italians, and Russians will decide their own fate."

She was countering my arguments with common-sense solutions, and I felt my position weakening, but at least the stubbornness had softened and she was back in the conversation mode. I had to start playing my aces.

"Mom, Malcolm and LeRoy both wrote that if I enlisted now and requested sea duty, it would be almost certainly granted. LeRoy has been in the Navy less than four months and he is already on maneuvers in the Pacific on the battleship USS *Oklahoma*. Malcolm was on the same maneuvers on the battleship USS *Colorado*."

"Peter, talk to your son. Tell him how foolish this is. I don't want all of my boys going off to the ends of the earth. A mother needs her children close by."

"Now, Gertrude, you know you can't hang on to the boys forever," Dad said. "They need to make their own life. We can't afford to send them to college, and there's not enough work here on the farm to make a living for us and a grown boy. LeRoy and Malcolm had to go off and work for President Roosevelt's New Deal recovery program with the CCC (Civilian Conservation Corps) before they enlisted, just to help us out so that we could get through the Depression. Randolph will probably have to go off to the city to get a job soon, so he'll be away from home anyway."

Good ol' Dad. I knew I could count on him. He probably hated to see me leave home as much as Mom did. We were a very close family, all working together on the farm while I was growing up. I think Mom hated to see me go because she never had any daughters, and now her boys were leaving one by one.

"Dad, I'd rather take my chances on learning something useful in the Navy while I see the world, than getting a job in Appleton or Milwaukee and be stuck there for the rest of my life," I said. "You've got Clayton and Robert here to help you out on the farm until they grow up."

"Peter!"

"Now Gertrude! Your boy is becoming a man and sometimes men have to do what men have to do. I'm so proud of the other boys and they seem to be having such a good time. Let's sleep on it and talk again over breakfast in the morning."

It was a long, sleepless night for me, and I suspect for my parents as well. It was as if all of our futures hung in the balance, depending upon the decision or non-decision that would emerge. At breakfast the silence was eerie. No one wanted or dared to speak. The only sounds were of spoons and forks nervously scraping plates and cereal bowls. The solemnity belied the tenseness in the air that was so thick you could cut it with a knife. Mother cleared her throat and began to speak slowly and deliberately, choosing the clearest and simplest words she could muster.

"Randolph, your father and I had a long discussion last evening after going to bed," she began. "The darkness and quiet of the night somehow made it easier to think clearly. We also prayed together that any decision we made would be the right one that would be the best for all of us, but especially for you."

I was holding my breath as dad looked at both of us with his usual stoic pride showing faintly through his expressionless face.

"Randolph, your father and I have decided …"

Oh God, what was she going to say? I sat motionless in eager anticipation.

"… that we would be sincerely pleased and proud if you would enlist in the Navy and join your brothers in the pursuit of your goals."

Momentarily shocked, I couldn't move, but then leaped off my chair into the air, spilling my milk all over the table and floor. I hugged and kissed my mother and shook the hand of a now glowing and smiling dad, as the cat cleaned up my milk from the floor. After the shock wore off and my tears had dried, dad said his first words of the morning.

"As soon as the Navy recruiting office at the courthouse in Waupaca opens, I'll drive you over and make the arrangements. Your mother and I decided you should go into the Navy because you, LeRoy, and Malcolm have always been so close and have done everything together while you were growing up. It didn't seem right to keep you apart when you are all becoming adults."

A thoughtful and profound decision. I should have expected nothing less from these salt-of-the-earth, religious, caring people. On that day, the trip from New London to Waupaca, a mere ten miles away, was the longest trip I ever took. The recruiter provided me with all the forms to fill out and confirmed that the Navy did, indeed, have slots available. If I was interested in pursuing this, he would send the paperwork on to the Great Lakes Naval Training Base. Was I interested? I said my first, "Yes, sir," so fast that it drew a smile from my dad and the recruiter. He told me to report to Great Lakes the following week for induction into the Navy. I was delighted, but for the first time a little scared. Had I done the right thing? Did I really want to leave home? Did I have what it takes to be a good sailor? Would I get homesick? Would I "wash out"? Would I get seasick?

The trip back to New London and the farm was a blur, as was the whole next week. Relatives and friends were coming around to say goodbye. Priests and teachers called to wish me luck. A final going away party was hosted with neighbors as guests. My dad gave me a new safety razor as a present. I guess this confirmed me as a man in his eyes and in my own. My mother gave me a new crucifix and a prayer book. The days came and went swiftly and now on a hot August morning, Mother and Dad, in silence, drove me to Appleton where I was to catch the Chicago and Northwestern train for Milwaukee and then the North Shore Railroad to Great Lakes. The train was late and the long goodbye was gut-wrenching for all of us. The moment came and went, and I was on my way. The umbilical cord had been broken.

I enlisted in the U.S. Navy at Great Lakes on August 27, 1940, three-and-one-half months after LeRoy and Malcolm had enlisted together on May 8, 1940. The basic training was difficult but fun, and I met many great guys. I learned to march, carry and present arms, practice basic seamanship, stand for inspections, and listen to lectures about the "Navy Way" of doing things. I literally memorized the *Blue Jacket Manual*. My buddies and I were able to go into Chicago on a weekend liberty once. We didn't have any money, so mostly we drank Cokes, ate hot dogs, and walked the streets. I realized I wasn't in New London, Wisconsin, anymore—but I loved it.

The days passed and the time came for us to receive our assignments. I had requested assignment to the Pacific Theater and to be aboard ship, hoping to get close to where Malcolm and LeRoy were. I even informed the chief petty officer of my desire to be near my brothers. This was rather bold, but something must have worked right because, when the assignments came out, I got my first choice. I was assigned to the USS *Colorado* in the Pacific. This was the same ship that Malcolm was on. What luck! A short furlough at home was followed by more sad goodbyes as the separation from family and friends grew wider and wider. The train trip to San Diego was long, tiring, and difficult, as we slept or sat upright in our seats for two days and three nights. We survived on sandwiches, donuts, and coffee. I saw the vast expanse of America that I had only imagined existed up to this point. The troop transport trip from San Diego to Hawaii was a slow and boring six-day trip and, yes, I did get seasick!

After processing, at the personnel office on Oahu, we were given our assignment and taken aboard ship. Because the ship was getting ready to put out to sea, we were busy. It was days before I could try to locate Malcolm, but I finally found him. The reunion was happy, but tearful, and we were grateful to be together again. Malcolm paraded me all around, introducing me to all his friends, with a "Hey, guys, I want you to meet my little brother." I was elated to be accepted by my fellow sailors so soon after arrival aboard ship.

Later, when we were alone, Malcolm confided that he had talked with LeRoy a couple of weekends ago on shore leave. LeRoy had encouraged Malcolm to attempt transfer to the USS *Oklahoma* because it was such a super ship, with excellent crew quarters and facilities. LeRoy stated that his ship had a great crew and the best cooks. Sailors worked eight-hour shifts on the *Oklahoma* instead of twelve, as was usual on other ships. They also had pool tables and other recreational facilities on

USS *Oklahoma*

board. He noted that when they were at sea during exercises, the power of this battleship could really blast the targets. The ship would move thirty feet in the opposite direction every time the guns fired. It sounded great. Malcolm and I put in for transfer to the *Oklahoma*, and to our surprise we both were accepted.

The next year can be summarized in one word: drills! We had general quarters combat drills, fire suppression and crash recovery drills, lifeboat and abandon ship drills. There were target practice gun firings and lectures on combat maneuver tactics. We were becoming combat ready. Every man knew his job and what was expected of him. Fortunately, we did get some shore leave to relax on the beautiful beaches of Waikiki. As I lay in my bunk reflecting on my time in the Navy and especially on this ship, I decided to write a letter home.

USS Oklahoma, Sunday Morning
December 7, 1941

Dear Mom and Dad,

I'm up early, just like on the farm. It's a great day here in Hawaii, but I have to admit, I miss Wisconsin. I suppose its pretty cold there now. Here it's 80 degrees and sun every day. I'm sorry I haven't told you previously how we all got together.

I don't know how LeRoy and Malcolm did it, but they finagled transfers and tactical orders, and the next thing I knew, our wish had become reality. Malcolm was transferred to the battleship USS Oklahoma on 8/27/40 and I got my transfer after we returned from maneuvers at sea on 11/11/40. Man, what a ship! It would engulf the whole city of New London and cast a shadow north and south to Sugar Bush and Bean City! It is huge. When I came on board, Malcolm and LeRoy received permission to give me a tour. The USS Oklahoma is truly a behemoth of a warship. Its fire power is enormous. I was lucky to get this assignment, and the three of us were so happy that the brothers were finally all together again. We have been in and out of port repeatedly on maneuvers over the past year, and the experiences were fantastic.

After we came back from maneuvers last week, Malcolm,

LeRoy, and I decided to have our picture taken together in uniform to send home to you for Christmas. I was so excited and happy that the three of us could enjoy liberty together in Honolulu and have the picture taken.

We're back on ship and tied up at Pearl Harbor now, along with a lot of other ships, awaiting our orders. Malcolm and LeRoy think we will probably leave port for extensive maneuvers in the South Pacific sometime later in December. It will be good to get out to sea again.

Well, that's it for today. I'll send this letter ashore with my roommate. I've got to get showered and dressed in "dress-whites" and join Malcolm and LeRoy for Sunday mass. I hope you like the picture.

Your loving son,
Randolph

Peter Barber had been a World War I combatant and had feared for his sons' safety. A few weeks prior to the attack on Pearl Harbor, he had asked the Navy Department that his boys be separated to different ships, so they would not be together in case of a catastrophe. He had not received a reply to his letter.

Peter Barber was quoted as saying, "When their young brothers are old enough, I'm sure they will avenge their deaths. I'm glad they died like men and I'm proud that they gave their lives to this country."

A brand-new destroyer escort, named in honor of the Barber brothers, the USS Barber, was christened by Gertrude Barber on July 4, 1942.

Clayton Barber was sixteen years old when his brothers were killed. He enlisted in the Navy in 1943 and served on the USS Barber as a gunner's mate. Robert Barber was nine years old at the time and carries with him the burden of this family tragedy. He and his wife continue to live on the farm where the Barber boys grew up near the Wolf River south of New London, Wisconsin.

The Most Precious Blood Catholic Cemetery on the south edge of the town of New London, Wisconsin, proudly displays a commemorative marker honoring the Barber brothers. It is next to the graves of Peter and Gertrude.

THE SUN ROSE CLEAR

The Veterans Service office in the courthouse in Waupaca, Wisconsin, displays the service medals posthumously presented to the Barber brothers. Each received the Purple Heart, the American Defense Medal, the American Campaign Medal, the Asiatic Pacific Campaign Medal, and the World War II Victory Medal, as well as the 50th Anniversary Commemorative Pearl Harbor medal. A document written in honor of each of the Barber boys proclaims:

"He stands in the unbroken line of patriots who have dared to die that freedom might live, and grow, and increase its blessings. Freedom lives, and through it, he lives – in a way that humbles the undertakings of most men."

Franklin Roosevelt,
President of the United States

The story of the Barber brothers is based on fact. Dates, locations, and names are correct. The narrative is the author's depiction of the Barber family, based on recent conversations with the only surviving brother, Robert, and his wife, Judy, at the Barber farm. The Barber farmhouse burned a few years ago and all memorabilia were lost except for what had been donated to the Veterans Service office.

THE SULLIVAN ACT
As told by
Lowell Peterson

On November 13, 1942, five Sullivan Brothers from Waterloo, Iowa, were aboard the light cruiser USS *Juneau* when it was torpedoed by a Japanese Submarine (683 sailors were lost on the USS *Juneau*). Four of the five brothers went down with the ship, and the fifth died at sea after several days in a life raft, the victim of exposure, delirium, and shark attacks.

A congressman proposed a law known as the *Sullivan Act* prohibiting siblings from serving together in battle or at sea. This proposal was never passed into law. In April of 1943, Mrs. Sullivan christened a new ship, the USS *Sullivan*. She proclaimed, "Our boys are back at sea now. Our boys did not die in vain."

THE CAMEO BRACELET
As told by
Peggy Ebben

My name is Peggy Ebben. My mother, Alyce O'Connell Drath and her parents were very good friends with the Barbers. LeRoy Barber was "sweet" on my mother and had written her many letters while stationed on the USS *Oklahoma*. In fact, his Christmas gift to my mother was the only gift, other than the picture for their parents, that the boys were able to mail out before the bombing. It was a cameo bracelet and arrived shortly after he died.

It has been sixty years since that fateful day in Pearl Harbor. Mother recalled that they did not know right away on December 7 if any of the boys were killed. But a short time later when Mr. Barber received the news, he came over to their house to tell my grandparents and my mother that all three of the boys had perished. My mother still cries at the mention of it. It must have been very traumatic for her.

For years mother kept all of LeRoy's letters. Unfortunately, she threw everything away several years ago, except for the cameo bracelet. She still keeps that precious gift in a box in her dresser drawer. Mother said that in one of LeRoy's letters, he mentioned that the Japanese were getting too close for comfort. That fateful day at Pearl Harbor changed the course of my mother's life. She met the man who would be my father sometime after Pearl Harbor. They were married June 24, 1944. My father passed away eleven years ago, and although they had a good marriage, I am sure she always had a spot in her heart for LeRoy.

A few years ago, my mother gave me all of her old photo albums. She said after learning of the Barber boys' fate, she and her mother wrote many photography studios in Hawaii in search of the pictures of the boys in uniform that they mentioned in their letters. I am enclosing an enlarged photo of the three boys in uniform taken in Hawaii.

THE CAMEO BRACELET

Killed in Pearl Harbor attack 12-7-41

TYPHOON: RAIN OF STEEL

CORREGIDOR
As told by
Werner Jensen

The attack on Pearl Harbor occurred on December 7, 1941, but the Philippine Islands are across the International Dateline, so for them the attack occurred on December 8, 1941. Within the next twenty-four hours, the Japanese attacked targets along a three-thousand mile front that included Shanghai, Malaya, Bangkok, Singapore, Guam, Hong Kong, Burma, Java, Sumatra, Borneo, Celebes, Gilbert Islands, Timor, and the Philippine Islands.

I enlisted in the Marine Corps in 1939. I had tried in 1938, but I was only five feet, seven inches tall and they wouldn't let me join the Corps (you had to be five feet, eight inches tall). They said, "You may hear from us. Things are going to change." Well, in March 1939, I got a notice to come back. They lowered the standard to five feet, six inches tall, so I was in. After getting out of boot camp, I was a traffic director for the U.S. Naval Hospital in San Diego.

Suddenly, one evening in September 1939, the Marine Corps told me to have my bags packed and be down at the flagpole at 0800. I was being transferred, and I had no idea where I was going. They didn't tell you. I boarded a transport, the USS *Henderson*, and we traveled up the coast to load supplies in San Francisco. I was so seasick, I could hardly move. The sergeant came around and said, "My God, man, we've got a long way to go and you're already sick!" We left San Francisco and went to Hawaii and then, of course, we hit them all—Midway, Guam, the Philippines, and Shanghai, China.

We disembarked at Tientsin, the port of entry to Peking, which was at one time the location of the emperor's palace. When I arrived there in 1939, the Japanese and Chinese had been fighting for a couple of years already, and the Japanese had pretty well established control of things. The Italian garrison had already left and, of course, the German garrison left before I got there. That was when Hitler was moving into Poland. The only garrisons left were the French and British, and I wasn't there a year when they left.

THE SUN ROSE CLEAR

I had the privilege of walking on the Great Wall, traveled to the Gobi Dessert, and saw the Forbidden City and the Temple of Heaven. What the Chinese couldn't take with them when they retreated, the Japanese stole and took to Japan, so all I saw were the buildings.

By late 1941, I had served two years of duty in China so I figured I was going home. We boarded a transport to leave China and I thought it was kind of odd that everything was painted black. The portholes were black. No smoking on deck, and we moved at night. I thought, "This is just like wartime conditions."

We arrived at the Philippines and disembarked there. They weren't prepared for us, so we were dumped off on the beach. We had to put up field kitchens and tents and sleep on the sand.

On November 28 and 29, the remaining 750 to 800 Marines were evacuated out of Shanghai on the USS *President Harrison* and the USS *President Madison*. A skeleton crew was left to clean up the details. Well, you know what happened to them. They never got out of there. The Japanese either took them prisoners or executed them.

About a week after the Shanghai Marines arrived in the Philippines, we were awakened in the middle of the night and told that the Japanese had bombed Pearl Harbor. I couldn't believe this. I said, "How can this be?" We had been acting as if we were at war for the last six months and we were bivouacked under war conditions. I thought, "How could we be caught so flat-footed?"

On the following day, December 9, 1941, the Philippines were attacked and bombed in strength. The commanding officer of the U.S. Army Air Force at Clark Air Base was afraid of sabotage, so he moved all of his airplanes out in the middle of the air field and bunched them together so they could be guarded. Well, on the first day, the Japanese came in there and wiped the whole works out, with nothing left.

A squad of men and I were evacuated to Southern Luzon to a Navy base, where they kept PBY flying boat observation and rescue planes. I was assigned to guard duty at the Cavite Navy Yard, which was a submarine base. We called the PBYs the flying coffins. They could land on the ocean and pick up survivors and bring them back, but every time they went out and came back, we were one plane short, two short, and in about two weeks none of them came back. There weren't any more. The Japanese had shot them all down.

I spent Christmas Eve 1941 in a foxhole near Manila Bay. The next morning, we boarded a mine sweeper and were on our way to Corregidor, a rocky island at the mouth of Manila Bay. We stayed in Manila Bay all day because the Japanese had planes overhead all the time. We just ran around in circles trying to keep away from them. When night approached, we were able to dock at Corregidor, which we called "The Rock". The Rock had been set up as a beautiful fortification, with all of those big, 16-inch guns pointing out to sea, protecting the harbor. Unfortunately, the enemy was over on the flank, out of the line of fire, and the guns could not be turned. They were useless. The only thing the Marines had to fire at the Japanese positions were mortars. The .155-caliber artillery guns that the Army had on the island had to move every day, because as soon as they'd shoot off a few shots, the Japanese returned fire on their position.

A handful of us, I guess you'd call it a squad, were detached to General Douglas MacArthur as couriers and personal guards. He was up on top of Corregidor, in the old Army barracks at his headquarters. That duty only lasted about five days. Then the Japanese got brave. They dropped a bomb, and it went right down through the barracks and exploded in the basement! General MacArthur said, "I guess it's time to go down to the tunnel." He moved his headquarters into the tunnel and didn't need us anymore, so we were detached to the Marine Corps on Monkey Point, the point toward Cavite Navy Yard where Manila Bay could be accessed. Corregidor is nothing but a gigantic rock with tunnels all over the place where supplies and the hospital were contained. At night we strung barbed wire in the water out in the bay and had to lay low during the day because the Japanese could see all the movement on the island. We noticed we were losing weight and getting awfully hungry. We didn't realize it, but General MacArthur had put us on half-rations: two meals a day and one canteen of water is all we got. It gets pretty hot in the Philippines in summertime, and these meager rations were just not enough to sustain us.

We could see that neither Bataan or Corregidor were going to get any help from anywhere. The "scuttlebutt" (rumors) came around that we were just a bunch of dead fish! They weren't going to relieve us, they weren't going to send us any supplies, and when we lost something, it was gone. There was no replacement. If you lost a man, it was one man less. There was nobody to take his place. This went on for five months.

They were fighting hard at the Bataan Peninsula. The regular Army, the Philippine scouts, and the Philippine Army were able to hold the front lines on Bataan. One of MacArthur's strategic maneuvers had been to bring the troops to Bataan, where he could have a front line that wasn't too long and hold off the Japanese. They did a good job at it.

The last month, when Bataan fell, was the worst. If you took field glasses and looked over at Bataan, you could see the commotion. The Japanese had set up their artillery and started to blast both of us. Bataan fell April 6, 1942, and on May 6, 1942, we fell. That whole month the Japanese shelled us twenty-four hours a day. I think anybody who has been in a war knows what shelling is. It was continuous and never let up. During the day, it was impossible to move. I've seen World War I pictures where they show the no-man's land between the trenches. Well, that's the way "The Rock" looked. There wasn't a leaf. There wasn't a thing there.

Food was a problem while we held off the Japanese. We ate the monkeys, although I didn't care for the monkey soup. We ate the Army mules. We ate the Army horses. We ate anything. I learned to eat lizards. The Filipinos with us knew how to cook and feed us, so at least we got something to eat, but the rations got worse and worse and we went down in weight. We were just a bunch of skeletons.

During the shelling siege, we would go to get something to eat and all of a sudden they'd start shelling, so you'd look for the nearest foxhole you could find and jump in. Well, I happened to jump in one containing a big snake, and I don't like snakes. I pulled my .45 and was going to shoot it. I let off one shot, then I said to myself, "Whoa, you damn fool! You shoot yourself in the foot, you're good for a court-martial for a self-inflicted wound." So I got out of there, even while the shelling was on, and looked for another foxhole. I looked in that one before I got in it.

Finally, "The Rock" surrendered. I was out on Monkey Point, and we were going to push 'em right back in the "drink". This we could handle. But then they would come back again tomorrow or the next day. "Skinny" Wainwright (Lieutenant General Jonathan Wainwright), who was in command after General MacArthur evacuated to Australia, called surrender. There were some problems. The Japanese moved in and took control, but they wouldn't accept the surrender until the large island of Mindanao, which was down south, would also surrender. General Wainwright kept telling them he did not have jurisdiction over the people down there, but the Japanese wouldn't listen. So for about forty-eight hours we sat "on the fence", not knowing if the Japanese were going to push us off a cliff or let us live.

After the capture, things started getting worse. The Japanese moved us from "The Rock" to Manila and paraded us down main street. The transport craft we arrived on didn't want to get too close to shore, so they dropped the ramp down in the front and we had to jump. Well, we jumped into eight to ten feet of water and had to swim to shore. Some of the men couldn't swim, and the Japanese left them there. I was taken to Bilibid Prison, a big prison in the Philippines. It was full of small cells like our top security federal prisons such as Alcatraz. I was fortunate because I didn't have any wounds. Those who were wounded were in big trouble. No medication, no help, no nothing.

Eventually, we were taken to Cabanatuan, which is in central Luzon. The Japanese had three camps up there, Camp I, Camp II, and Camp III. Camp I had the prisoners from Bataan. Of all the prisoners that were on the "Bataan Death March," about 1,700 didn't make it. The "March" was seventy miles long in steaming jungle heat without access to food or water. They dropped by the wayside, and as soon as they faltered, they were bayoneted or shot. The Japanese guards didn't mess around. A lot of prisoners were just jerked right out of their hospital beds and told to march. The Japanese showed no respect for them. The casualties were so high because they weren't fit to march in the first place.

We were moved from Bilibid prison to the prison at Camp II, and I was sent on work details over to Camp I to dig trenches to bury the dead. Men were dying faster than we could dig the holes. It wasn't too nice a job. We took those who had died during the night, retrieved their dog tags, put the bodies in this pit, and covered 'em up. The next day, we'd do the same thing.

We were forced to work on Clark Airfield also. While we were up there busting rocks with sledge hammers for the airstrip, some of the boys tried to escape. The guards caught four. I have no idea if they were really escaping or whether the Japanese just wanted to teach us something. They made us stand out there and watch the escapees dig their own graves and then they executed them right there on the spot. They said, "We'll have no more of this, and from now on, we're going to number you off in tens. If one of you is missing at roll call, the other nine are going to get it." After that, we kind of shaped up a little bit. We didn't think we were so macho anymore.

We were getting thinner and thinner because we were on a rice and soup diet that we weren't accustomed to. It wasn't enough to eat in the first place.

In September 1942, I was called to take a physical, and because I had no wounds and was able to work, I was set aside and put on a transport for Japan. I called it a "hell ship", and that's what it was. The Japanese liked horses, and they still had their cavalry, so they carried their horses around in these transports. They put us down in the hold, but they forgot to clean it out after they took the horses out, so you can imagine the stench. They jammed sixteen hundred of us down in the hold of this ship, and we had to lay down in shifts because there wasn't room for everybody to lay down at the same time. We had a bucket in the middle of the floor to use as a latrine, and if we hollered loud enough, they'd finally let us haul it out. That way you could get on deck once in awhile. I got on deck a couple times.

We were quite concerned about the American submarine outfits. We were leery that they might find us out there, because we were traveling on a Japanese Army transport, with no indication that we were aboard. We made it to Formosa and stayed there for about a week while the Japanese awaited destroyer escort to continue on into Japan.

THE SUN ROSE CLEAR

I have a short diary entry that one of the fellows wrote. In it he wrote:

November 26, 1942.

Our group of 400 arrived at our final destination on this day. For record purposes, we were under the very able leadership of Major William Reardon. When they unloaded the ship, they split us in groups of 400. A total of 46 officers and 354 enlisted men of all branches of the service were in our group.

Upon arrival in Japan, we disembarked at Kobe, boarded a train and went to Osaka, to our living quarters in the center section of a factory. Needless to say, we were very disgruntled, tired, cold, hungry, and hating our present predicament more by the minute. The very military, young, Japanese lieutenant, who later turned out to be our camp commander, kept us out in the cold for three hours. Now, to emphasize this, we had just come out of the tropics and here we were in Japan in the latter part of November. It was cold and we suffered.

We listened to this Japanese lieutenant, and following the speech, there was a class on Japanese commands. We were compelled to learn "forward march," "halt," "eyes right," "salute," and "attention" in Japanese. Freezing in our Philippine dress, we were a dissenting lot and needed lots of coaching and some persuasion at the end of a very determined Japanese bayonet. We then had to swear that we would not attempt to escape. Now, that's ridiculous! Where were we going to go in Japan? We don't look like Japanese. There's no place. In the Philippines, you could escape and get away with it, but not in Japan. But we had to swear allegiance that we weren't going to try to escape and to the best of our abilities we would perform faithful discharge of our duties.

Our new camp had quite a title, which, of course, we were supposed to memorize in about three minutes. It was called "Osaka Prisoner of War Camp, Yotogawa Branch Camp, Osaka, Japan." We called it "Yotogawa Boonsho." Assisting the lieutenant was a young and very personable Japanese sergeant and his name, as nearly as I can translate it, is something like Yoshima Orsowa.

Our quarters were large, very airy, and located in a remote corner of a barrel factory. Comfort during the daylight hours was very difficult, due to the cold. Our bodies couldn't stand this weather on the diet we had been forced to submit to. The interpreter, a half-brain individual, stated that "America shall soon lose the war because of food shortage," maintaining that the rice in the States was being rapidly used up. He told us that soon we would be in more comfortable quarters and they were in the process of being built. We hoped so. The balance of our total strength of 1,600 went in other directions. We all wondered how many of them we would see again.

The treatment was pretty rough. If you didn't do what you were told, they could beat you within an inch of your life, and they didn't hesitate to do it. We were suffering from dysentery, diarrhea, beri-beri, and malaria. This took its toll. By the time we moved from that camp to another camp of the 400, we had lost 167, in spite of the fact that we were supposed to be physically fit. We had been sorted out down in the Philippines because we were in the best condition and would be able to work for the Japanese. The beri-beri was an especially bad one. That's when the feet swell and the skin breaks and it turns into gangrene. We had a navy corpsman there who acted as a doctor, and he would go around and clip the toes off when they rotted. The fellows would sleep at night without blankets covering their feet, even though they were freezing. The rats would come along and eat the toes right off their feet. They wouldn't even feel it.

As a man died, he was put in a coffin. Can you imagine putting a six-foot soldier in a Japanese coffin that is five feet? There was nothing you could do but break his legs and stuff him in there. We had to have guard duty at night. Somebody would have to stay up and sit on the coffin all night or the rats would chew their way right into the coffin.

Another bad experience was during meals. You'd get your bowl of rice, and you'd sit there and nurse it along. You'd shiver but you wanted to get every kernel you could. As soon as a guy got up at the end of the table, there was a rat sitting there taking his place, and the rat kept moving down the line and cleaning up each bowl. The rats were just all over the place.

During the day, those of us who were capable were forced to work in a steel mill in Osaka. This mill was eventually bombed out by the Americans, so we were moved to a new camp in the foothills to work in the nickel mines.

THE SUN ROSE CLEAR

We also were taken down to the harbor to unload ships that were bringing supplies from Korea and China. We would be down in the hold of these large ships, lifting and carrying bags of rice, and we would hear planes overhead. We knew they were American planes that were there to bomb the ships and the harbor, so we would drop everything and run up the ladders to get off the ship. The guards would try to keep us down in the hold of the ship, but we would run right over them and get ashore. It was funny that they didn't shoot all of us. The guards were probably more scared than we were and wanted to get off the ships also. We would sit up on shore and cheer as the planes dove in and bombed the harbor. We were encouraged that the war must be coming to an end, because we could see that these were carrier-based American planes, and therefore our Navy must be close by.

We were not too far away from Hiroshima, but we were totally unaware that the atomic bomb had been dropped.

At war's end, American transports flew over our camp at low level and dropped food supplies. Well, this was like being bombed. There were tin cans flying through the air everywhere and we had to run for cover or get killed. The whole works splattered all over the hillside. The ground was painted every color in the rainbow by peaches, tomatoes, beans, etc. It was quite a sight! The transports finally came back with large parcels of food on parachutes, but it didn't matter, we couldn't eat it anyway. We had been on a rice diet for so long that this food was too rich for us and it made us sick.

We were finally liberated and taken to Tokyo by train, where we were processed, deloused, bathed, and given new uniforms. The U.S. brass fed us a big meal, which I promptly vomited.

Our group of liberated prisoners spent one week on the battleship USS *Indiana*, in Tokyo Harbor, at about the time of the signing of the surrender on the battleship USS *Missouri*. I was then sent home by airplane via Iwo Jima and Guam to the United States.

It was over.

> *Gunnery Sergeant Werner Jensen (see photo in color section) returned to his home town of Waupaca, Wisconsin, after almost three-and-a-half years as a prisoner of war.*
>
> *He was fortunate, unlike many others, to find his high school sweetheart waiting for him upon his return. While he was still in uniform and on active duty, Jensen married Eva Mae Bender and then traveled to the Great Lakes Naval Base in Illinois for his final physical examination prior to discharge, with plans for a honeymoon upon his return. At Great Lakes, he was told, "You're not going home; you've got tuberculosis; you're going directly to a sanitarium at a naval facility in Samson, New York." Sergeant Werner Jensen spent the next nine months on a "honeymoon" alone in New York.*
>
> *Jensen was eventually discharged from the sanitarium and from the Marine Corps*

with a ten percent disability. The U.S. Government, fifty-plus years later, tried to revoke his disability because he was told that he had never cultured positive for tuberculosis bacteria, even though his chest x-ray was abnormal.

Jensen was finally reunited with his new wife and they spent the next 52 years together, until her death. They had two wonderful children, one of whom survives. Jensen worked for more than thirty years as a bookkeeper/accountant.

Failing health in latter years has not daunted Werner Jensen's spirit. His sly, humorous, quick smile rises quickly out of a poker face. The short Marine haircut has been replaced by thick, gray, curly hair. The memories have been softened, but not erased, by the passage of time. Jensen is still barely five feet, seven inches tall, but will always be a very big man in the eyes of his family, friends, and fellow veterans.

THE TB TRAIN
As told by
John H. Steiner, M.D.

In early 1946, I was at the Great Lakes Naval Base awaiting assignment to a military hospital to fulfill my obligation to Uncle Sam. The war was over, and the Navy didn't know what to do with newly-drafted doctors. After a period of inactivity, I was issued orders to report to Seattle, Washington. I arrived there and discovered that I had been assigned to care for troops returning from Japanese POW camps. They were malnourished, barely skin and bones, and were horribly ill with one disease or another. Most had tuberculosis. I, along with another doctor and several corpsmen, were to accompany a trainload of more than one hundred of these men across the country to the tuberculosis sanitarium at Sampson, New York. It was a nightmare caring for these horribly sick young men on such a long trip. En route we lost at least four patients, who hemorrhaged to death from their lungs and drowned in their own blood. The train stopped in Chicago and picked up more tuberculosis-infected troops (including Werner Jensen), who had also returned from POW camps. The whole trip was a sickening experience, one I would never wish to relive.

THE BATTLE OF THE PHILIPPINES
As told by
Numeriano Hollero, M.D.

This story contains graphic descriptions of atrocities. Proceed to the next story if you prefer.

On December 7, 1941, the military defense force of the Philippine archipelago, a democratic protectorate of the United States, consisted of nineteen thousand U.S. Army troops, a few Navy and Marine detachments, twelve thousand Philippine Scouts, and one hundred thousand Philippine Army troops under the command of General Douglas MacArthur.

In May 1937, General MacArthur had noted in an interview by Malcolm Rosholt, reported in the China Press in Shanghai, that "I doubt very much whether any nation on the Pacific has any sinister designs on the Philippines, despite all talk to the contrary." He also stated, "We feel that a Philippines prepared to defend itself will be a stabilizing factor in the Pacific."

Just four-and-one-half years later, the attack on Pearl Harbor changed everything. At the same time that the Hawaiian Islands were being attacked, a Japanese task force was on its way to attack the Philippines. Most of the two hundred U.S. aircraft at Clark Field were destroyed on the ground by Japanese bombers.

In January 1942, the Philippine and American troops withdrew to Bataan and Corregidor to establish a line of defense, but with the Pacific fleet in ruins at Pearl Harbor, there was no hope of supplying reinforcements. Southeast Asia and Malaysia were also rapidly coming under Japanese control and, therefore, General Jonathan Wainwright was placed in command of the Philippine forces as General MacArthur was ordered to withdraw to Australia to build an army for defense of the Southwest Pacific. As MacArthur was secretly evacuating on March 11, 1942, he promised the Philippine people, "I shall return."

With the fall of Bataan on April 8, 1942, and Corregidor on May 7, 1942, the Japanese now controlled Manila Bay and Subic Bay, which they used for staging further advances into Malaysia and the South Pacific. Ten thousand Filipino and United States prisoners-of-war (POWs) died or were slaughtered by the Japanese on the sixty-mile march from Bataan to the confinement camps (The Bataan Death March).

The following story is told by Numeriano Hollero, M.D., who lived through the Japanese occupation of the Philippines.

THE SUN ROSE CLEAR

The island of Panay was occupied by the Japanese on April 16, 1942.

I was six or seven years old when the Japanese occupation began. My father was the mayor of the municipality where we lived, and my uncle was the police chief. We lived on Panay in the city of Iloilo.

Our city had a population of three hundred thousand, and each household was guarded during the occupation by a squad of Japanese. Their officers periodically would come and wake us up and search the houses. They were looking for Philippine flags, American flags, and radios. We often had all three, but my father was very lucky because he was the mayor, and the Japanese officer, a colonel, had known my father before the war. He would say to the soldiers, "I know them," and we would not be searched. Oh my God, we were lucky! Summary execution upon discovery of any of the three articles was the standard order.

The Japanese forced us to go to school. They switched the national anthem to Japanese and they switched "God Bless America" to "God Bless the Japanese." The flag was Filipino and Japanese combined. We had to recite and count in Japanese and, of course, we had to bow. Under Japanese rule, the Philippines had a puppet government. President Jose Laurel was their puppet, with the main Japanese headquarters in Manila.

The men detained by searches or collected at the whim of the Japanese, as well as any boy age fifteen and older, were gathered in a park that was all concrete and forced to lie down. It gets very hot in the Philippines, and you could watch the men who had been detained lying in the heat of the sun. They were given no water, so their children would try to carry water to them, but the Japanese would kick the children, grab the water, and throw it on the concrete, laughing and kicking the detainees while they tried to lick the water off the concrete. It was just terrible. The Japanese would then line up all the people whom they had detained and a truck would come, loaded with Filipino people who were traitors. We called them "fifth columnists" (native Filipinos paid or threatened by the Japanese to work against their own people). If these traitors pointed at somebody, the Japanese would kill that person whether there was reason or not. Throughout this time, you had to watch yourself very carefully, because you never knew which Filipino was a traitor, and if you did not watch what you said, some day you were going to get visitors.

My father thought we should leave the town to avoid the Japanese, so he said, "Let's go into the mountains." So we drove with our car into the mountains, but the Filipino guerrillas stopped us and commandeered our car, and we ended up walking. We stayed in the mountains for a while and then decided to return to our city. The Japanese had increased their control and made everyone go to designated areas and bow to them at their every command. Bowing to them really "bugged" me. The Japanese considered themselves the superior race in Asia. Nobody else counted. Just for forgetting to bow, you could be beaten, put in jail, or killed.

One old man of our city was told to go to a designated area by the Japanese. He said, "I've lived here all my life and I'm not going to go." He never went to the area they designated. The next time we visited our home, this man had been burned at the stake.

A new neighbor, age thirteen or fourteen, befriended me. He was a gambler and would take me to the casinos, even though I was only seven years old. We were barefoot kids, but he would win and I would hold paper bags full of money for him. The two of us would then go and eat in first-class restaurants. My mother caught on to this and said, "You're not going with that kid anymore." The kid started losing, and then he began to steal, even selling his sister's Singer sewing machine, so he could go gambling. His brother-in-law was Japanese, a sergeant assigned to our street and a reputed bad guy. Oh my gosh! This guy brought this kid into the middle of the street and used martial arts on him. I was so afraid that the kid was going to squeal and tell them that I was one of the gamblers and thieves. If there is anything the Japanese hated the most, it was stealing.

When the Japanese first arrived at our city, they lined up many of the young men just because they were males and killed them one after another. They were lined up next to a well and beheaded. My uncle and my fifteen-year-old cousin were in the line. My uncle noted that just before the executioner would strike, he would yell "Hie." My uncle told my cousin that when he says, "Hie," ("Yes", in Japanese) turn your head quickly so he hits your jaw and not your neck. My uncle went first and did just that, not making a sound, and they kicked him into the well, thinking he was dead, but he was still alive. My cousin did the same as my uncle, but he became frightened and began to scream. My uncle whispered at him to "shut-up." At that time, the bodies were really piling up, but the Japanese were able to reach my cousin and bayonetted him while my uncle watched. The Japanese performed this ritual all over the Philippines.

My brother was in the Philippine army, a guerilla officer living in the mountains. We could not have contact with him, but he would come to the city selling tomatoes in a basket so we would know it was him, and he would pass messages to us or talk to us. Throughout the war, my brother and cousins were all guerrillas and actively fighting the Japanese. The Resistance Movement was active. The Japanese were afraid to go out in the "boondocks," so they stayed close to the cities and villages. U.S. submarines would drop by at a pickup point and unload guns and ammunition for the guerrillas, as well as shoes and clothes. One guerilla had never had shoes, so when a fly landed on the toe of his shoe, he tried to shoot it off with his new carbine and shot off half his foot.

THE SUN ROSE CLEAR

For awhile, to avoid the Japanese repressive attacks, we went to another island, but later on we came back to our city. We then went into the mountains, traveling at night, to a farm that we owned way out in the boondocks. My God, we could not see anything; there were no lights, no flashlights. It was pitch black. We were just stumbling all over the rice paddies. We stopped along the way and people would feed us, and then we would go on. The tenant who cared for our farm, built us a house. We were not bothered by the Japanese in this remote area, and it was like paradise, because we also had rice. Our rice is like gold.

Before the U.S. invasion came, the Japanese knew they were "going to get it." Therefore, they rounded up all the women in Manila, including the nuns, raped them, and then lined them up and strafed them with machine guns. Those in the back survived because they dove to the ground right away.

Also, when the Japanese knew the Americans were coming, they tossed kids up in the air and would catch them on their bayonets just for fun. After these atrocities, most of the perpetrators would commit suicide to avoid the inevitable reprisals by the Americans and Filipinos.

We were in the rural area at this time, and we would know when the Japanese were coming because we had bamboo signals. We would all run to the swamp and submerge part of our body under water. You could see everybody doing the rosary. The Japanese never found us.

My uncle, who was in a surgical residency training program, was also secretly helping the guerrillas; my aunt provided anesthesia to his patients. They did their surgical procedures under a mosquito netting. My uncle had a good reputation as a surgeon, so he was called in to operate on an American guerilla advisor who had appendicitis. He did it and saved his life, but the news spread and the Japanese heard about it. They captured my uncle and tied his hands and arms behind his back and above his head for many hours. He had also been a good pianist, but after this experience and the injury to his hands, he could not play the piano or do surgery anymore. The Japanese were going to kill him, but he escaped. Helping an American meant certain death. Later, my uncle became a pediatrician; in his eighties, he and my aunt have celebrated their sixtieth wedding anniversary.

We heard that the Americans were coming, and there were more airplanes overhead daily. There were bombings and dogfights. I would go out in the field on our farm and watch the dogfights like watching a movie, never thinking I could get hit. When we heard that the attack was coming, we were told to get far away from the city, so we walked and walked for a whole day until we were in the mountains near the seashore. One day, I walked down to the seaside port. The Japanese were lining up people on the dock, having them bend over, and chopping their heads off. I watched this about four times, and then my mother saw me and chased me home. At other times, we also saw Japanese pilots lying dead on the beach at low tide with their ears "lopped" off. The Filipinos were getting even.

My first experience with a GI was funny. I could hardly speak English and did not understand it well. The GI wanted me to bring him some drinking water, so he gave me a chocolate Hershey bar. I was about to eat it, but he suddenly grabbed it away from me because there was some white stuff on it. He said, "No, no, no." I was just sick because he threw the candy bar away.

When we got back to our house in the city, our next door neighbor's house had been burned down. We were lucky. We had a big house, and some mango trees had protected our house from the fire. The Japanese had taken all of our library books out next to our house and covered them with gasoline also trying to burn our house down, but the fire did not catch. Our house had been used by the Japanese as a sugar warehouse. The inside of the house was piled high with sugar, and the Japanese tried to burn it to deny the supplies to the Americans. The Japanese also killed all the horses and animals so the Americans could not use them for food. The Japanese martial arts experts who did this then committed suicide because they knew they were doomed.

Eventually, American MPs came in and liberated the Filipino prisoners who had been beaten badly on a daily basis by the Japanese just for practice. Two prisoners bribed the American MPs to hand over one Japanese soldier, and with revenge in mind, nailed him to the floor. Of course, he was writhing in pain, so the two liberated Filipino prisoners said, "Oh, you've got appendicitis" and sliced his belly open.

All of us were looking up to General MacArthur as our savior. All of us. My father and all of my uncles revered him. He was their hero. Before he came back, we knew he was coming. Airplanes were dropping boxes of Chiclets® with his picture on them and the saying, "I shall return." He was like a savior to us. Even after MacArthur was fired by President Truman, the Filipinos would never agree with what President Truman had done.

- *In October 1944, the United States and allied forces returned to the Philippines with air and sea attacks. Admiral Halsey's Third Fleet and Admiral Kincaid's Seventh Fleet destroyed seven hundred Japanese aircraft, three battleships, four carriers, ten cruisers, and nine destroyers. As the Naval forces escorted the U.S. Sixth Army invasion force to the first onshore landing at Leyte Island on October 20, 1944, the U.S. lost three carriers and three destroyers in the Battle of Leyte Gulf. Admiral Oldendorf engaged and stifled the Japanese Southern and Centre Forces in the Battle of Surigao Strait on October 25, 1944, preventing the Japanese Navy from disrupting the Leyte landings. These engagements comprised the greatest and most decisive naval battles of World War II and of all naval history. The Japanese lost 10,500 sailors and airmen in this battle.*

THE SUN ROSE CLEAR

After securing the island of Leyte and the neighboring islands of Mindoso and Samar, the U.S. Sixth Army moved on to invade Luzon, the island location of Manila, the Philippine capitol. U.S. troops reached Manila on February 3, 1945. The ground war in the Philippines continued right up until the end of the war on August 15, 1945. Securing the Philippines from the Japanese cost the U.S. Army 146,000 casualties.

When General MacArthur returned to the Philippines in October 1944, he spoke to the country by radio: "People of the Philippines: I have returned! By the grace of Almighty God, our forces stand again on Philippine soil—soil consecrated in the blood of our two peoples. Rally to me!"

Dr. Hollero continues:

After the war, I continued my education and was living on the neighboring island of Negros, about two hours by ferry from Panay. I was frustrated with my professional schooling and did not feel I was learning enough, so I decided to take a test to qualify for study in the U.S. My brother notified me, "You passed," so I said, "I'm going." I sold my share of the land to my sister and left. My education in the Philippines included an Associate Degree in Arts from the University of the Philippines and a Doctor of Medicine with Honors from the University of Santo Tomas. After my arrival in the United States, I did various surgical residencies and a general practice residency in Chicago and Milwaukee before starting a family practice in Iola, Wisconsin, in 1966, which I continue to this day. My brothers and sisters are all still alive in the Philippines and very successful. I visit there at least once a year.

Mabuhay ka, Pilipinas na bayan!
Long live the Philippines!

EARLY PHASE OF THE PACIFIC WAR 1941-42

As told by
Lowell Peterson

Information contained in *Guadalcanal* by Richard B. Frank, Random House Inc., 1990, exquisitely describes the events that occurred during the early phase of the Pacific War.

The devastating destruction dealt to the U.S. Navy at Pearl Harbor on December 7, 1941, led to a new American military strategy in the Pacific. President Roosevelt named Admiral Chester W. Nimitz to the position of commander in chief, Pacific Fleet (CINCPAC), and appointed Admiral Ernest King as commander in chief of naval operations (COMINCH). General Douglas MacArthur was named commander of the Southwest Pacific Area, which included Australia and the Philippines and Admiral Robert Ghormley was appointed commander of the South Pacific Area. Admiral Nimitz remained in complete control of the Northern and Central Pacific Areas. All operational land and water-based aircraft in the South Pacific area were placed under the control of Rear Admiral John S. McCain Sr. (grandfather of Senator John McCain), and all seaborne forces were controlled by Vice Admiral Frank J. Fletcher. A South Pacific Amphibious Landing Force was established and spearheaded by the First Marine Division, commanded by Major General Alexander A. Vandegrift.

On April 18, 1945, a surprise bombing raid over Tokyo by Lieutenant Colonel James Doolittle and sixteen B-25s launched from the aircraft carrier *Hornet* shocked the Japanese military. On May 7 and 8, the Battle of the Coral Sea dealt a heavy blow to the Japanese Navy, but the U.S. losses were also heavy, with the loss of the carrier *Lexington* and sixty-six aircraft. The battle, however, prevented the Japanese from taking Port Moresby on the southern coast of New Guinea and damaged two large Japanese carriers, preventing their participation in the Battle of Midway. The Battle of Midway, although costly to the U.S. in loss of ships and aircraft, was devastating to the Japanese, with the loss of four carriers and 250 aircraft.

At the end of June and into early July 1942, to strengthen their area of control, the Japanese decided to build a series of airfields on several islands including

Guadalcanal. The island of Guadalcanal, ninety miles long and twenty-five miles wide, is a part of the Solomon Islands northeast of New Guinea. The United States countered the Japanese move by giving Guadalcanal top priority, code name "Cactus". The United States quickly built an airfield on the island of Espiritu Santo to stage daily B-17 raids on the unfinished airfield six hundred miles away. All Japanese aircraft on the ground at Guadalcanal were destroyed as the native airfield construction workers disappeared into the jungle.

On July 22, 1942, the ships carrying the amphibious First Marine Division left Wellington, New Zealand, for Guadalcanal; on August 7, 1942, the U.S. Amphibious Force approached Guadalcanal, undetected under the cover of darkness, rain, and a heavy cloud cover. Part of the task force continued north to attack Tulagi. Shortly thereafter, the First Battalion, Fifth Marines, followed shortly by the Third Battalion, landed at "Beach Red". A beachhead was established, and the U.S. Marines began to move inland through the mosquito-infested jungle, also securing the airfield.

The defeat of a United States Navy task force, with the loss of five cruisers and four destroyers in the Battle of Savo Island, by the superior nighttime tactics of a Japanese task force, changed the American strategy overnight. The U.S. Marine infantry battalions ashore were suddenly converted from an offensive operation to a defensive posture, to prevent the loss of Guadalcanal to a Japanese counterattack. The airfield was completed by the Americans on August 18, 1942, and christened "Henderson Field". On September 8, 1942, Major General Kiyotaki Kawaguchi landed at Guadalcanal with the Thirty-Fifth Japanese Infantry Brigade, and marched toward the ridge overlooking the airfield.

The battle for the ridge raged through September 12 and 13, 1942, but the Marine's First Raider Battalion, "Edson's Raiders", repelled three attacks by Kowaguchi. After the last Japanese attack, the Raiders had only three hundred men left, but they held the ridge and the Japanese retreated into the jungle. Colonel Merritt "Red Mike" Edson and his second-in-command both received the Medal of Honor for their heroism. Henderson Field remained under the U.S. flag.

After a successful raid on the Makin Islands, "Carlson's Raiders" of the Second Raider Battalion, commanded by Lieutenant General Evans Carlson, landed at Guadalcanal on November 4, 1942. During this jungle campaign, the charismatic Carlson coined the American slang word "Gung Ho", meaning "working together" in Chinese.

Extensive, almost continuous land, sea, and air battles for control of Guadalcanal continued for the next two months. Sea battles in the area saw the loss of the carrier USS *Hornet*, but the carrier USS *Enterprise* escaped. An all-out decisive battle by November 15 had Admiral Halsey committing his entire force to

EARLY PHASE OF THE PACIFIC WAR 1941-42

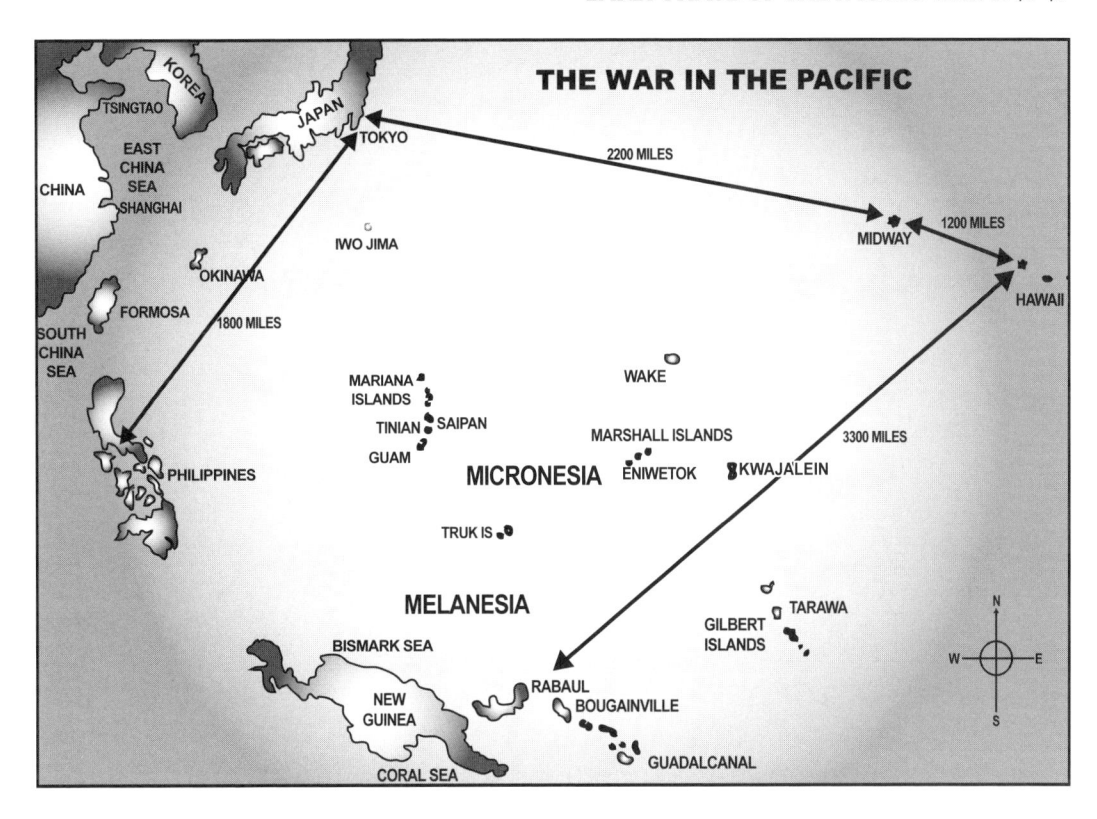

battle. In spite of its superior strength, the Japanese Task Force was defeated, and no counterattack at Guadalcanal was possible.

The Japanese withdrew from Guadalcanal on December 31, 1942. The total casualties for the United States at Guadalcanal were 7,100, and for the Japanese 30,347. The air, land, and sea battle of Guadalcanal inflicted a costly, irreparable setback to the Imperial Japanese Navy and the Imperial Air Force, from which they would never recover.

This narrative is the background for the story that follows.

THE USS *HORNET* AT "IRON BOTTOM SOUND"

As told by
Leonard Duescher

As I look back now, I realize that the legacy of the Hornet *and its men was that it was the ship that held the line in the battle of the South Pacific.*

After I graduated from Aero Industries Technical Institute in Los Angeles, I was employed in the experimental department of Consolidated Aircraft in San Diego, California. The Depression was still a recent memory, so, getting a job of this importance was special—at least my parents and friends back in Wisconsin thought so. On April 14, 1942, I enlisted in the U.S. Naval Reserve as a skilled enlistee who, along with others with special skills, received a rating above that of other recruits. I was rated an AM3c, which is equivalent to a sergeant in the army.

I decided to take an exam to be an aviation cadet and was one of three sailors of six hundred who passed. The three of us were then given a much more thorough physical examination for Officers Candidate School and I found out, to my surprise, that you had to be circumcised to be an officer in the Navy. When I was born in September 1920, the doctor came to our home for delivery of twin boys. He returned later to circumcise us, but I was told that my twin brother cried so much that my father would not let the doctor "hurt" the other twin. I was sent to sick bay to comply with Navy regulations.

I returned to active duty on June 8, 1942, and found that my company had been shipped out, so I was assigned to a "nest unit" to await my orders for Pilot Training School. I was sent to Hawaii on the USS *Betelgeuse* and was told, "Your papers will catch up with you." On the way to Hawaii, I found out that the cargo on board was aviation gas, bombs, and ammunition. The third day out of San Diego, we came under submarine attack, but fortunately the accompanying destroyers sank the Japanese sub. Going to general quarters, assuming our combat duty stations, and preparing for torpedo attack made this a memorable first experience of war at sea.

When we arrived at Pearl Harbor, I was sent to Ford Island, where the Chief announced that he needed volunteers for VT6 at Kaneohe Air Base. I quickly stepped forward and was soon on my way to VT6, a torpedo squadron stationed at Kaneohe. I thought I had it made, until I found out that we were at a Carrier Air Service Unit (CASU), which regrouped air squadrons for aircraft carriers after battle duty at sea. I was a replacement for battle losses from the Battle of Midway. I started to realize that what I was told by sailors in San Diego was true: "You should avoid volunteering for anything."

After the Pearl Harbor attack, the beautiful sand beaches of Oahu were now filled with barbed wire, and swimming was only allowed in a creek emptying into the ocean. After a farewell luau by the river with lots of beer, we returned to reality and made preparations to go aboard the aircraft carrier USS *Hornet*, which was freshly refurbished following the battle of Midway.

I was assigned to supervise a group of sailors handing canned goods down from the hanger deck as we helped provision the ship. Some cases broke open, and contents filled with fruit and fruit juices were salvaged and hidden. I was told, "Before the cruise is over, you will be eating the food hidden by the sailors." I recall vividly about two months later, when the ship's stores were empty, we retrieved the hidden cans and secretly ate the contents. This was a real treat compared to regular chow, which by now was mincemeat pie, beans, and green, dehydrated, scrambled eggs.

When we sailed out of Pearl Harbor in the middle of August 1942, we were in full blue dress wool uniforms, although the temperature was about eighty degrees. This was done to indicate to anybody watching that we were going north. The carrier USS *Hornet* proceeded on its mission as part of Task Force 17. Two days out of Pearl Harbor, the loudspeakers announced, "We are on a mission of war to the South Pacific," and shortly thereafter other ships joined Task Force 17, as we headed for Guadalcanal and Tulagi. The Air Group assembled twenty F4F fighter aircraft that had been loaded and stored in gallery spaces under the superstructure supporting the flight deck. Each bay of the gallery could hold one disassembled aircraft.

On the thirty-first of August, the aircraft carrier USS *Saratoga*, was hit by several torpedoes and had to return to Pearl Harbor. The *Hornet* was now alone, the only operational carrier in the South Pacific. Nonflying members of VT6, like myself, had air duty fourteen hours every day, repairing the planes and keeping the torpedo bombers airworthy. My job was as a metal worker. One day, I found out I was on the list to fly a scouting mission. While we were airborne, the *Hornet* had to change course because of submarines, which made our pilot search for the ship on our way back. After some time, he said over the intercom, "If we can't find the ship soon, we will have to sit down on this island," as he pointed to a small island.

Needless to say, I was happy when we spotted the *Hornet* and landed safely.

In early September, one of the VT6s returning planes sighted a sub near the *Hornet*. The pilot warned the *Hornet* and did some fancy flying, opening his bomb bay doors and dropping a depth charge near the sub, which had already fired several torpedoes at the *Hornet*. From the deck we could see the torpedo wakes in the water as they narrowly missed the *Hornet*. The talk aboard ship listed the number of torpedo misses at over fifty since we had arrived in the combat zone.

Everyone aboard was happy when the battleship USS *North Carolina* joined Task Force 17, because she had a lot of antiaircraft fire power. The carrier USS *Wasp* and her escorts joined Task Force 17 about September 13, 1942.

On a very warm and humid day, AM1c John Bullock and I were working on one of the TBF torpedo bombers, when we decided to get some fresh air. We walked to the Port Quarter and were leaning on the rail looking at the *North Carolina* when there was a tremendous explosion. We saw the screening destroyer, the USS *O'Brien* aft of the *North Carolina* take a torpedo meant for the *Hornet*. The torpedo blew the bow section completely off the destroyer. A geyser of water and smoke rose several hundred feet in the air off the port side, as the destroyer seemed to disappear. The battleship *North Carolina* took a second torpedo meant for the *Hornet* near midship on the port side. The torpedo would have hit right below where we were standing. The destroyer and battleship were positioned to protect the carrier from torpedo attack. The men on the starboard side of the *Hornet* yelled, "The *Wasp* is hit."

Bullock, who had been on the USS *Panay* when it was sunk on the Yangtze River in China and on the aircraft carrier USS *Lexington* when it was sunk in the Battle of the Coral Sea, became very alarmed as we watched, stunned by what was happening. We saw the carrier *Wasp* disintegrate as the gasoline, bombs, and torpedoes on the flight and hanger decks exploded sending parts of the flight deck high in the air. I was later told that the *Wasp* was fueling and arming its planes at the time. The damaged *North Carolina* moved in close to protect the *Hornet*, the only remaining battle-ready carrier in the Pacific. We were alone against the enemy who had six battle-ready carriers in operation. It was at this time that we became known as "the ship that held the line". The date was September 15, 1942. At that moment I realized that I was in the very center of the war in the Pacific. The destroyer USS *O'Brien* that had protected the *Hornet* sank as the result of its battle damage while attempting to return to the U.S. for repair.

We were low on supplies and the food continued to be mincemeat pie, green eggs, and beans, along with bread and dumplings from beetle-infested flour. In October 1942, we headed for Noumea, New Caledonia. We were in harbor for less than a week, taking on whatever supplies were available when we got word that the Japanese were on the move. The *Hornet* departed Noumea early.

The flight deck of the *Hornet* was painted a deep blue for the attack of April 18, 1942, when Lieutenant Colonel Jimmy Doolittle and the B-25 bomber crews embarked on the retaliatory bombing raid of Tokyo in response to the Pearl Harbor attacks. This was because the color of the North Pacific was deep blue, making the ship harder for the enemy to identify from the air. The Japanese knew that the *Hornet* was also responsible for the numerous attacks on them in the Solomon Islands, and they were determined to get "Blue Base" (the *Hornet*) at any cost.

We again sailed to the area known as "Iron Bottom Sound" off Guadalcanal. The area was christened with this name because of the many Japanese, American, and allied ships and airplanes sunk there. The weather turned ominous with dark clouds, so Admiral Murray ordered the *Hornet*, the heavy cruisers *Northampton* and *Pensacola*, as well as the antiaircraft cruisers *Juneau* and *San Diego* to proceed north to attack the Japanese bases at Bougainville, Rabaul, and Rekata Bay, leaving the destroyers and slower ships behind. We raced north at thirty knots and early the next morning, attacked these bases, interfering with the troops assembling to reinforce the Japanese garrison on Guadalcanal. When our planes returned, the *Hornet* was already heading back toward Guadalcanal to defend Henderson Field from the expected Japanese attacks.

During the early weeks of October, the *Hornet*'s F4F fighters shot down a number of large Japanese four-engine seaplanes. These planes were equipped with internal fuel tanks to increase their flying range, and they would explode when hit. There never were any survivors. I was told that the *Hornet* captain would at times give false headings in a misleading direction by radio to other ships and would then order the F4s flying air cover to attack the Japanese planes lured into the trap.

On the *Hornet*'s one-year birthday, October 20, 1942, the galley cooks surprised everyone by making a birthday cake and serving chicken, turkey, and dehydrated potatoes. AM1c Bullock and I decided that we would go to the last chow call, relax, and enjoy the meal. We sat down to enjoy the best food in weeks, but were soon interrupted by a combat alert with bells, sirens, and loudspeakers proclaiming the sounding of "General Quarters". We had to leave our food and rush to our battle stations. The food was dumped, as the mess hall became an ammunition handling area. The radar had picked up unidentified aircraft, but it was a false alarm. The planes were later determined to be some of General MacArthur's B17s on a bombing run.

On October 23, we were being refueled by a tanker along our starboard side as lines were sent over and hoses were connected to take on aviation gas, fuel for the boilers, etc. At the same time, either a cruiser or destroyer would pull along our port side and take fuel from us. I was told to send one hundred, one-hundred pound bombs to the tanker. I had about ten sailors doing the loading, and late in the process the word was passed, "Prepare to cast off in fifteen minutes." One of the sailors said to me, "When are you going to send the fuses over?" I thought the bombs were already fused. So the next load to the tanker was the crates containing fuses. My lack of training in the use of weaponry was apparent.

During the bomb offloading, a yeoman of VT6 came with orders for me to return to the States for pilot training. Some of the VT6 men said that I should wait for the next tanker, as it was a new one that would return directly to the States. I knew this rusty old tanker, after breaking from us, was headed for Guadalcanal, where it would unload aviation gas, bombs, and other supplies, with a good chance of being sunk on the way in or out. I decided to wait for the new tanker, which would meet the *Hornet* in about a week. With the fueling over, we were on our way back to Iron Bottom Sound.

On the twenty-fourth day of October, Task Force 16 was joined by the carrier USS *Enterprise* and the new battleship USS *South Dakota*, with even more fire power than the departed *North Carolina*. This was a very welcome addition. We were advised that the combined Task Forces 16 and 17 would now be known as Task Force 61.

On Sunday, the twenty-fifth of October 1942, I attended church services on the hanger deck. We must have been at general quarters at the time, as later on the hospital ship USS *Solace*, I found the church bulletin folded in one of my lifejacket pockets. I still have that bulletin. Wearing a lifejacket when the temperature is eighty degrees is like wearing a fur coat to a Fourth of July picnic. The *Hornet* and the other ships stayed at general quarters through the night because we were planning to attack the much larger Japanese task force on Monday morning, October 26, 1942.

Then came the last day of the aircraft carrier *Hornet*: Monday, October 26, 1942. The two carriers, *Hornet* and *Enterprise*, had about 170 planes against the Japanese 500 planes. The Japanese also had land-based bombers available nearby. As soon as our scout planes reported finding the enemy task force, the *Hornet's* air group was ordered to take off. After our planes had departed, Bullock and I went forward to the bow to look for a safe place for the expected counterattack. Suddenly it was announced, "Enemy aircraft twenty-seven miles out and approaching." We knew they were probably flying at about 180 mph, or were nine minutes away, but as we started walking at a fast pace toward the bow of the ship, our antiaircraft guns started firing. The announcement had been late. Bullock yelled above the noise, "Hit the deck!"

THE USS HORNET AT "IRON BOTTOM SOUND"

Oct 25, 1942
Day before we were sunk

Divine Service

Sunday Sunday 25, 1942.

CHURCH CALL...Bugler

CALL TO WORSHIP...............(Cong. Stand).....Chaplain

OPENING HYMN...86 Onward Christian Soldiers.

LORD'S PRAYER...(Remain standing... Chaplain and Cong.

RESPONSIVE READING..Sel. 31 "The Fear of the Lord".

SCRIPTURE LESSON

GLORIA PATRI..Page 8 in Hymnal..(Cong. Stand.)

APOSTLES CREED. Page 8 in Hymnal.(Chaplain and Congregation)

    Chaplain....O Lord, show thy mercy upon us.

    Cong........ AND GRANT US THY SALVATION.

    Chaplain....O God, make clean our hearts within us.

    Cong........AND TAKE NOT THY HOLY SPIRIT FROM US.

MORNING PRAYERS..(Cong. seated and bow in prayer.

HYMN...116 'Jesus, Lover of my soul.'

SERMON..."Warm Middle Ground".

CLOSING HYMN..1st verse of Hymn... 'Eternal Father'.

BENEDICTION......................................Chaplain.

* * * * * * * * * * * *

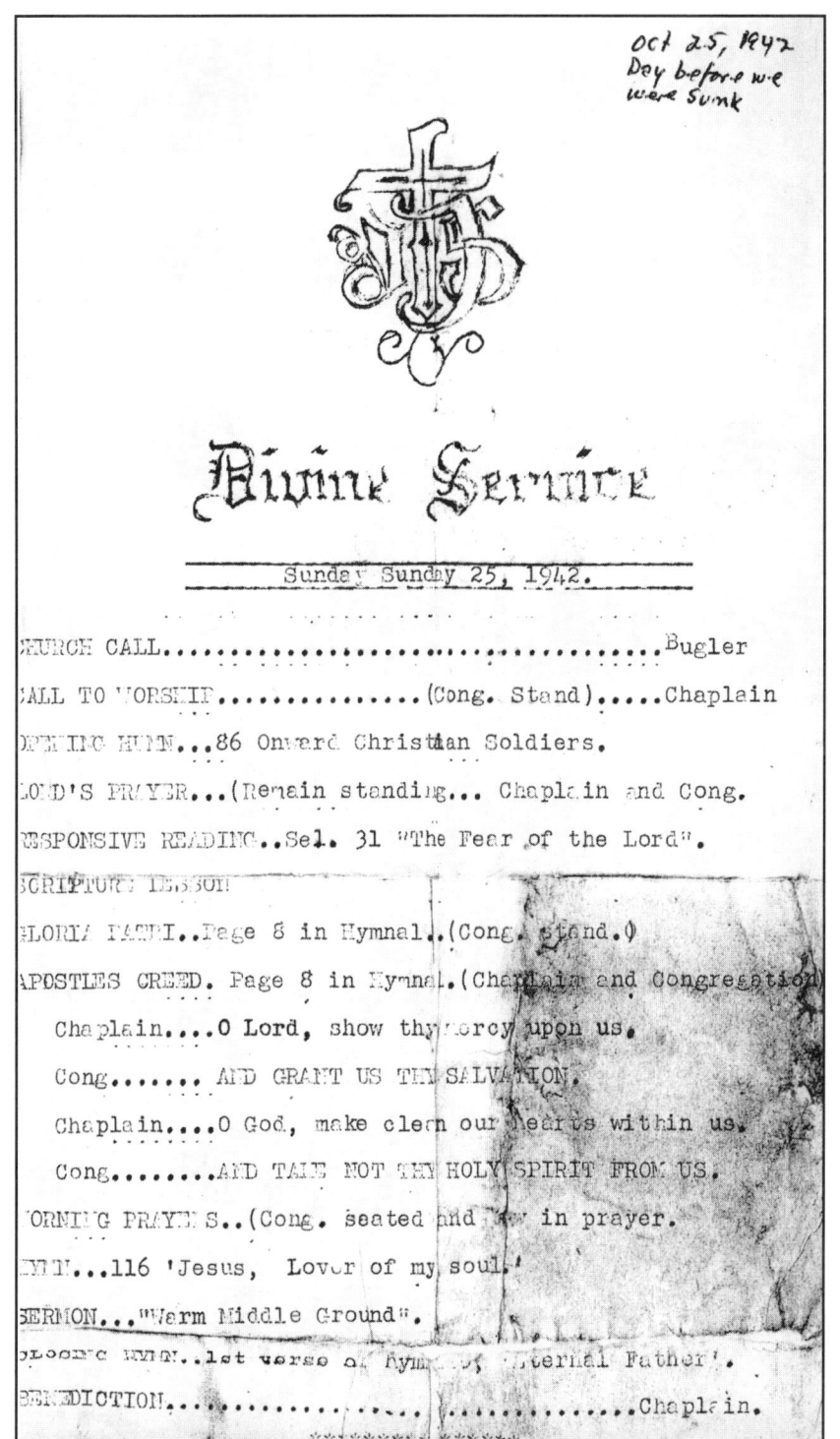

The church bulletin from the Sunday, October 25, 1942, church services on the hanger deck of the USS Hornet during general quarters. Leonard Duescher found the bulletin in his life jacket pocket after transfer to the USS Solace hospital ship.

THE SUN ROSE CLEAR

Shortly there was a bomb hit and explosion forward and a second five-hundred pound unexploded bomb landed in one of the ready rooms, which was an air-conditioned room with leather chairs used for briefings of the squadron aircrews. Some of our crew carefully rolled the unexploded bomb to a nearby passageway and braced it so it could not roll around and explode. Within a very short time, the *Hornet* received five other hits. Two of these were also five-hundred pound bombs. One penetrated to the fourth deck down; the other hit aft of the island, killing thirty Marines who had been manning pompom guns, as well as killing several sailors who were on the starboard aft flight deck. The bomb also penetrated just far enough through the flight deck to kill several sailors on the hanger deck below. Shrapnel from this bomb also cut the cables holding a spare SBD dive bomber stored overhead, which crashed to the hanger deck about twenty feet in front of us.

Seaman Stone, who was responsible for fueling our TBFs and securing the gas line when under attack, was flash blinded by this bomb. Bullock and I were hit with shrapnel and falling debris. Shrapnel from the bomb entered my right leg and knee joint, so that I couldn't walk. Over the noise, I could hear Bullock, only inches away, say, "Are you hit?" and I replied, "I am." He said he had been hit in the chest. The ragged edges of the shrapnel, as it passed through the kapok lifejacket into his chest, picked up a small handful of the fiber, which also entered his chest, stopping just short of his heart. The kapok fibers saved his life. Earlier, when we went to general quarters, he had complained that someone had stolen his "Mae West" inflatable life jacket, which was cooler to wear and still met the requirements of general quarters. He now had a bulge in his chest, but thanks to the thief, he was still alive.

Also hit by the exploding bomb and fire was a sailor we called, "Dagwood". He was married and the father of two children and, whenever we went to general quarters on the *Hornet*, he always put on his flash clothing and a steel helmet, and carried his gas mask. He loved his family. He was perhaps eighty feet aft of us when we came under attack, and the shrapnel from the same bomb that hit us also hit him just below his steel helmet, killing him instantly.

Shortly after that the hanger deck heaved up as two torpedoes hit the starboard side in the engine room area just aft of the island. The hanger deck now buckled and bulged several feet in many areas. The ship immediately took a fifteen-degree or more list to starboard. Bullock became alarmed that we were about to capsize and told me to get some rope to tie our lifejacket bottoms securely between our legs to prevent neck injuries when we jumped into the water. All power had been knocked out, so the word was passed person to person to abandon ship. The list of the *Hornet* continued to increase, but then slowly the ship started righting itself as engineers flooded compartments on the port side. A second order was passed canceling the abandon ship order. Many sailors in heavily damaged areas and areas on fire had already jumped into the water. Some life rafts had been cut free and were in the water along with a lot of debris.

The cruiser USS *Northampton* attempted to take the *Hornet* in tow. The heavy steel cable had just been secured when another attack occurred. This required cutting the line, so the *Northampton* could maneuver and defend itself. The *Hornet*, dead in the water, unable to maneuver, was hit by another torpedo. From bow to stern, the damage to the ship was extensive. Bullock and I were taken to an area of the hanger deck near the metal shop, which now was serving as a first aid area because the hospital area on the ship had suffered a bomb hit and was unusable. Bandaged, we now lay among a number of other wounded sailors. We were told that all wounded would be taken off the carrier. We were no longer needed aboard the *Hornet* and, secondly, the sharks would be attracted by blood in the water.

A destroyer, the USS *Russell*, came along the port side aft. A rope net was put over the side of the *Hornet*, and the wounded were lowered to the deck of the destroyer. The sea had a six-foot swell, which made the transfer difficult, plus the destroyer kept rolling into the side of the *Hornet* and the flying bridge was damaged. The levers used to release depth charges were hit, releasing a large depth charge. Sailors were screaming. The captain over the loud speaker system on the *Russell* said simply, "SILENCE," and everyone was quiet. I had never heard that order before, but I understood. The captain then said that the depth charges had been secured and the fuses were on safe. Bullock said, "We're going to be okay."

An event occurred on the destroyer *Russell* that still haunts me to this day. The destroyer had stopped to pick up sailors in the water, when we came under another air attack. The horn sounded general quarters as the ship got underway. As our speed increased, the sailors who were still in the water hanging on ropes, crying for help and trying to get aboard, had to let go. The help they wanted could not come. When the air attack was over, the destroyer returned to the sailors in the water and took aboard those few who remained alive. Meanwhile, during the attack, many had drowned or been killed by sharks. Other destroyers also picked up survivors. The *Russell* circled the *Hornet* for the last time looking for any survivors and found none. I could see where the torpedoes had hit the *Hornet* on the starboard side. One hole appeared large enough to drive a train through. The *Hornet* capsized in Iron Bottom Sound shortly after the *Russell* left the area.

The destroyer was now so overloaded with men that it was actually low in the water. The wounded were put in the bunks of the crew, and others were put below deck to conceal their presence in case of another air attack. Some men died during the night, among those some of the wounded marines from the *Hornet*. The ships formed a circle for burial. The sailors were buried at sea, committed to the deep, in accordance with Navy practice, and the marines were also buried as the "Marine Hymn" was played at a fast tempo. There were no dry eyes. I knew that I could easily have been among their numbers.

I was placed on a stretcher with a wire cover so I could not fall out and hauled by lines between ships to the cruiser USS *Northampton*. A chief pharmacist mate met me and took charge of my medical needs and dressed my wounds. The loudspeaker system on the *Northampton* was playing the song "Intermezzo," from the movie by that name. It is one of my favorites. I asked the chief if they would play it again. It is a beautiful, calming piece of music.

A few days later in the harbor at Noumea, New Caledonia, I was transferred from the *Northampton* to the hospital ship USS *Solace*, which was filled with survivors from the aircraft carrier *Wasp*, many of whom were serious burn cases. I was told I had two choices. I could stay aboard and end up in Australia or, as an ambulatory case, I could board the S.S. *Lurilene*, a peacetime passenger ship converted to a troop transport, and return to the States. Bullock, Stone, and I chose going to the States. We received a sterile tweezers to remove the kapock from Bullock's chest. We were told, "When you get to the shrapnel, call for a doctor, who will remove it." When we located the shrapnel, we called for a doctor and he removed the piece and gave it to Bullock as a souvenir. A mess attendant came each day with a quart of water per man. Seeing the wounds of Stone and Bullock, he felt sorry for us and each day we got an extra quart of water. As many as a thousand wounded and sick marines from Guadalcanal were also on board. One day when we went to chow, one of the civilian mess people growled at Stone when he did not take the food tray. I was behind Stone and Bullock was in front of him to guide him. I said, "Stone is blind," and the mess attendant then apologized and said, "Take him to a table." He served us there at every meal from then on until we arrived in the States.

As the *Lurilene* approached San Diego, we were met and escorted into port by destroyers. I sat and recalled and recorded all that had happened to me. I realized that I had been on five different ships without ever setting foot on dry land. The ships were the *Hornet, Russell, Northampton, Solace,* and the *Lurilene*. This had all happened in a five-month period of time.

I was allowed liberty to go to downtown San Diego. I made some long distance calls for other sailors who were unable to and then called my parents collect because I had only one dollar left. I was well acquainted in San Diego and had decided to go to the U.S. Grant Hotel for a drink. There, I ran into three of my buddies from VT6. They, like many others, had become separated in the water and were picked up by different ships. They were happy to see that another sailor from VT6 had made it safely home. As drinks were twenty-five cents each, I ordered them a drink with my last invasion currency dollar. Our dollars were stamped with the word Hawaii, just in case the Japanese invaded. These dollars could then be declared invalid and void.

I was then ordered to go to Seattle and reported to the hospital there in January 1943. I received an Honorable Discharge from the Navy hospital on April 3, 1943, about a year after I had enlisted. The chief pharmacist that handed me my discharge said, "Do you remember me?" I said, "No," and he then asked if I was the sailor who came aboard the *Northampton* and requested that they play the song "Intermezzo" again. I said, "Yes," and he replied that they wore the record out in the few days it took to get to the hospital ship *Solace*. He also said the *Northampton* was sunk about two weeks later. She also went down in Iron Bottom Sound.

I was told later that on October 26, 1942, our Task Force had shot down 179 Japanese planes piloted by battle-experienced Japanese pilots who had been flying in the war against China. The Japanese were unable to replace these losses with skilled pilots, which became evident later in the war at a battle near Saipan, called "the Mariana's turkey shoot", when American pilots shot down 426 Japanese aircraft in two days. As I look back now, I realize that the legacy of the *Hornet* and its men was that it was the ship that held the line in the battle of the South Pacific.

When I left the Navy hospital, I returned to Wisconsin and worked in the Machickanee forest fire tower. This gave me an opportunity to think. My father had been sheriff of Oconto County and, because of my firsthand knowledge of law enforcement, I wrote an exam for State of Wisconsin beverage and cigarette tax investigator and was ranked number one for the position. I worked in state law enforcement for about thirty-two years, the latter years working as a special agent for the Governor's Office, the Attorney General, and the Department of Justice. I moved to Waupaca, Wisconsin, in 1965.

On May 30, 2000, Senator Russell Feingold presented me with the Purple Heart at the Wisconsin Veterans Home at King, Wisconsin. I received the World War II Victory Medal, the American Campaign Medal, and the Asiatic Pacific Campaign Medal in October 2000. The Navy and the country were busy fighting a difficult war in 1942 and 1943, and it never bothered me that they had not awarded the medals at that time. When I think about this now, I feel lucky to have had fifty-eight good years since WWII, even without the medals.

STORM CLOUDS IN ASIA

CHINESE - JAPANESE RELATIONS 1850-1945

As told by
Lowell Peterson

World War II in Asia can be better understood from a historical perspective on the basis of the following information. It provides the foundation for the story that follows.

The superior, "colonial master" attitude of the European imperialists of the early nineteenth century forced Asians into the humiliating position of sociopolitical inferiority. Western ideas were perceived to be a menacing threat to their honored ancient Asian cultures, but at the same time, the trade and industrial advancements of the West were envied and desired.

In the latter half of the nineteenth century, Japan's ports were opened to trade, a marked westernization occurred, feudalism was abolished, nationalism flourished, and a decline of the Buddhist religion occurred. The Tokugawa Shogun period (1603-1867) ended in Japan, the Shogun was deposed, and the Meiji era (1868-1912) began with restoration of the Emperor to the throne. Shintoism, a secular "religion" taught that the Emperor was the son of heaven and also "Bushido", the way of the warrior, now permeated the national consciousness. Honor and unwavering loyalty were inviolate.

In the Russo-Japanese War of 1904, Japan took control of Korea and conquered half of Manchuria, giving the Japanese an influential foothold on the Asian mainland. The rest of Asia, especially China, realized that Japan, having defeated an Eastern European power, Russia, was now an imperialistic country similar to the European nations.

At the Paris Peace Conference following WWI in January 1919, Japan received rights to the German concessions in China and the German controlled islands of the north Pacific. At the conference, China tried to eliminate all foreign concessions within its territory and abolish all foreign extraterritorial claims, but received no assistance or support. The Chinese walked out of the conference.

THE SUN ROSE CLEAR

Japan had developed a stable infrastructure in the last half of the nineteenth century and advanced rapidly in science and technology, while designing its strong army similar to Prussia's and its navy like Great Britain's. In contrast to Japan's political consolidation and economic growth, China underwent a revolution.

In 1912, Sun Yat-sen overthrew the two hundred-fifty-year-old Manchu Dynasty and proclaimed a new Chinese Republic, with its capitol at Canton. Sun believed in a benevolent dictatorship and government by "the able" rather than a Western-style representative democracy. After the 1917 Communist revolution in Russia, Sun strengthened his revolutionary government in South China with the help of Russian Communists, establishing a coalition with the Chinese Communists as well.

Sun Yat-sen died in 1925 after two terms as leader of the revolutionary Kuomintang party, and control passed to his brother-in-law, Generalissimo Chiang Kai-shek. After securing and stabilizing his control in the south, Chiang launched a northern military expedition on July 9, 1926, conquering and securing Changsha, Nanchang, Nanking, and Shanghai from warlord control. The Kuomintang moved its government headquarters to Nanking, but unfortunately, the party split internally into a right-wing nationalist group and a left-wing communist group. The Generalissimo dealt with this by expelling left-wing members, thus eliminating dependence on Russia and allowing him to ally with the West. The Communists reorganized and established their capitol at Hankow in the north of China.

In 1931, Japan, which had maintained a presence in southern Manchuria since the Russo-Japanese War, now with increasingly militaristic leaders, seized Chinese Manchurian arsenals at Mukden in retribution for what they called "Chinese economic warfare" and in 1932, without provocation, the Japanese landed seventy thousand soldiers in Manchuria in an act of open aggression seizing all of Manchuria and much of northern China. The Chinese sought help from the League of Nations, but the League failed to act. In February 1932, the Japanese proclaimed the independence of Manchuria, which they renamed Manchukuo, and staged a well-publicized coronation of a puppet governor, "The Last Emperor", Pu-yi, naming him the successor to the Manchu Dynasty.

Erh Ch'i (the double seventh: the seventh day of the seventh month), July 7, 1937, was chosen by Japan for the full-scale invasion of China. The Japanese army that had landed in Manchuria now marched in force across the Marco Polo Bridge near Peiping, with plans to conquer China in a matter of months, against expected very weak resistance. However, the Chinese warlords, Chinese Communists, and Chiang Kai-shek's Nationalist army joined to resist the Japanese attack.

In the first year, Shanghai and Nanking fell to Japan, forcing Chiang to move the government to Hankow. On the day known as "Bloody Saturday", August 14,

CHINESE - JAPANESE RELATIONS 1850-1945

Nationalist Chinese Chairman, Generallisimo Chiang-Kai-shek and General Claire Chennault. (Photo from the personal collection of Malcolm Rosholt.)

1937, thousands of Shanghai Chinese were killed. Canton and Hankow fell to Japan, forcing Chiang-Kai-shek to move his government a thousand miles to Chungking, while the Communists established their capitol at Yenan. In the next seven years, 20 million Chinese civilians and military personnel would die as a result of the war, while another 50 million became refugees.

The U.S. Air Force effort early in the war in China was surreptitiously under the control of the Tenth Air Force headquarters in India, but was composed of volunteer mercenaries, the American Volunteer Group (A.V.G.). This unit was replaced by the China Air Task Force (C.A.T.F.) on July 5, 1942, which was deactivated March 9, 1943. On the fifteenth of March 1943, the Fourteenth Air Force was created from the C.A.T.F., separating it from the Tenth Air Force in India and Burma. The Fourteenth Air Force was placed in the capable hands of Major General Claire Lee Chennault. Chennault flew no missions in China because of his age, but he commanded his squadrons as a tight ship, and had the unwavering respect of his men. They became known as "The Flying Tigers", a name originating from a story in a Chinese newspaper. The main airfield for supply of the

THE SUN ROSE CLEAR

Fourteenth Air Force was near Kunming and the forward tactical base was at Kweilin. The Flying Tigers of the Fourteenth Air Force flew P-40s and P-51s, but the lack of fuel, parts, and good maintenance often kept the planes grounded. To support the combat effort with fuel and supplies, the C-46 and C-47 cargo planes and B-24s flew the dangerous trip across "The Hump" from India.

The Japanese army, one hundred thousand strong, fought south from Changsha, past Hengyang, toward Canton, and then diverted southwest toward Kweilin, the capitol of Kwangsi Province. The Japanese conquered Changsha on June 10, 1944, and Hengyang airfield on June 26, but the Chinese Tenth Army resisted further advancement until August 8, 1944. The Japanese then moved forward, taking Kweilin and Linchow in November 1944. The Americans and

A successful group of fighter pilots of the "Flying Tigers" with a P-40 "Shark" fighter plane. (Photo from the personal collection of Malcolm Rosholt.)

Chinese workers pulling a concrete roller to pack down the crushed rocks on the airfield runways. (Photo from the personal collection of Malcolm Rosholt.)

Chinese at the air base at Kweilin were evacuated and as they left, the Chinese destroyed runways and hundreds of buildings, thus denying their use to the Japanese. The retreating Chinese army and its U.S. Airforce support group moved south to bases at the rear.

The starving, ill-equipped Chinese army and the Chinese people, in spite of being isolated by blockade, and facing overwhelming odds, had resisted the enemy. The Chinese army knew how to strategically retreat. The will to survive had not faltered. The Japanese army had failed in its attempt to win a quick, decisive victory in China, and failed to win the ultimate victory over a determined people. China never surrendered to Japan. The eight-year struggle ended with the unconditional surrender of Japan to allied forces in September 1945.

THE SUN ROSE CLEAR

Chinese lady, with baby on her back, carrying baskets of rocks used to build runways for American pilots. The rocks were crushed by women with hammers. (Photo from the personal collection of Malcolm Rosholt.)

CHINA SERVICE
As told by
Malcolm Rosholt

"Malcolm Rosholt personifies the spirit of the Flying Tigers. He is a recognized authority on China's war of resistance against Japan and on WWII, as well as on the history of aviation in China. His fluency in the Chinese language made him uniquely qualified to serve as liaison officer attached to the Chinese War Headquarters in South China, and coordinator for the Air Raid Warning and Rescue System, in Japanese dominated areas of the China mainland."

Wayne G. Johnson, Past President Flying Tigers
Flying Tigers of the 14th Airforce Association
50th Anniversary Issue, Vol. 4. 10 March 97

THE SUN ROSE CLEAR

In 1928, I had visited China and Japan on a student tour conducted by Upton Close. I returned to China in 1931 and worked as a journalist until 1937. My wife, Marge, my one-year-old daughter, Mei-fei, and I left China because of the Japanese hostilities that were intensifying around Shanghai.

On December 7, 1941, I was sitting eating spaghetti and meatballs in a basement apartment in New York City with a fellow writer, Ron Hubbard, who, many years later, would found the *Church of Scientology*, and a pulp fiction writer, Arthur Burks, when the announcement came on NBC that Japanese carrier based torpedo bombers had attacked Pearl Harbor. Ron and Arthur were reserve officers in the Navy and Marines, respectively, and left immediately to report for duty. I returned to San Francisco to organize a bureau of information and commentary for the *Chinese News Service*. In August 1942, I decided to apply for a commission in the Army Air Force and was accepted with the rank of First Lieutenant. Basic training in Miami Beach was followed by combat intelligence school in Harrisburg, Pennsylvania, and three months at Camp Savage language school, south of Minneapolis, to study the Japanese language. In September 1942, due in part to my command of the Japanese and Chinese languages learned from tutors, and also because of my familiarity with the Asian culture, which I had nurtured as a journalist in Shanghai with the *China Press* from 1931 to 1937, I was held in rather high regard by my superior officers.

My first assignment was to the Seventh Air Force at Hickham Field, in Hawaii. There were a dozen officers qualified for overseas intelligence duty, but I boldly asked my colonel for orders, stating, "I think I belong in China." He agreed. I sailed for the Far East from San Diego across the South Pacific to New Zealand, and from there to Perth on the West Coast of Australia, before proceeding through the Indian Ocean to Bombay, India. I was then posted to Karachi, India (now Pakistan), before flying across India to Assam. I crossed the Burmese mountains, commonly called "The Hump", to Kunming, China, in the nose of a B-24 and witnessed an awesome, never-to-be-forgotten, view of the Himalayan Mountains before turning southwest and crossing into Yunnan (south of the clouds) Province, landing at Chengkung, about seven miles south of Kunming Air Base, on October 26, 1943. I was assigned to the Headquarters Squadron of the Fourteenth Air Force ("The Flying Tigers"), commanded by Major General Claire Lee Chennault.

After three weeks of briefing, I was sent to join the Chinese Army headquarters of the Sixth War Area at Enshih as a liaison-intelligence officer. In this capacity, I, along with my Alert-Net Liaison Team, and other fine radio teams stationed at Changsha, Hengyang, Kweilin, and Chihkiang (straight river) coordinated U.S. Air Force strafing and bombing strikes against the Japanese Army, as they advanced into central China. Chihkiang was near where the last battle of World

War II was fought in China. I spent ten months in the "boondocks" with the Chinese Army. In September 1944, I was advanced to the grade of Captain by General Chennault. During my tour of duty, I was decorated three times by the Chinese and received the Bronze Star and the Legion of Merit from the U.S.

Throughout late 1944 and early 1945, I was placed on detached duty with the Office of Strategic Services (OSS), the forerunner of the CIA. My new post was in southeast China with the Third War Area. I was able to obtain intelligence about Japanese troop movements and forward this information by radio to headquarters. My Chinese spies, however, were often unreliable, and disappeared after I had trained them, clothed them, given them money, and furnished them with radios. By this time, the OSS had taken over all east China intelligence operations. In January 1945, we found evidence that the Japanese Air Force in China had been ordered to "stand down" since Japanese planes and pilots were unable to fly because they were short of fuel. As a result, several hundred Japanese aircraft were idled on the ground in the tri-cities triangle of Hangchow, Shanghai, and Nanking.

I was ordered to leave China in 1945 along with my radio operators and civilian missionaries as Japan threatened to complete its conquest of China. Some refused to leave, including John Birch, later the namesake of the John Birch Society, who, in April - May 1945, moved north to assist in the Nationalist attack on Japanese ground forces. His zeal led to his demise at the hands of the northern Communist's guerrillas. I was in Nanking at this time and never saw Birch again. I left China secretly, by way of Nanking, leaving the city by river sampan, because roads were bombed out or controlled by the Japanese. The cockroaches about picked me up and threw me overboard! By October 1945, the war was over and I was on my way back to the United States.

Malcolm Rosholt (see photo in color section) was discharged from the Army Air Force with the rank of Major on December 13, 1945. He returned to his home in San Mateo County, California, and later the family moved to Rosholt, Wisconsin, a village founded by his grandfather, J.G. Rosholt.

Malcolm Rosholt and his wife made a career of writing about Wisconsin's state and local history, and in addition, he has written about the Fourteenth Air Force, and Chinese aviation history. Rosholt has written a total of twenty-five books.

Now at the age of ninety-four, Malcolm Rosholt resides at the Wisconsin Veterans Home at King, Wisconsin. Next to his bed is a typewriter with a half-filled sheet of paper, awaiting further inspiration, for his next book which details his interesting journey through the twentieth century.

HEAVY STORMS

DUNKIRK
As told by
Lowell Peterson

The British policy of appeasement toward Hitler was dealt its final blow when Germany invaded Poland on September 1, 1939. In response to this unmitigated, naked aggression, Great Britain and France declared war on Germany on September 3, 1939. This response surprised Hitler, who had hoped Great Britain would continue to follow the policies of Prime Minister Neville Chamberlain which had allowed Germany to swallow up Austria, Czechoslovakia, the Rhineland, and other areas without major objection. After the declaration by France and Great Britain, Hitler was faced with having to fight a war on two fronts.

The French fortified the heavily bunkered Maginot Line along its border with Germany, while the British sent thousands of troops to Northern France. Unfortunately, the Maginot Line did not extend along the BeNeLux countries (Belgium, The Netherlands, Luxembourg) for political border reasons, and because of the engineering difficulties inherent in these low countries, with high water tables.

The German army of 1939 did not initially express an overt interest in invasion of the Western Front, and therefore the British and French maintained only a defensive posture in what was called, "The Phony War". Meanwhile, Germany was busy securing its southern border through a pact with Italy, securing its northern border by invading Norway in April 1940, and concluding a nonaggression pact with the Soviet Union on the Eastern Front. The BeNeLux countries remained neutral, confident that the Germans would honor and respect that neutrality.

On May 10, 1940, Germany unleashed a Blitzkrieg attack with thirty divisions against the West, conquering Luxembourg in one day and the Netherlands in five. King Leopold surrendered Belgium to the Germans against the will of his people on May 28, 1940.

The British and French forces were not as well disciplined or as well equipped as the Germans, lacking a coordinated commonality of command. The French had

THE SUN ROSE CLEAR

seventy-two divisions, three of which were armored and Great Britain had ten divisions with one armored brigade on the Western Front. The Belgians had twenty-three divisions, but by the time the Allied forces joined them, ten divisions had already been destroyed by the rapidly advancing Germans. As the attack in the west began, the British and French raced north to meet the attack in Belgium, but this allowed the Nazis to unleash the main thrust of forty-five divisions south through Luxembourg and the Ardennes Forest, outflanking the British and French forces. The French and British armies were trapped and defeated by the flanking force.

The French and British soldiers, cut off from central France, were forced to retreat to the coast at Dunkirk (Dunquerque, Dunkerque). A massive British evacuation flotilla of a thousand vessels liberated 338,000 French and British troops to England between May 26, 1940 and June 4, 1940.

Fifty thousand Allied troops were eventually captured by the German army and Dunkirk surrendered on June 4, 1940. The German army moved on to conquer Paris on June 14, 1940, and the French signed a humiliating armistice with Germany on June 22, 1940. French General Charles De Gaulle, spirited out of France to England, broadcast via radio to the French people throughout the war maintaining their spirit of resistance. The events that occurred at Dunkirk provide a background to the story that follows.

THE ESCAPE
As told by
Pierre Dehay

    In 1942, German industries, stripped of their workforce by the wartime conscription of soldiers, needed workers. They encouraged workers and laborers in occupied countries without jobs to come and work in Germany for a salary. At least they now could eat. As the war progressed, this deportation from the occupied countries became obligatory, but the salary was maintained. In France, this was called services obligatoire du travail, the infamous "S.T.O." The workers could only come back in their country if they were ill or members of their immediate family were ill, and to do so they had to present a medical certificate from a physician countersigned by a German military physician. To return home to their country, the worker needed three things: his personal passport, his letter of permission, and a railway ticket. Workers who were able to obtain permission to go back to their native occupied country very often did not return to Germany. Many hid and then worked for the Resistance Movement. These resistance workers would then smuggle their passports to prisoners of war in German Stalags so that these documents could be used for escape.

    This story, told by Pierre Dehay, describes his escape and the escape of his comrade, Maurice Parent, who used the name on his confiscated passport, Maurice Cogis, during the escape. They had been captured at the battle of Dunkerique (Dunkirk) and were being held at a German prisoner of war camp, Stalag VIII C in Breslau (Wroclaw), Poland. Pierre, an artist, painted decorations, designs, and paintings for the opera house. He also used his talents to forge the stamps which were necessary on the passports for individuals to pass "control points". All of the stamps of these two prisoners and many others were drawn by Pierre Dehay's hand.

    Maurice Parent worked in the daytime at a vegetable store for a greengrocer. At night the two were obligated to return to the Stalag where they secretly planned their conspiracy to escape.

Breslau, Friday night, May 19, 1944.

    In the halls of Haupt'bahnhof (main train station), we are three Frenchmen lost in the German crowd-Maurice Parent and I, who will try the great adventure and also Leon Leplatois, who wishes he could accompany us. We are all good friends. Leon, on this evening, is our "witness-reporter". If things turn bad and

THE SUN ROSE CLEAR

Maurice and I are arrested at the first control, Leon will immediately warn our conspirators. If our escape plan works and after forty-eight hours we are in France, he will tell the other prisoners of our escape. The escape has been prepared for a long time, but only a few of our trusted, intimate friends know of the project.

With a detached casual facial appearance, we show our passport, our leaves of absence, and our tickets at the first control point. We had purchased the tickets yesterday. Without paying attention to the papers, the traffic warden punches a hole in our ticket, guffawing, "Ach! Zuruk, Frankreich!!! Gross Paris! Ach so." (Ah! Returning to France!!! Great Paris! Oh, I see.) He adds, in German of course, "Platform No. 3, change in Berlin." We already knew this. On the ground floor of the Breslau station there is a huge hall with its wickets, its cafeteria, its newspaper stalls; on the second floor, open to the air, are the railroad tracks. For the moment, we are safe. We return to Leon, who shakes our hands vigorously and wishes us well. We say nothing. The less we talk, the better it is. We climb the stairs. Maurice has a suitcase and I have a haversack.

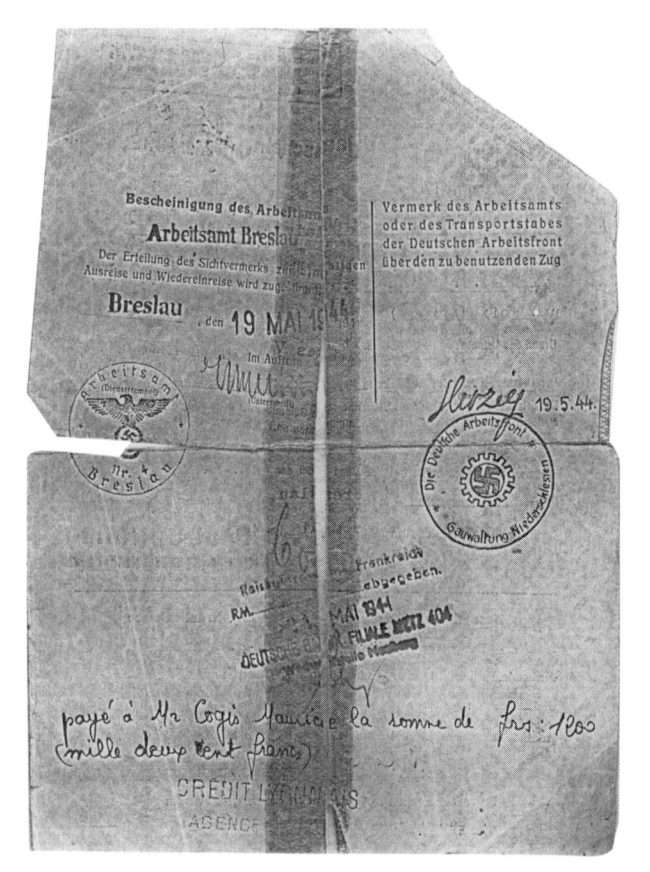

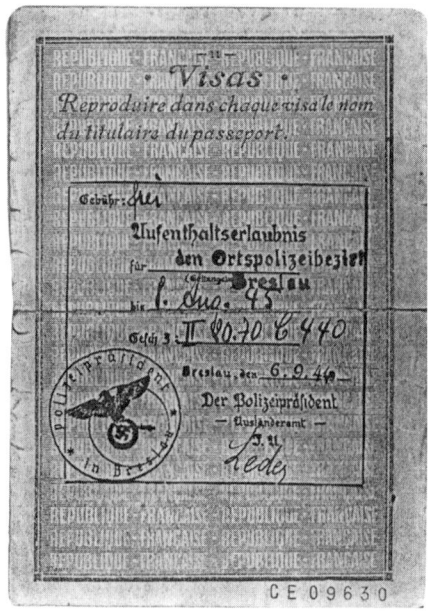

Documents forged by Pierre DeHay.

What hour will our train arrive from Poland? On this point, my memory fails. I only remember the tone of our feeling: We are now between "dog and wolf": no turning back. It was just before nightfall, about 8:30 p.m.

As we arrive at the quay (platform) No. 3, things become more complicated. The other platforms are almost deserted, while ours is crowded with people. The huge crowd departing in advance of the war front, combined with the metro rush hour, make it impossible for us to advance even six feet toward the rail line in twenty minutes. The speaker announces the train's arrival, but the train is already full. By bad luck, it stops with the coach directly in front of us. It is impossible for us to reach the doors at the front or at the back. Even by jostling people, we will never reach the doors.

But, as a good rugby man, Maurice, with use of his great shoulders, knocks clear a passage. A pathway opens and an obliging "gretchen" (colloquial nickname for a native German girl) takes his suitcase. Maurice continues his advance to the opening, turning his face to be sure I follow him. Nine feet of a compact crowd separate

Documents forged by Pierre DeHay.

the two of us. It is an impossible obstacle. I shout to him, "Go ahead! Leave without me!" Without hesitation, he gives up and recovers his suitcase and we find ourselves again like two idiots in the middle of a lot of people on the quay, as the vociferous employees in uniform make an effort to shut the doors of the train.

This is a great bit of bad luck! We could not imagine such things happening. We imagined twenty delays and checkpoints, but not this one. We knew, like all the people, that in front of the Russian army advance, the Germans of "Greater Deutschland" would return to the fold, but we could not have imagined this crazy disorder. What to do? We could not go back "home" as children do after an escapade. Could we renounce our "beautiful plan" caressed for such a long time? Could we reverse the future? Not at all! It's now or never!

First, we had to stay where we were. We had to await the dispersal of the passengers and think deeply about our problem. We sit on a bench at the end of the quay in the obliged blackout darkness, as we talk under our breath.

Let's see! Our original plan called for changing trains in Berlin. Yes, this was really the bad part of our plan. Waiting two hours in the station in Berlin is always dangerous. We must choose a new itinerary, and for this we must go down and look at the time schedules displayed in the main hall. Maurice understands this at once.

"For you, Pierre, it's too dangerous; all Breslau knows you," he exaggerates.

It's true that "Der Franzosischer Kunsmahler des Operhaus" (the French artist painter of the opera) is as recognizable and is as obvious as a "white wolf". My presence here in the middle of the night risks that I will be recognized.

"I will go there, Maurice says, nobody knows me and, with my German hat, I can seem German."

It's true. Maurice, with his Tyrollean felt hat with its feather, seems more German than a native.

"You wait here for me, okay?" he asks.

"Okay, good luck," I reply.

I stay alone with the collar of my overcoat turned up and my hands in my pockets. The night is brisk and the waiting is interminable. In fact, it lasts only a quarter of an hour. In this time, I relive our last month of captivity like a movie.

"Was machen sie hier? Papiers, bitte! Schnell, mensch." (What do you do here? Your papers, please, quickly, man.)

I jump. I am torn out of my dreaming and stand up in a bound. The police! I'm taken!

In the black, I recognize, with great relief, Maurice's laughter. He saw my peaceful dreaming and made a good joke.

"Have you become crazy. What is this about?" I ask.

"Forget about it, friend. We are going. I found a train that passes here at five past seven a.m. It reaches Leipzig at half past midday. A quarter of an hour later, we can board a train to Paris."

"Bravo! It's fine," I reply, overjoyed. "We avoid Berlin and the waiting is short. Let's only hope that we don't miss the connection."

"Yes, let's hope that all the way we don't have to hesitate. It's the only available scheme. Believe me, I studied the time schedules," Maurice assures me.

Hours pass. We sit down, we stand up, we wander back and forth to warm ourselves a little. We talk. The risk of a delay disturbs us. It's the war, and railways are often destroyed by the night bombings. Anything is possible. Let's hope God will be with us this once.

Recollections of P.O.W. life, "Kommando 811" by Pierre Dehay, 1945. (From the collection of Pierre Dehay.)

THE SUN ROSE CLEAR

"Le Beaux Di Marches" (The Nice Sunday) by Pierre Dehay, 1945. (From the collection of Pierre Dehay.)

Time progresses and things take care of themselves. Our fears subside. We deal with all sorts of practical details. We avoid being together, and don't speak to people, and obey lots of orders that we more or less follow. In our excitement, we speak only about our return to France. Maurice will call his wife, Mathilde and his parents, who have an electric materials store in Meudon, a suburb of Paris. I will call upon my mother, who will be totally surprised, and I will also call on Paulette. I have exchanged letters with Paulette for many months, becoming more and more affectionate with her, and I desire to know her better. The night passes. Nobody comes to detain us.

About 6:00 a.m., the station comes alive. On Platform No. 3, there are now only a few persons. Some are workers easily identified by a small wallet under their arms containing their midday snack, but there are also passengers carrying luggage. Nothing appears upsetting.

Five past seven and the train is on time. It is full, just like the one of yesterday. We get on, however, without too much difficulty, and we crowd together, standing near the door. We take a last look at the roofs emerging from the fog of sleeping Breslau. We slowly leave Breslau and depart into the industrial suburbs, where the chimneys of factories stand tall. After this, we are in the Silesian Plain, monotonous, punctuated only by fir trees.

Our train is as slow as a wheelbarrow! Halts follow halts. Workers get off. After several stops, we are able to find places to sit. We are being judicious and, according to our plan, prepared in advance, we choose two different compartments. This will give each one a chance if the other is arrested.

Precisely, after one hour along the way, the first ticket collector with a marine blue uniform and gold braid approaches. It does not seem very dangerous. He is still sleepy and gives back the tickets of the other passengers with a distracted air. It's now my turn. "Ach! Franzose! Zuruk Paris!" (Ah, Frenchman! Returning to Paris!) He fears that I don't understand and he translates with a frightful accent. "Paris, schonestadt. Belleville, Montmartes, (a section of Paris where the Moulin Rouge is located) bedides madames!" (Paris, beautiful city. Fair city, Montmartes, loose women!) He is winking slyly and returns my papers, laughing, "Permission; aber Zuruk Deutschland nicht permission?" (Permission; however, not permission to return to Germany?) I affirm to him my intention to come back certainly to work for the great Germany. He laughs, and it seems to him that it doesn't matter. Not a very good Nazi, I imagine.

Ten minutes later, I walk down the corridor to Maurice's compartment. I am immediately reassured. He's all right. Encouraged by this first success, we chatter for a time looking at the landscape, which is uniformly flat. The monotonously similar villages, with the same clean lines, neat, like a clay model, and also the similar isolated farms, surrounded by trees, are seen repetitively.

The halts are becoming less frequent and the train takes on some speed. Another ticket-taker comes by and Maurice and I resume our respective places. We have nothing to worry about again this time and hopefully thereafter as well.

Everything seems all right. Our mental attitude is good. At about 11:00 a.m., like obeying a dumb signal, in all compartments, the Huns unpack slices of bread and margarine and large dry sausages that they eat with great application. We imitate them while conversing in the corridor.

We are approaching Dresden. We now see damaged farms and the town itself, the victim of terrible aerial bombing, is completely destroyed. In our carriage, all the conversations stop. Tension is general. At this moment, two men of the Gestapo appear at our end of the corridor with submachine guns under their arms. We quickly return to our compartment. No mistake, things are becoming serious! The Gestapo soldiers take their time checking identity cards and the ausweiss (passport) with meticulous detail. It's my turn. I constrict my buttocks. The sweat runs down my back. "Franzose? Freiwillige arbeiter?" (Frenchman, volunteer worker?) "Jawohl," (Yes, indeed) I respond. The Gestapo interrogates me as follows: Surname, name, birth date, date of arriving in Germany, profession, etc. Fortunately, I know my lesson perfectly and don't make a mistake. My face is confronted with my photograph. They evaluate my height. Distressing moments drag on. Without any further commentary, the soldier gives me back my pass, my urlaubsshein (title of permission), and my ticket. Phew! That was a close one! For the question, "Beruf?" (profession), I nearly answered "kunstmahler" (artist painter) by habit, instead of "urhmacher" (watchmaker), which appeared on my identity card.

After the cross examination is finished, euphoria overcomes us. Following this control check, made by Gestapo (secret police) specialists, everything is quiet. From now on, it's in quietude that we wait for control checkpoints; however, it's difficult during an escape to keep a serene mood for very long. New anxieties replace past ones. Now, it's a question of time. We have twelve hours to go to make our connection at the next train, and we do not know how far it is to Leipzig. No signs indicate the distance to us. We look at our watches frequently. Twenty past twelve, twenty-five past twelve, half past twelve, and still nothing is in view. Our train is late. Will we arrive in time for our next connection? Twenty-five minutes to one. Now we see the bombed suburbs of a great town. Is it, at last, Leipzig? God bless, we are here. It must be about twenty minutes to one when the train stops in the station.

Jostling all the people, we rush onto the platform and sprint, crossing the rails, without taking the subways, to arrive two platforms over, where the panel indicates

THE ESCAPE

"Toward Frankreich-Paris," (Toward France-Paris). Some minutes later, our "Train of Liberty" arrives. The crowd here is almost as congested as in Breslau. This time, the tension is greater, however. We must get on this train or risk a high probability of capture. Maurice, like a bulldozer, rushes, saying to me "You follow me, okay?" Head lowered, following his heels, I become swallowed up into the open passage until we grip the handle of a door just at the time when the train starts. We are the last to get in. In the door of the compartment, we are being crushed. I have all the difficulty in the world closing the door behind me. Maurice holds his suitcase on his head with his two hands, as it is impossible to move. One hour passes in this uncomfortable situation. At the next station, by some miracle, a few persons get off. We are a little less compressed, but remain restrained. I have an idea. I locate a dining car two or three carriages forward. Should we go there? Maurice approves and slowly, very slowly, we arrive there at last. Here is a change of scenery. The room is full. All the tables are occupied, but it is calm. At the end of the carriage, four persons stand up and we replace them before the table is cleaned. We relax in happiness. I pat a pipe and Maurice lights a cigarette.

The landscape marches past. We cross a country devastated by the war. For long intervals, ruins remain in smoke. A factory is in flames and the firetrucks are busy. The night was probably very hot here from the bombing.

An impeccable barman with a white jacket gives us the menu. We still have lots of food tickets. We can have a good meal! The menu is made up of kartoffel (potatoes), Swedish turnips, and red cabbages. The bottles of beer accumulate in front of us. Our emotions are as thirsty as our bodies! The site is pleasant, and we linger a maximum time. As we relax, we have ersatz coffee (substitute burnt barley), of course.

Then, two Nazi SS officers, a colonel and a captain, enter. They are very inquisitive and ask us about the weather. The two places across from us are unoccupied, and they settle down near us after the usual salutations. We find ourselves becoming a little anxious. We'll have to act convincingly! We soon know our worry is needless. Our two SS soldiers are returning to their garrison and are not inquiring policemen. Seeing that we are Frenchmen who have nothing to hide, they ask us where we come from and where we are going. "Ach, Breslau!" They want to know whether the town has been bombed. They receive our negative answer with satisfaction.

They then change the subject to "Ach, Paris! Prima, Paris!" (Oh, Paris, terrific Paris.) Soon we have to listen to the usual tourist folklore, which, for the Huns, describes Paris as the most beautiful town in the world: The Eiffel Tower, Notre Dame, the great boulevards, le Musee Grevin, and, of course, Montmartre, le Moulin Rouge, and the "petites femmes" (small, petite women). With ardor, they remind us during the conversation of the Reine Pedauque and Maxime's (famous restaurants). These two Nazis seem to have retained a memory acquired during their occupation years in France, and they are not very ashamed to reminisce about their experiences in France, leaving thoughts of their wives behind.

A ticket collector arrives asking for the tickets at all the tables. He stops at our table, hesitates for a moment, and goes on his way. It must seem to him inopportune to disturb SS officers. Our unintentional companions have helped with something!

Maurice speaks German much better than I, so he does the talking, avoiding my stammering. The talk becomes more spirited by the moment, such that I cannot even understand it, but suddenly I perk up my ears. They are speaking about the war. We must be careful not to make any mistakes in our conversation! They ask, "Do you believe in the British-American landings and do you believe they will succeed?" (Of course we believe in it, because the imminence of the invasion has encouraged us to escape and to take advantage of our false documents.) Maurice gives an evasive answer, evoking "the formidable Atlantic wall," the power of the German army, etc. In short, he does not do badly. It is curious that our Nazi friends seem a little less optimistic. They don't profess any faith in German victory and become more quiet. The conversation fails. We take advantage of the pause and get up to leave. They stand up, always courteous as the Germans usually are, and wish us a pleasant stay in France. We acknowledge them and say, "Also to you, sirs."

As we leave the dining car, a pleasant surprise is waiting for us. The train is half empty. In the corridor where we are walking, there is nobody standing, and in the carriage, some seats are unoccupied. We also have a new surprise. In a compartment, two French soldiers are nibbling sandwiches. Surprised, we sit down near them. Immediately, they explain to us that they have been officially released from their prison camp and show us lots of papers covered with official stamps that are different than ours. At this stage of the war, this astounds us. There aren't any releases that we are aware of, but as is always true with the Huns, anything is possible.

We are sad to deceive the French soldiers, but we remain loyal to our plan, which appears to them as not very glorious. We maintain our false role as French workers, volunteering for work in Germany, enjoying a permission of ten days' leave, just like our urlaubsschein (pass) shows. They ask, "Is this true? You come here to work for Hitler of your own accord?" We answer in the affirmative and indicate to them that we hope our effort will help shorten the war. We receive a contemptuous answer. "You must really be silly to believe such tales! You would be better to have remained at home." After that, they turn away, disguising weakly the contemptuous feelings they have for us. The situation is very tense and unpleasant, but we accept it without stumbling, although we are laughing up our sleeve.

A ticket collector again arrives. It seems as if it rains them. The railway employee doesn't bother us. Indeed, he gives us back our papers without a word, but, oh, irony of destiny, he carefully scrutinizes the papers of our soldier companions, and after he has barked the order for them not to budge, he goes to find the chief of the train. Our two fellows seem dazed and roll their frightened eyes. At the next station, we see them taken off the train by the feldgendarmen (military police) who arrest them. Maurice and I are very surprised. We have unknowingly been talking with other escapees.

To this day, I still cannot believe it. No prisoner breaking out of a Stalag or a prisoner working on a farm or at a factory would dare risk escape in a French uniform on a German train. They had probably not received an obligatory stamp on their ausweiss (identification card). Our ausweiss stamps are absolutely false, since they were drawn by me, but they are "right" in any case. We have passed six controls since Breslau, seven with the first evaluation in the station of departure. The quality of my stamps bring us the evidence of our success. I have always kept these papers and the stamps as a relic. Whenever I contemplate them, it's with a retrospective fright, noting that they are too perfect, too neat, and without any blot of ink. I can hardly believe that they deceived the Gestapo's expert vigilance.

Our friend, Ostoya, who managed a successful Resistance Movement during the occupation years, told me years later with conviction: "You had the luck of an unfaithful husband. We would never have dared send an agent on a mission with likewise arranged documents." Our luck in this matter was principally our innocence. We wouldn't have tried the adventure if we had doubted. Neither would all of the other prisoners or deportees who tried, with papers that came directly from my forgery.

Without notable incident, the trip continues, but I only retain a confused memory of it. I don't remember the names of the towns we went through. Did we go through Kassel? Probably. Through Koblentz or Frankfurt? I don't know. For us, it was not important. The itinerary in wartime is sometimes odd and complicated because the right of way may have been destroyed by bombing. The only thing that was important and certain was that we were approaching the west and liberty.

From time to time, without obvious reason, our train stops in the country or lingers in a small station. Sometimes, we see war prisoners with such odd dress that it is impossible to know their nationalities. They were probably deported to Germany with the dress of convicts, striped blue and white, and given work to maintain the railway stations and tracks. We see military troop trains more and more frequently. All branches of the German army blend together. They are all

THE SUN ROSE CLEAR

hurrying to the east, to the battle.

A whole train load of Panzer (armored) units passes by with their antiaircraft guns pointed to the sky. We stop a long time near a half-destroyed station while a seemingly endless train, packed with a whole division of equipped infantrymen with field boots and helmets, goes by in cattle wagons. Tired, thin, poorly shaved, clothes worn threadbare, they look nothing at all like the triumphant German army that four years earlier had invaded France. That earlier German army, the armored division of which had hurled itself upon the British-French lines at the Canal Albert, had caused Dunkerque to fall. Dusty trucks had stretched out along the roads of Flanders, as the conquering Germans carried away me and the rest of our lamentable flock of prisoners. At that time, we saw them parade, stand up on the trucks, joyous, sure of victory, shouting "nicht Paris, nicht Paris" (not going to Paris). Time has passed, and today it is we who are going west to Paris, but without fanfare or pomp. The current German soldiers we see moving east are coming from Paris, but they are reluctantly on their way to a slaughterhouse. The greater part of them seem tired, silent, and already resigned to their fate. Among them we see old men who are more than fifty years of age and more still, adolescents, barely out of school. Each great army sooner or later, as it faces defeat, has this appearance.

The train empties itself more and more as passengers get off, but nobody gets on the train at the stations. We are now alone in the compartment. When night falls, we lie on the seat benches and sleep comes. Speakers wake us up. I don't understand what they're saying. Maurice translates for me. "It's the border; we must get off and let our luggage be searched." Where are we? A sign says, "Neuburg-an-der-mosel." This name tells us nothing, but the name "moselle" lets us presume that we are in Lorraine (a province of France near the border).

On the platform, we receive orders. "Assemble! Shape a column! You have to change your German money and to show your papers!" In single file, under the close watch of a feldgendarme, we go to the end of the platform, enter a small feebly lighted room, a shabby suboffice of the Reichbank (German Bank). I give my papers to the wicket gatekeeper, who hardly can see them in the dim light. I also give him my last German marks and, in exchange, I receive French money, about twelve-hundred francs. We are then marched farther. I quickly count that we are about a total of thirty. There are soldiers in feldgrau (gray German uniform) and three or four civilians. We maintain our practiced scenario. I leave Maurice and put myself ahead of him, separating us by eight permissionnaires. Swinging his electric torch, the feldgendarme marches us away into a dark corridor, to a door, which on his order, we go through in single file. When he gestures to me, I am taken into a dark office and placed in front of a table, where I put down my papers.

Two Gestapo men review them absentmindedly. They speak words that I don't understand. The wait is short. They affix a stamp on my passport. It states, "Deutche grenpolizei, 21.5.44. Aureise" (German police, May 21, 1944, permit to travel in railways). This authenticates my false papers. I leave quickly and am again on the platform in almost total blackness.

Behind me, I count the others coming out, five, six, seven, eight. It is now the turn of Maurice. A fellow comes. It isn't him! Another fellow comes, but never Maurice. Mechanically, I carry on the count and arrive at the fateful number of thirty. No more are coming out. The panic overwhelms me! What has happened? I am sure that Maurice has been arrested. We are so near our object. What to do? Should I return to the compartment? Is it prudent? Is it our luggage that betrayed us? That is silly. There is nothing inside our luggage to cause suspicion and nothing to even prove that it is ours. I hesitate. Should I leave the train and take off on foot? In Lorraine, I should be able to find some help, but how could I locate the partisans? Without the rails, alone in the country, I might turn the wrong way and wander back into Germany. I am completely confused and lost!

Abruptly, the door opens and Maurice appears. I run to him: "what happened? I was afraid."

"Oh, nothing! One of the policemen is from Breslau and he has not been home since last year. He wanted to know whether the town was damaged and what was the morale of the people. I had to give him a total description!"

Everything is okay. I can smile again. We return to our carriage and our luggage is there. It has not been searched.

The continuation of our trip is without incident. On our seatbench, we sleep quietly, and when we awaken, the day is upon us. After washing our hands and faces quickly, we eat our last snack and press our noses against the glass to fill our eyes with the familiar landscape. Without a doubt, we are in France. The names of the towns we pass through prove it to us. We recognize villages with roofs and the typical architecture of the buildings arrayed in a sort of pleasant disorder. "We are at home." People are moving slower, their attitude is less tense, and everything seems different, even the cows!

At Nancy, (a city in eastern France) passengers board the train, speaking French instead of German. When they enter our compartment, they hesitate. "We will not sit in here; there is a Hun," they seem to say to themselves. They go away. We look at each other and burst out laughing. It is Maurice's feather hat that identifies us. We don't wish to tell them the truth, so we keep the door closed. This solitude does not last long. Two "grey mice" (German Waffen-SS combat soldiers) move into our compartment with authority and immediately begin talking to us. We simulate that we don't understand what they are saying. Our attitude doesn't seem to rebuff them. They persist, becoming playful, brushing themselves against us. We are very upset. Fortunately, the next stop rids us of their obnoxious presence.

A Frenchman, about forty years old, enters our compartment after these ruffians have left. He has an intelligent, beckoning face that portrays trust. Ten minutes later, forgetting our prudent determinations and without thinking, we reveal to him that we are trying to succeed at an escape. What's the matter with us? It is a mystery! I don't remember to this day which of us revealed this first. The man, surprised, looks around in all directions with a suspicious appearance and signals to us to keep quiet. With a very low voice he says, "Mind you! You believe you are sheltered because you are in France? You haven't any idea of the number of dirty dogs we find here. It's lucky you fell on me." He is right. How could we be so silly to confide to an unknown? It's difficult to explain. Success must have clouded our heads. No other possible reason exists. The fellow gets off at the next station. We look at each other and are not very proud. The lesson is good. In the future, we will watch our tongues.

After we pass through Champagne, the Ile de France, we are impatient to arrive at our destination. Now, as we say in France, we can "smell the stable". Paris is in the distance, and then suddenly Paris is in view. We are at the eastern station of Paris! Terminus! All the people get off. The control, now completed by a French railroad employee is pure routine. The German policemen standing near him don't interfere. It's five minutes to eight o'clock.

A gigantic picture of Doriot (a French collaborator of Germany), striped in the tri-color flag, hangs in the hallway with this inscription, "Doriot, the only chief of the party who doesn't fight the war with the skin of others." Nazi propaganda posters are everywhere, dedicated to the glory of the French volunteers fighting with Germany or fighting against Bolshevism. On one poster a martial-appearing Hun, his finger pointed forward, enjoins us: "Comrade, the Waffen SS waits for you." We are faced with the curiosities of Paris and the reality of wartime.

We leave the station quickly, and when we are outside in the open air we can smile to ourselves and experience a touch of satisfaction. It's finished! We won!

Maurice proposes that we go and have a coffee. He says, "I must phone my wife, Mathilde. No, it is you, Pierre, who must call. I am afraid to surprise her too brutally. You will do it gently. Here is the number."

I call Meudon (a suburb of Paris). A man's voice answers. "I want to speak to Madame Parent, the young Madame Parent."

He answers, "She is not here. Who is calling?"

I say, "A friend of Maurice."

He persists, "What friend? Who are you?"

THE ESCAPE

I reply, "A friend from captivity, Pierre Dehay." I feel, in the phone, the elder Parent begin to tremble. I am also trembling. I lose my thoughts. I don't know what to say. I cut in brutally, "Wait, I pass you to Maurice."

Maurice begins, "Hello, Dad?"

When Maurice finishes the call and hangs up, he explains to me: "We are unlucky; Mathilde is in Ariege. She will not be here for a few days. It isn't important. I'll wait for her at home."

Pierre Dehay, 1983

This story, written in French by the hand of Pierre Dehay, has been kindly translated by my friend, Jean-Louis de Firmas, and his lovely wife, Nicole, who is the daughter of Maurice and Mathilde Parent. Alix, daughter of Jean-Louis and Nicole, was this writer's AFS exchange student daughter in 1987-88.

—Lowell Peterson

Lowell Peterson's daughter, Linda Peterson, talking with Mathilde Parent. December 1992.

THE SUN ROSE CLEAR

EPILOGUE

After the return, Pierre Dehay was hidden in a Parisian suburb by partisans. Maurice Parent, whose family was very well known in Meudon, quickly understood that he was going to be denounced by the villagers because of jealousy and risked return to prison. Paris and France were under German occupation at this time. The Allied invasion of Europe and the liberation of Paris were still a month or two away. Maurice, therefore, left the Paris suburbs and went to join his wife, Mathilde, in Ariege, a region in the south of France, at his parents-in-law. On this trip, between Toulouse and Foix (pronounced Fwah), on the train, there was a young man who smoked blonde tobacco, which was then totally unknown in France. The French only had black tobacco. Maurice thought the stranger was probably an allied pilot who had been shot down and was trying to cross over the Pyrenees to Spain, with the help of the French Resistance. Upon reaching Foix, Maurice approached his in-law's house with caution. Nicole, a young girl six years of age at that time, had never known her father. Maurice asked her, "Is Madame Mathilde Parent here?" Nicole answered, "Sir, who are you? Why do you ask for my mother?" The reunion was a happy one.

Mathilde worked for the French Resistance during the war, secretly carrying letters and secret papers from her occupation at a suburban Paris post office to Foix. In order to be able to make this journey, she would send herself a telegram with a false message stating that Nicole was very ill and that Mathilde must come immediately to Foix. The trip from German-controlled France to the free area of southern France also required passage through German control points. Mathilde would place the contraband documents under seat cushions on the train until the control points had been passed, while she played upon the sympathies of the guards, with her story of traveling to see her sick daughter.

Mathilde continues to live in Faux at the age of ninety. Maurice died in 1965 at the age of fifty-three. Pierre Dehay lives in Paris to this day.

Jean-Louis de Firmas, M.D.

DANGER IN THE NORTH ATLANTIC: THE NAVY ARMED GUARD

As told by
Lowell Peterson
(Name of interviewee withheld by request.)

With the fall of France to the Nazis on June 21, 1940, the Kriegsmarine (German Navy) established U-boat submarine operational headquarters in Paris and gained control of the French ports of Brest, Lorient, St. Nazierre, and La Pallice, on the Bay of Biscay. The German U-boat Wolf Packs roamed the Atlantic Ocean from the French ports and feasted hungrily on US Merchant Marine supply ship convoys. In the period from June 1940 until October 1940, 217 ships and 1,395,298 tons of shipping were lost to the German attacks, and the loss continued at greater than 264,000 tons per month. At this rate of loss, Great Britain would soon be bankrupt and unable to sustain the war effort against Germany.

The "Lend-Lease Act" (HR-1776) became law in March 1941, allowing President Roosevelt, at his discretion, to supply military materials under a lease agreement to any allied nation. The sinking of merchant marine supply ships intensified and, therefore, Congress revised the Neutrality Acts (Public Law 294) in November, 1941, less than one month prior to Pearl Harbor, allowing the merchant ships to be armed. Navy seamen and armament were placed aboard the merchant ships and by the end of 1942, 1,813 ships had been armed. Thus was established the Navy Armed Guard.

I was seventeen years old when I enlisted in the U.S. Navy in 1939. I was sent to Great Lakes, in Waukegan, Illinois, for basic training, and then to Norfolk, Virginia, for gunnery school, where I was trained on the five-inch, .38-caliber antiaircraft gun, and on a three-inch, .50-caliber antisubmarine weapon. I was then assigned as a welder to the Brooklyn (New York) Navy Yard until the war started. The navy was asking for volunteers to join the "armed guard". I volunteered, because I thought I could contribute to the allied cause, and hopefully make a difference. What more could a small-town boy do under the circumstances?

The merchant marine ships transporting supplies to the war, were called Liberty Ships and they were embarking from ports at Brooklyn, San Francisco,

THE SUN ROSE CLEAR

New Orleans, and Virginia. The hulls of the ships were made of only one-quarter or one-half inch steel plate, welded together rather than riveted. Industrialist, Henry J. Kaiser was building these ships in California, sometimes building an entire ship in less than ten days. We called them "Kaiser's Coffins".

I served on four different merchant marine ships: the SS *Thomas U. Walter*, the SS *Andrew Moore*, the SS *Ted Rafferty*, and the SS *John Andrew*. As many as thirty-eight navy guards were assigned to each ship. We stood watch for up to sixteen hours at a time.

Our life was truly one of hours of boredom, interrupted by moments of sheer terror. When we went to General Quarters, things got very exciting. If submarines were detected in the area by our escorting cruisers and destroyers, or by our sailors on watch, we immediately were at General Quarters. An eighteen-ship convoy would normally have three to five destroyers and cruisers as escort. The cruisers stayed in front of the convoy, using their sonar to detect the subs, and the destroyers would then move in to protect the convoy, using depth charges to try to sink the submarines. On board the Merchant Marine ship, the armed guard sailors would look for the wake formed by the sub's turret or periscope, which had to be above water to get bearings for firing torpedoes at us. We shot at anything that even came close to resembling a wake from a sub. If we saw a wake of a periscope, we would aim at it and try to disable it. Sometimes, if we were lucky, the subs would have to surface, and then we would get them with our five-inch, .38-caliber guns, which could penetrate their armor.

The German submarine Wolf Packs traveled in groups of seven to eighteen submarines per pack. If they detected a convoy, they would form a perimeter around the border of the ships, and then a few submarines would try to get right inside the convoy and break it up, scattering it to make it easier for the perimeter subs to pick off individual ships. On one occasion, we were under sub attack by two subs just sixteen miles out of Brooklyn. We called in fighter bombers, and they sank both of the submarines.

The trip from Brooklyn to England took twenty-two to twenty-four days, eighteen if we had good weather and no harassment by submarines; the trip from England to Russia took four days. In 1943, we hit a hurricane only one day out from Brooklyn, and when it was over, we realized we had been blown backwards almost to Brooklyn. I went on the trip to Murmansk, Russia, from England, three different times. In spite of the fact that we were bringing necessary war supplies to Russia, and at some significant danger to ourselves, the Russians treated us very poorly, and were downright rude. They probably resented our generous supply of cigarettes, food, and luxuries that they did not have. They also wanted to keep us away from their women, who were providing services to our crews in exchange for food, cigarettes, and clothing.

In December 1942, the SS *Andrew Moore* was sunk by torpedoes, and in March, 1943, the SS *Thomas U. Walter* was also sunk. After the torpedo sank the *Andrew Moore*, I was rescued within hours by one of our escort cruisers. The sinking of the *Thomas Walter* would prove to be quite different. We were in a life raft for twenty-nine days in the treacherous North Atlantic. Although we were in a large life raft, in the high seas we capsized twice. We started out with twenty-eight sailors in the raft, but only nine of us would survive. I feel very fortunate to be one of them, but I have flashbacks and nightmares to this day, reliving that experience. Wounds, drownings, and exposure to the cold without adequate food and water took its toll.

When I was not aboard ship, I was expected to do shore duty as an SP (Shore Patrol). I did this in England, Italy, and Africa. In Italy, some U.S. WACs (Women's Army Corp) had set up a thriving business in what could be called a "house of ill repute." We had to raid the place, and one of the irate GI customers, unhappy at being shortchanged from services rendered, shot me in the leg.

I entered the service as a seaman first class, and ended my career as a gunners mate first class. I could have made chief gunners mate, but I turned it down. I did not need the rank, and did not want the responsibility. I just wanted to do my job for my country and go home when the war was over. After all, I only had a sixth grade education.

I remain convinced that in WWII we took part in a just cause and saw it to a just finish. I remain deeply dedicated to the cause of all veterans who have served their country with pride.

> *Nearly 150,000 Navy Guard sailors would serve on 6,236 merchant ships. One thousand ten were killed, and numerous others would be wounded. Twenty-seven hundred merchant transport ships would be built during WWII and, between 1942 and 1945, 710 ships were sunk.*
>
> *In 1942, the Kriegsmarine transferred most of its U-boats from France to Norway to operate against convoys supplying the Soviet Arctic port at Murmansk. Convoys braved the treacherous seas, carrying supplies fifteen hundred miles from Iceland or Scotland to Murmansk. In 1942, 8,333,000 gross tons of allied shipping was sunk by the Germans. By January 1943, one hundred U-boats were at sea at all times. In early 1943, twenty-two percent of all allied ships and material were being destroyed each month.*
>
> *In the spring of 1943, the German code was broken and the location and tactics of the U-boats became an open book to the allies. In May 1943, forty-seven U-boats were sunk. From that time forward, the U-boats suffered eighty percent casualties, and the supplies began to get through to Great Britain and Russia. Twenty-eight thousand, two hundred U-boat crewmen lost their lives and seven-hundred and eighty-five of the one thousand, one hundred and sixty-two U-boats built were lost at sea.*

TOWARD FIRST LIGHT

FROM D-DAY TO V-E DAY
As told by
Roland H. Vogt

War is hell and a terrible waste. Combat leaves an indelible mark on all those who are forced to endure it. The only plus side was my men's incredible bravery and devotion to each other. We had a loyalty to each other, and, yes, love. Until countries cease trying to enslave others, it will be necessary to accept one's responsibilities, and be willing to make sacrifices for one's country, as my fellow soldiers did.

I was drafted out of college into the Army in November 1942, and sent to Camp Phillips, Salina, Kansas, for basic training with the Ninety-fourth Infantry Division. In a period of time, I became a corporal, went on three months of maneuvers in the Tennessee Hills, made "buck sergeant", and moved to Camp McCain, Mississippi, to prepare for combat.

Roland H. Vogt

THE SUN ROSE CLEAR

I arrived in England at Chippenham as a staff sergeant and moved to Southampton for what was supposed to be a three-month tour of duty. A number of us volunteered to join the battle-hardened First Infantry Division, which had just arrived from the Italian Campaign in Sicily, Italy. After only seven days in England, we were, to our dismay, on our way to the invasion of Fortress Europe at Omaha Beach, Normandy, France, D-day, June 6, 1944.

We had been told that there would be four German battalions in fortified positions on Omaha Beach, but it turned out there were eight battalions waiting for us, who fought doggedly from their fixed positions on the top of the high perpendicular cliff above us. We had been taught that the goal of every attack on every battlefield was to gain momentum. However, every instinct, especially among young and inexperienced soldiers, is to take cover under fire. There was no cover. This primal instinct is reinforced when bodies, and parts of bodies, of others who also found no cover and became casualties, lie all around. Under these circumstances, it takes a considerable act of will to persuade your body to act and move forward.

On Omaha, the inexperienced Twenty-ninth Infantry Division, facing combat for the first time, deprived of many of its officers and noncoms due to casualties in the first hours after landing and dismayed by its losses, became dangerously paralyzed. The First Infantry Division, veterans of the fighting in Italy, were on the left flank of the Twenty-ninth Division, and because of their combat experience, fought much better. Without the "Big Red One", the battle would have likely been lost. The beach was covered with men, dead and wounded, together with disabled and burning vehicles and tanks. The Twenty-ninth Division suffered over two thousand casualties on the first day of the Normandy Invasion on the beachhead called "Omaha".

Stevens Point Daily Journal

FORTY-NINTH YEAR — FULL LEASED WIRE SERVICE OF THE ASSOCIATED PRESS — STEVENS POINT, WISCONSIN, TUESDAY, JUNE 6, 1944 — 12 PAGES

ALLIES INVADE FRANCE

Supreme Headquarters, Allied Expeditionary Force, June 6—(AP)—The Allies landed in the Normandy section of northwest France early today and by evening had smashed their way inland on a broad front, making good a gigantic air and sea invasion against unexpectedly slight German opposition.

Prime Minister Churchill said part of the record-shattering number of parachute and glider troops were fighting in Caen, nine miles inland, and had seized a number of important bridges in the invasion area.

Four thousand ships and thousands of smaller landing craft took the thousands of American, British and Canadian seaborne forces from England to France under protection of 11,000 Allied bombers and fighters which wrought gigantic havoc with the whole elaborate coastal defense system that the Nazis had spent four years building. Naval gunfire completed the job, and the beachheads were secured quickly.

Allied losses in every branch were declared to be far less than had been counted upon in advance.

The Germans said the landings took place from Cherbourg to Le Havre—a front of about 100 miles, and that a strong airborne force was fighting as far inland as Rouen, 41 miles east of Le Havre.

A peaceful Omaha Beach long after WWII. (Pointe du Hoc is on the horizon.)

I remember lying on the beach under fire behind some Rangers. I had taken cover behind some motionless, obviously dead bodies. It was the only cover available. The Rangers hollered, "What do we do, Sarge?" I was so scared. It was a good thing I was lying halfway up my body in the surf, because I'm sure I had wet my pants. I said, "You guys lead on, you're Rangers; I'll follow." They said, "You're a sergeant, we'll follow you."

So we headed for the cliff. The first group to reach the cliff threw grappling hooks with knotted ropes onto the top of the hill. We climbed the cliff with the help of the secured ropes, using the knots for holding our grip. The Ninety-fourth Division was now attacking in force and beginning to break out from the beachhead. We slowly gained ground inch-by-inch and were able to hold it. A handful of courageous leaders and small groups of armed men found a way around the German strong points guarding the "draws" or exits from the beach area, as we forced our bloody path away from Omaha Beach. We fought our way into the hedgerow farmland of Normandy, as we headed southwest toward Brittany, France, where 400,000 German Armed Forces awaited us. I was twenty-years old and already a veteran of combat: one hour or one day of being shot at, facing mortar and artillery fire, made you a veteran.

In Brittany, I joined up with Company I, Second Platoon, which had just arrived from the U.S. to join the Ninety-fourth. Of the 160 men who had trained in Kansas to form this company, only two of us would survive the entire war, due to attrition from death, wounds, and repatriations. The Ninety-fourth Infantry Division proceeded from Normandy to Brittany via St. Lo, Avranches, Rennes, Chateaubriant, and Nazay, and now approached the German stronghold of St. Nazaire.

Colonel Benjamin Thurston had joined the Ninety-fourth Division at Camp McCain, and when he arrived in France and found that I already had three months of combat experience, we became trusted friends. From then on, I went on at least eleven reconnaissance patrols with him. Colonel Thurston, a West Point graduate, was loved and respected by all of his men. It was a privilege to serve under him in combat. He brought many of us home who would not have made it without the benefit of his brains, bravery, and concern for his soldiers' lives. I pray in thankfulness to God to this day for Colonel Thurston's leadership.

We spent some months in the St. Nazaire area, advancing along the Brest-Nantes Canal, in the area of La Pessouis. As we dug in on the high ground beyond the town, we began to take artillery fire from both sides. The artillery from the Three hundred-second U.S. Infantry across the canal began firing at us, and at the same time, the German artillery was also firing at us. We were finally forced to withdraw, and the Germans reoccupied the town. Fortunately, only one sergeant was killed by the artillery fire. At this time, I was a platoon sergeant and saw our inexperienced platoon leader, a lieutenant, cowering in a shallow slit trench, trembling and crying out for everyone to retreat, which we reluctantly did.

During that night, word came to me to report to Captain Watkins and Lieutenant Jacques. They informed me that they anticipated an order to recapture La Pessouis and the high ground beyond. Colonel Thurston had been informed of the situation and late that night received orders from the command post to recapture the ground immediately. Early in the morning, October 6, 1944, Colonel Thurston joined I Company and met with Captain Watkins and Lieutenant Jacques, Kelly, and Arenaz, and informed me that I was leading the attack. Colonel Thurston told us that in support, we would have Battery C of the 919th Field Artillery Battalion, plus another battery from the same battalion, as well as a battery of assault guns, in addition to 60 and 80 mm mortar support.

As we moved out, I was directly behind the point of the attack, and to my surprise, Colonel Thurston joined me as we followed the road leading into the village. I sent out two scouts ahead of my platoon, with the main body of the battalion's two thousand men about two hundred yards behind. We passed over a stone bridge spanning a brook, and as we progressed, I sensed movement to my right. A group of Germans was fumbling about, trying to set up their machine gun less than fifty yards away. I whispered to the Colonel not to look, informing him that Germans to our right were frantically trying to get their machine gun in operation. I then yelled to my men to hit the dirt, pointing out the Germans who were at our right flank.

Most of the platoon flopped on the left side of the dirt viaduct leading from the bridge and began to fire at the machine gunner, as more Germans began to pour out of the farmhouses. Perhaps as many as seventy-five to one hundred Germans began to return our fire. I grabbed and pulled the Colonel down. He had been standing up firing like General Custer, and was struck by fire twice before he hit the ground. Colonel Thurston had a shot land between his legs, spattering him with gravel up into the crotch. A second bullet caught the tip of his .45 pistol, deflecting the gun downward, setting off a round in the chamber, wounding him in the leg and penis. If the German bullet hadn't hit the .45, it probably would have torn the Colonel's leg off, or worse yet, killed him. "Medic! Medic! The Colonel's been hit!," I yelled.

A few of my men had now reached the buildings in the hamlet, sheltered there while firing, but most of us lay out in the open, against the viaduct, firing at the enemy, who were darting about as the machine gun was still having its troubles and not firing. I sent my third squad around the German flank to wipe them out. The Colonel continued moving around and would not stay put until all was in order. Two of my men to the right of the Colonel and two to the left were hit, with the bullet "thunks" being unmistakable. All four men died before my eyes. With the Germans firing at us on three sides, Colonel Thurston called Lieutenant Jacques to try and move the First and Third Platoons across the brook, with the intention of smothering the Germans.

The Colonel was then evacuated, as he was covered with blood, wounds in the crotch and in his right arm and leg. The lieutenant who was supposed to lead the men across the brook at the Colonel's order had disappeared, so I led the platoon to the other side of the stream. We were able to force the Germans out of the village and off the high ground. They suffered heavy casualties. We lost more men that day but accomplished our mission. The Colonel rejoined us in a few days, despite his wounds. They could not keep him away from the battalion. We were glad to see him once again, a bit pale, but ready for action.

Sometime later, I was summoned to the office of Colonel McClune at Regimental Headquarters, who told me that Colonel Thurston had recommended a commendation for me for saving his life. Colonel Thurston thanked me for spotting the German machine gun nest, and shortly thereafter I received my battlefield commission. When I reported to Captain Emeis, battalion adjutant, he told me that all of this came about because of Colonel Thurston's recommendation. I was ushered into the regimental commander, Colonel McClune, who, when I entered, never looked up as I came to attention, saluted smartly, and received in return a "wave" salute. McClune set me at ease, then gruffly said, "Sergeant Vogt, you have been put in for the Congressional Medal of Honor or a commission. What do you say?" I was sure he was being facetious, so I said, "Sir, I can't eat a medal, so I'll take the commission." He looked up, grunted, and said, "That's what I thought; you're excused." Again, I saluted, made a smart "about-face" and left him, to be greeted by Captain Emeis, who put his arm around me, gave me a Second Lieutenant's bar, and sent me back to my unit. I was keenly aware that front line first and second

THE SUN ROSE CLEAR

Statue of General Dwight Eisenhower, Supreme Commander, Allied Expeditionary Forces, Europe (located near Caen, France).

lieutenant casualty rates were extremely high throughout the entire European campaign. General Patton's insistence on the officer's rank being displayed on his helmet did not help matters any.

During February and March 1945, following the Battle of the Bulge, frantic action occurred on the Western Front. It was General Eisenhower's plan to destroy the German Army west of the Rhine; therefore, the American Third and Seventh Armies were assigned the task of destroying the enemy within the Saar-Rhine-Moselle Triangle. The 376th Regiment, of which I Company was a part, was on the east bank of the Saar River just south of Trier.

General Dwight D. Eisenhower, Supreme Commander of all Allied Forces in Europe, then ordered General George S. Patton Jr., Commander of the Third Army, to attack and take the key German town of Trier. Under Patton's command were five armored tank divisions and nine infantry divisions, with the Ninety-fourth Infantry Division being one of them. Most of this strength was concentrated in the VIII Corps and the XII Corps, which were engaged in closing the Battle of the Bulge. After the "Bulge", only three armored divisions remained, with the Third Army and the other two were transferred to the First Army. General Eisenhower ordered Patton not to use the armor unless a clear breakthrough had been made. That restriction placed the burden of the breakthrough right on the shoulders of the Ninety-fourth Infantrymen.

However, General Walker, Commander of the XII Corps, to which the Ninety-fourth Division was attached, had managed to come up with a tank battalion of twenty light tanks to be attached permanently to the Ninety-fourth Infantry Division. This unit, the 778th Tank Battalion, was of great assistance to the Ninety-fourth in breaking through the remaining pillboxes and bunkers of the Siegfried Line. By February 19, it was clear to the corps and division generals that the Ninety-fourth, fighting as ever in snow, cold, sleet, rain, and against fierce German opposition, had penetrated the Siegfried Line.

I was with Colonel Thurston when we checked out the terrain on a reconnaissance mission before the attacks at Nennig, Borg, and Weiss. It was during the fighting in and around the town of Nennig that Axis Sally gave the Ninety-fourth its nickname of "Roosevelt's Butchers". As one after another German counterattacks were repulsed by the 376th Regiment, of which I Company was a part, the bodies of the German dead became a problem. Fortunately, the winter cold kept them refrigerated, but there was no way to evacuate them. Finally, we piled them neatly in rows near abandoned houses.

It is a veritable truth that "the best laid plans of mice and men often go awry". Such was the experience of this twenty-one year old lieutenant, who, in retrospect, finds an element of humor among the horrendous memories of combat that might best be forgotten.

Pointe du Hoc, Normandy.

THE SUN ROSE CLEAR

There was a lull on the battlefront prior to moving toward the Rhine River, with our ultimate goal being the large town of Ludwigshafen. I received word to report to battalion headquarters to meet with Colonel Thurston, third battalion commander, early in the afternoon of March 15, 1945. The Colonel informed me that Company I and my platoon would spearhead a night attack on the town of Grimburg. I was going to ask, "Why me?", for the other officers in our Company were OCS graduates and I had received only a battlefield commission and momentarily felt unqualified. However, on thinking it over, I figured I had more experience in the field than the other officers, as they were only recent replacements.

The regimental captain informed me that the strength of the Grimburg Garrison was maybe five hundred, a thousand, or more Germans. I received maps to study, and after a few hours of absorbing and attempting to memorize as much detail as possible, the Colonel informed me that a platoon of light tanks from Company D of the 778th Tank Battalion would support us. Again, I was about to protest, for everyone knows that tanks can be heard thundering along for miles. This was supposed to be a sneak attack. The Colonel anticipated my protest and ordered me to move out, stating, "I'll be about one hundred yards behind your lead platoon, and we'll cross the IP (initial point) at 2000 hours." The men were issued extra ammunition and K-rations to last a week, and told to rest until zero hour. I could not relax, for this was the first time my platoon would lead a night attack. We had led daylight attacks, but never under the cover of darkness.

At 2000 hours, on the evening of March 15, Third Battalion with Company I and my platoon as point, set out on foot to take the first objective, the town of Grimburg. Walking alongside the tanks with two scouts ahead of me, the attack began. Entering the heavy woods, we encountered roadblocks created by the Germans who had neatly severed fifteen, three-to-four-foot-in-diameter pine trees, which were over one hundred feet tall, dropping them over the road, making it impossible for the tanks to continue. I said a silent prayer, thankful that we could proceed with the attack without the noisy tanks. As we were on radio silence, I sent a runner back to the Colonel asking him for further instructions. I received word to proceed on foot with the attack; the tanks were to catch up as soon as the engineers had cleared the trees from the roads.

After conferring with the Colonel, it was decided to leave the main road and head cross-country, following logging trails to Grimburg, to make up for lost time as a result of the roadblocks. I brought along two maps, and one of them did show some of the logging trails. The lead scout had trouble finding the proper trails because of the darkness in the dense forest. In order to maintain complete blackout conditions, I took my raincoat out of my backpack, which the scouts then held over me, while I lay on the ground to study my map and compass, using my flashlight with the red emblem from a package of Lucky Strike cigarettes inside the lens to diffuse the glow.

The route meandered over hills and across streams, and I had to refer to my map, under cover of the raincoat, three more times. In places, the dense foliage completely shut out any moon or starlight, and we often had to hold on to one another's belts to maintain contact. After groping along for some time, we suddenly came to a stream, only to find that the water was flowing in the wrong direction. So, under the raincoat again! My suspicions were right. We were going downstream, when we should have been going up. We were going away from Grimburg! Well, from that point on, I relied only on my compass and not the maps.

We started to retrace our steps and, as I approached the Colonel, he asked what was happening. I hesitantly whispered, "Wrong turn, Sir." He didn't say a word, thank God. There were over four thousand men strung out along this trail, and now we had to turn them all around and backtrack. The black night was filled with griping, grousing, and grumbling. This would be what was called an Army Snafu (Situation Normal, all Fouled Up). This wrong turn cost us over two hours of marching time, but we were finally heading toward Grimburg.

The Colonel now dropped back to be with the main body. It took another one and one-half hours before we came into a clearing, and there was the town. I sent my runner back to report to the Colonel, who then deployed the main body of men around the town while I Company moved in. The sneak attack had taken the Germans completely off guard. No alert orders had been given to the sentries, because local German commanders hadn't the faintest idea that there were any American troops within miles. As the outposts were rounded up, their only apparent emotion was that of complete astonishment. Company I searched each house, rounding up the town's garrison, all of whom were found in their beds, either sleeping or being entertained by the local Fräuleins. Apparently, more anxious than their soldier-protectors, the citizens of Grimburg were all awake, assembled in the most strongly reinforced cellars.

By 0300 hours, the town was completely cleared. A perimeter defense was set up, and those troops not actually manning the outposts found suitable barns and sheds, and settled down for some much-needed sleep. Colonel Thurston sent a runner asking me to report to him. "Oh, oh," I thought. "I'm in trouble." Imagine my surprise, when he shook my hand, and hugged me so strongly that my helmet flew off my head. With the words, "Lieutenant, a job well done," he smiled and winked at me. This, coming from a West Pointer, really pleased me. I had always admired this man as a true leader of men.

He also told me, that because not a shot was fired and not one life was lost on either side, he was especially proud of me. One of the platoons actually had been fired upon by a sentry, and our boys returned the fire, wounding him. However, this all took place after the town had been secured. Colonel Thurston made sure I received a commendation, though I was embarrassed, for I felt the Lord was looking over me and all those men that night. Had it not been for the German road block earlier that evening and the "wrong turn", we would have hit the town around 2200 hours by using the main road, with noisy, armored, tank support, rather than after midnight, when all was calm and peaceful.

Without an announced purpose, all the officers and noncoms from the Ninety-fourth Infantry Division were called from the front combat lines and assembled in the town square in front of the Hotel De Ville, Borg, Germany. General Patton arrived with great pomp in a caravan, strode forward, and gave a blistering abusive castigation of the Ninety-fourth Division because of a large number of nonbattle casualties (e.g., trench foot). General Patton criticized the Ninety-fourth for having more men captured than any other division in his Third Army. He then said he did not want any commander who flubbed a mission to come back alive, that when a battalion or regiment got into trouble, its commander must get right into the midst of the battle, straighten them out, or get himself killed in the effort. That is what field-grade officers—colonels, lieutenant colonels, and majors—were for. The General then complimented the Ninety-fourth for doing an outstanding job and gave some valuable advice on infantry tactics, etc. He said, "You are never to surrender, never retreat." Before dismissing the Ninety-fourth Division, he called for all battlefield commissioned officers to come forward (there were four, of which I was one). In colorful language, he said, "These are the true combat officers. You son-of-a-bitches from West Point and OCS should follow their true example of leadership." The General then presented me, Lieutenant Roland H. Vogt, Company I, 376th Infantry Regiment, with the Silver Star Medal. I was thrilled, but embarrassed, to be singled out by the general in front of my fellow soldiers. I was also awarded two Bronze Stars during my combat tour in Europe.

May 8, 1945, was declared as V-E (victory in Europe) day following the Nazi surrender to General Eisenhower in Reims, France, on May 7.

On June 13, 1945, we entered Strakonice, Czechoslovakia. The German forces we found there were made up mostly of young boys, as young as fourteen years old, and old men wearing only parts of a uniform and looking hungry.

One day, my runner came to me with the message that there were Germans on the radio from Prague begging for "Amerikaner" to answer their call. They wanted to surrender to the Americans and not the Russians. They said they would guarantee safe passage through Pilsen to Prague. I immediately told Colonel Thurston of this, and he relayed the request to Regimental and Division headquarters. We never heard a word from the "upper echelon". They probably suspected a trap.

Unfortunately, I did not have enough points to go home when the war in Europe was over because of receiving my battlefield commission. Officers needed more points than the troops, so I was destined to spend one more year in Europe. We did get orders to go to the Pacific for the invasion of Japan, but V-J (victory in Japan) came with overwhelming suddenness.

I was promoted as a captain to regimental staff on June 29, 1945, as liaison officer for Colonel H. H. McClune, regimental commander, whose command post was stationed in Strakonice, Czechoslovakia. I was billeted in the town of Klatovy, about twelve miles away and ninety-two miles from the large and beautiful town of Pilsen. After three months in Czechoslovakia, the Russians told us to leave because "Roosevelt and Churchill gave us this land." I then spent seven months in Oberammergau, Germany, where I moved twenty-nine officers into the Schilcherhof Inn. I also stayed there until I returned to the United States.

In the Army, we had been called ASTP (Army Special Training Personnel). In 1943 and 1944, a male who graduated from high school with a very high IQ was sent to Fort Benning, Georgia, with the intention of forming a special group for intelligence activities. However, the ever-increasing rate of casualties on the front lines in Europe and on the islands of the Pacific resulted in these boys being sent to both fronts as replacements. Of course, we were happy to have them, as we were constantly forty to sixty percent below our fully staffed regimental strength. But when I found out where these replacements came from, I could not believe the Army would send them out to be used as "gun fodder". Many of our recruits could not read or write, and yet these highly intelligent ASTP boys were thrown into this mix. There were ten ASTP boys in my platoon. At the end of the war, three remained. One, whom I had promoted to sergeant, went to West Point, and is now a retired full Colonel. Another, whom I had also promoted to sergeant in the field, was badly wounded when I sent him to lead a combat patrol. He lay, severely injured throughout the night, was rescued the next day, then sent to a hospital in England, and sent back home. He became a professor of physics at Yale University. The third became a sergeant also and later an electrical engineer for Boeing Aircraft.

I eventually returned to Appleton, Wisconsin, in January 1946, finished college, married, took over the National Guard Company, and went to work with a manufacturing company.

> My current reflections on my time in combat reveal that our experiences seem to set us apart, forever, from anyone who had not been in combat. We didn't want pity. We just wished that those back home could understand what we were going through and that any inconveniences that they had were trivial. There were times

THE SUN ROSE CLEAR

when replacements sent up to the front lines never had their names added to our units, because they got hit before we even knew their names. They came up, confused, frightened, and hopeful, got wounded or killed, and went back to the rear on the same route by which they came. They were faceless to us, like unread books on a shelf. They never had the chance to belong to the company, or make any friends, before they got hit. It's amazing that although Company I was outstanding, so few of the men were decorated for bravery. Uncommon valor was displayed so often, it went largely unnoticed, for it was expected of us. So many were awarded the Purple Heart, and it was my good fortune to be one of the few exceptions. This will always amaze me. The few men, like me, who never got hit can claim with justification that we survived the abyss of war as fugitives from the law of averages. To this day, I still ask myself, why me? I thank God each day for giving me one more day.

Roland Vogt died of heart failure, March 29, 2002, in Appleton, Wisconsin, at the age of eighty years.

German coastal defenses in Normandy.

German gun emplacement at Pointe du Hoc, Omaha Beach, Normandy.

HEDGEROW COUNTRY
As told by
Dr. Earl Spangler

The horrors of D-day and the early days of the invasion of Fortress Europe and the Atlantic Wall were now history. The march through France toward Germany had begun. The reality of casualties, wounds, pain, fear, and death quickly replaced the pre-invasion bravado. The need to get the job done, field-by-field, hedgerow-to-hedgerow, foxhole-by-foxhole kept the soldiers going, hoping and praying that they could survive and contribute to the success of the operation.

I was commissioned in the Army as a First Lieutenant through ROTC and served at Camp Wolters, Texas; Fort Benning, Georgia; and at Fort Leonard Wood, Missouri; before going on maneuvers in Louisiana for three months in 1944. I returned to Camp Breckinridge, Kentucky, and was placed on overseas orders for the D-day invasion of Europe. After several days aboard the SS *Susan B. Anthony*, I landed in Glasgow, Scotland, and began movement through replacement channels toward southern England, eventually boarding a British transport to cross the English Channel one-and-one-half weeks after D-day. As I waded ashore on Omaha Beach, I noted a sunken ship that turned out to be the SS *Susan B. Anthony*, which had hit a mine on D-day as it carried troops for the invasion.

I was placed in charge of thirty enlisted replacements, given a bivouac area, and told that eventually some front-line units needing replacements would come and get us. When the trucks arrived, we piled on, drove through shattered villages and forlorn fields, and were dumped off at a crossroads. I looked around and saw evidence of previous action, such as foxholes, but there was an eerie silence. I put out security and settled in. That night, tracer bullets went over us in both directions, along with other gunfire. This did not seem right. By morning, no one had come for us, so I decided to find out where we were and what was happening. Going back the way we had come seemed to be a good choice. I came to a command tent, presented myself to a major, and explained the situation. He said, "My God, Lieutenant, you are between the lines." That explained a lot.

I returned to our bivouac area, and in time, some more trucks came, picked us up, drove for awhile, and deposited us in a rest area. I reported to the company commander and was assigned as Weapons Platoon Commander, Company C, 116th Regiment, Twenty-ninth Infantry Division.

This was hedgerow country. Hedgerows are masses of tangled vegetation consisting of centuries old beech, oak, and chestnut trees, with intertwined branches and roots forming a solid barrier, separating field from field, pasture from pasture, and farm from farm in this northern province of Normandy, France. Tanks and infantry could not penetrate the hedges and were forced to pass through exits at the end of the hedgerows. The Germans had these exit paths well sighted in and could deliver

Hedgerow.

Hedgerow in Normandy.

mortar and artillery fire at a moment's notice on the advancing troops and tanks. Only squad- or platoon-sized units could operate in these congested small areas. There was no front line. Each hedge row and field, with its own troops, tanks, and artillery, operated independently of other units facing the same barriers. German and Allied military units were often just a field apart, and we were able to hear each other's movements and conversations. A foxhole next to a hedgerow was not a good idea. Digging into the roots was difficult, and artillery bursts in the tree branches above would drive shrapnel straight down. Wearing a helmet was mandatory.

If advances were to be made, units would have to solve the hedgerow problems. Attempts to climb over or use existing openings ended badly. Using mortars and artillery to destroy the hedges did not work. Tanks were stopped cold by the vegetation. Demolition charges did work rather well, but it was determined that it would take seventeen tons of explosives to advance one-and-one-half miles, so this plan was squelched. A tank driver in the 747th Tank Battalion suggested welding two pipes, four feet long and six inches in diameter, to the front of a tank and reinforcing them with angle irons. The tank would then hit a hedgerow, gouge out two holes into which explosives, packed in 105 mm Howitzer shell casings, could be placed and detonated, making a hole large enough for a tank to go through. Later, we were able to replace these pipes with solid steel prongs, which eliminated the need for explosives and let the tank punch through.

Once through, the tankers would spray the area with machine gun and other fire, and a squad or more of infantry would follow with .30 caliber light machine guns, lay down a base of fire, identify German positions, and clear the area so that others could follow. Such advances were measured in only short distances until the next hedgerow was reached, and then the whole process would begin all over again. In many cases, we only moved a few yards per day. This situation would continue in Normandy until late July and early August 1944, when St. Lo was taken and a breakout occurred, opening the way for the dash to Paris and the encirclement, capture, and slaughter of thousands of Germans in the Falaise Gap operation.

Shortly after arriving in Normandy, the company commander told me that there was a soldier in a nearby town who was causing trouble in a house and the lady of the house wanted him out, but he refused to leave. My mission was to get him out. When I met the lady, she left no doubt, in French and English, that she was unhappy. After trying reason, tact, and a direct order to no avail, the unruly sergeant grew more vocal and defiant. I unslung my carbine, flipped off the safety, leveled it at him, and told him to move, which he did. I reported back to the company commander, thus completing my first act of liberation in France.

In combat, you lose track of time. You eat when you can and relieve yourself when you can,

Lieutenant Earl Spangler in 1945.

hoping not to be spotted by a sniper in an awkward, pants-down, squatting position. On one occasion when it was fairly quiet, I decided to carefully go out into the woods, where I found a somewhat sheltered spot, lowered my trousers, and squatted. At the same time, I cradled my carbine in my arms the best I could. Things were quiet, and I reflected a bit on earlier days in my life when I went into the woods hunting and had been confronted with a similar urge.

My reverie was broken when I detected some movement in a tall tree forty yards away to my left. Was it a sniper drawing a bead on me as I sat rather awkwardly and somewhat helplessly on my haunches? This did not seem like the way I should meet my end. An infantry man should go out charging the enemy, weapon blazing, eyes focused. As I look back on it, what difference would it have made? If the worst happened, someone would find me, check my dog tags, throw me into a truck, and eventually deliver me, pants up or down. I slowly and hopefully unobtrusively began to raise my carbine and point it the best way I could to where the movement had occurred. I curled my finger around the trigger and

THE SUN ROSE CLEAR

began to squeeze. Just then, a flurry of movement occurred, the branches shook, and out flew a big black bird. This incident spelled relief in more than one way on that day in June 1944.

One of my most vivid memories of the march through Normandy was a church service held by a chaplain in an apple orchard. Soldiers knelt and prayed together, sang a hymn, and listened to a short message emphasizing the need to place their trust in God. No cathedral ever served its congregation better. It has been said many times that there are "no atheists in foxholes". The soldiers marched on from that apple orchard with a comfort and peace in their hearts that passes all understanding.

The Normandy French farmers had been under German occupation for four years, and most anti-Germans had left the area; therefore, we were watched with sullen and furtive glances and near-hostile attitudes. On occasion, a friendly Frenchman would furnish us with milk or vegetables, but this was rare. A drink of fresh milk from a farmer tasted better than any cold beer on a hot day had ever tasted. Occasionally, they would furnish us with Calvados, an alcoholic concoction. It was a triple threat. You could drink it, you could use it in your cigarette lighter, or you could run your Jeep on it!

Sleep deprivation is a given under most combat conditions. Even while sleeping, you are not resting well, as the enemy may try to catch you asleep and take your position and your life. The slightest noise will awaken you. There is no night or day, just time that you lose track of. In one period, to the best of my recollection, I got six hours of sleep in as many days. There probably were catnaps, but no solid sleep. Soldiers often break under the strain of sleep deprivation and under the constant exposure to danger, and death. I remember one evening when things were fairly quiet, suddenly, from a nearby hedgerow, a soldier came running across the field hollering incoherently and threatening to expose our position. I ran out of my foxhole, tackled him, got him under control, and passed him back to the medics. Some who reached their threshold of endurance either shot themselves or begged someone to do it so that they could get evacuated. The self-inflicted wound (SIW) was not that uncommon, but most were not categorized as such.

Units from the rear came to the battlefield to collect, identify, and remove the casualties. It was a gruesome task, and one learned to excuse these collectors if they were often drunk. The dead were laid out in rows or stacked like cordwood awaiting collection. They would be taken to the rear, identified further, registered by a graves registration unit, and placed in a temporary cemetery. Later, they would be removed to a permanent site or returned home.

In the field, there were good military leaders and there were bad military leaders. Some generals were known among the troops as "butchers" for exposing their troops constantly, and often unnecessarily, to danger for the general's personal aggrandizement. One day, I saw a two-star general walking around and in front of him, on a leash, was a bulldog wearing a red bandanna. It was our division commander. He seemed to have a propensity for putting the Twenty-ninth Division in any advances, attacks, or dangerous spots available, seemingly with no regard for the cost. On the other hand, there were majors, lieutenant colonels, full colonels, and generals who valiantly stepped into harm's way, as they led battalions, regiments, and task forces into battle.

I was eventually evacuated to the Forty-ninth General Hospital in Oxford, England, with battle fatigue and an infected pilonidal cyst. I was then transferred to the Ninety-sixth General Hospital near Malvern, England, and when my patient status ended, I was sent to a replacement facility at Litchfield, near Coventry, best known as Colonel Killian's Concentration Camp. Here, I took part in a disliked, abhorrent, and largely ineffectual policy. Colonel Killian wanted no food wasted and had officers at each mess hall to see that every person cleaned his plate under threat of court-martial. My policy was to turn my back to any garbage can so that if questioned, I could truly say that I had seen no waste. I was eventually returned to the Ninety-sixth General Hospital as head of the rehabilitation section and remained there until the end of the war in Europe. When the war in Europe ended, the Ninety-sixth was gradually dismantled, and I was sent home. I boarded the *Queen Elizabeth* and reached New York in three and a half days. Also on board was Rabbi Stephen Wise and Colonel Jimmy Stewart with his Air Force unit. As we debarked at Pier 90, we were serenaded by Cab Calloway and his band.

Lieutenant Spangler aboard the Queen Elizabeth returning to the U.S. after V-E Day.

I regard my service with pride and satisfaction. I respect and appreciate my fellow veterans. I have never found a WWII veteran I did not trust nor one who would not be helpful, should the occasion arise. Ninety-nine percent of them served honorably; loved their country; did their jobs competently; became good husbands, fathers, and grandfathers; served their community in other capacities; passed on their pride and perseverance as best they could; and became one of the most stable and contributive

THE SUN ROSE CLEAR

generations this country has ever seen.

Most Americans do not fight wars because they want to and do not memorialize wars for self-aggrandizement. But we did not shirk, and even now do not shirk our obligations. We hoped, in 1941, that what we had to do would be justified, successful, and meaningful. Today, we know that it was. In short, we just did our jobs.

> *Lieutenant Spangler was awarded the Bronze Star, the Combat Infantry Badge, the American Theater Ribbon, the European Theater Ribbon with one Star, the European Victory Medal, and the Medal of Liberated France. Upon returning to the United States, he was promoted to captain and was discharged from the army in January 1946. He remained in the army reserves until 1969, achieving the rank of lieutenant Colonel. In the meantime, he returned to graduate school, completed his doctorate, and became a professor of history and a college administrator. He taught at Macalaster College in St. Paul, Minnesota, and Carthage College in Kenosha, Wisconsin, where he was also academic dean, before retiring to Waupaca, Wisconsin.*

Lieutenant Colonel Spangler, Army Reserve, 1960.

THE BATTLE OF THE HURTGEN FOREST
As told by
Sid Miller

Sid Miller entered the U.S. Army in 1941 as a private, was progressively promoted to the rank of sergeant, qualified for OCS (Officers Candidate School), and was commissioned a second lieutenant. Battlefield promotions raised his rank to captain.

Sid Miller married Lillian Roesler, from northern Wisconsin, while he was stationed at Fort Wolter, Texas, in 1942. Their first son was born in March 1944, three weeks before Sid left for overseas.

Miller landed on a Normandy beach on D-day plus three, June 9, 1944, and fought through France, Belgium, and through the Hurtgen Forest into Germany. He was captured and became a prisoner of war on November 29, 1944.

THE SUN ROSE CLEAR

Sergeant Miller in 1941.

Day 1 (for F Company, Twenty-sixth Infantry, First Division, in the Hurtgen Forest)

After the street-by-street fighting in Aachen and the holding action at Verlautenheide, the initial entry into the Hurtgen Forest involved a whole new set of tactics. Adjustments were, out of necessity, made by the hour and sometimes by the minute. Due to the terrain, we had no tank or motorized equipment support. It was strictly up to the GI foot soldier adjusting to the prevailing conditions, and how much training each had received. The more experience he had, the better chance he had of surviving and contributing to the success of the operation.

My platoon was on the extreme right flank, and I was assigned to contact the Fourth Division. The area we took over was a pine plantation and a meadow with a small stream running through it. I looked across the meadow and could observe no movement of anyone where the Fourth Division was supposed to be. Thinking that I had better cross the meadow and try and make contact with the Fourth, I told my platoon sergeant to get three men, one with a set of wire cutters, and follow me across. I took off at top speed, jumped the small stream, crossed the trail, and lay there watching the others follow. I told the man with the wire cutters to cut a hole through the concertina wire, but then I noticed a GI about fifty yards to our right. After ascertaining that he was from the Fourth Division, I asked where his officers and noncoms were located, and he motioned that they were to his right rear. I ordered him to go back and report that contact had been made with the First Division on their left.

I took off and made it back across the meadow to the pine trees, and the sergeant followed. We were catching our breath when there were two explosions in the area we had crossed. Two of the men following us had stepped on shoe mines and sustained wounds to their feet and legs. I called for medics who went to the aid of the downed men. We found out that the trees were booby trapped, evidently by the unit we had relieved. The trip wires, shoe mines, and sniper fire held up our advance for some time.

Darkness comes early in November, especially in the woods. Our total advance that first day in the Hurtgen had been a mere 150 to 200 yards.

Day 2

It had just started getting daylight and, as was my usual practice, I put my helmet up even with the ground and, if no one took a pot shot at it, I would stick my head in it and look all around before exposing the rest of my body. I had begun to look around, when I saw Lieutenant Smith, second platoon leader, who had his foxhole about thirty yards from mine, put his hands on the side of the foxhole and raise his body half out. The sniper's shot came and down he went. This prompted a fuselage of shots in the direction where the shot came from. We dragged Smith out of his foxhole to find that he had been shot through the stomach, just above his left hip. He was evacuated to the rear.

We then moved out with E Company on the left, and I had the right flank platoon. We started receiving treebursts, artillery shell bursts in the treetops above, which would cause shrapnel to forcefully rain straight down. These treebursts took a heavy toll throughout the time we were in the Hurtgen.

The Germans had constructed bunkers of logs camouflaged with natural forest growth, built in such a way that the narrow openings they could fire from were level with the ground. Encountering this type of defense was new to the guys who had only experienced street fighting, and it took some thoughtful decisions to combat such new tactics. Evidently, these bunkers had communications with artillery and mortar units in their rear, because as soon as we overran one of a series of connecting bunkers, we would receive one hell of an artillery barrage, which inflicted heavy losses from treebursts. It was the German tactic to abandon these bunkers as we approached, let the artillery and mortars come down on us, and then, as we retreated, retake the ground with no opposition. In contrast, as soon as we overran one of these bunker complexes, I would tell the noncoms to keep moving forward, as in this way we got into a more or less neutral zone between the bunkers and the artillery.

I would like to mention two men who were unusual individuals among the many I had the pleasure of being in combat with. The first was Pop Chaney, an individual who was extremely quiet, but very combat wise. He was a PFC (private, first class) and, although I had tried to promote him several times, he would not accept any promotion. He just wanted to be left alone and do his duty as he saw it, *and* he knew what he was doing. Pop was a turkey farmer in Ohio prior to becoming a GI, and he had the facility to "smell" Germans. As we advanced through the forest, I made it a point to keep track of Pop and watch him. At one point, we came into a sparsely wooded area of oak and pines. Suddenly, Pop held up his hand and all of us in his vicinity stopped and looked. Right along the edge of the pines, not thirty yards from us, appeared seven German soldiers going in the direction from which we had just come. They never had a chance. How Pop knew they were coming was never determined, but by his actions he prevented many casualties on our side.

Another individual whom everyone respected was a PFC by the name of Cohen from New York. He always carried a paperback book in his back pocket, and whenever we got in a fire fight or under artillery or mortar fire, he would sit down, take out his book, and start reading. It was really a morale booster for the rest of the men to see Cohen sit there and read a book when it seemed as though the world was coming to an end. The last time I saw Cohen, he was walking to the rear to find an aid station to plug up the hole where he had taken one through the meaty part of his right thigh.

Day 3

The third day in the Hurtgen started out calmer than the previous ones, as I think we had gotten through the majority of log bunkers. We had advanced so far beyond our lines of communication, supplies, and units, which were supposed to be on our right and left, that we were ordered to hold up in the early afternoon, dig in, and set up a perimeter defense. We set up our machine guns, BARs (Browning Automatic Rifles) and surrounded them with riflemen in such a way that there was a good field of fire to our front.

No sooner had I finished checking my platoon for the way they were dug in and camouflaged and returned to where my platoon sergeant and I had dug in, when it seemed as though every gun that would fire had opened up from our troops. About fifty to sixty yards in front of us, a column of Germans three abreast had approached from our right front and were proceeding to our left. I would estimate there were between seventy-five to one hundred in the group carrying their guns and other equipment, as though there was no other person within one hundred miles of them. I am quite sure it so surprised our GIs that they held their fire until the whole column was within view.

What happened then should not have happened to any group of well trained soldiers. The Germans never had a chance. Not knowing the firepower that we had, some of the Germans charged up the slope right toward us. A few took refuge in the conifers, and we called in artillery fire on that area. There were few, if any, German survivors. It was determined that this was a column of elite Wehrmacht soldiers making their way to provide support for the village of Hamich, which was being attacked by U.S. units from the Sixteenth Infantry of the First Division. By eliminating them, we perhaps greatly assisted the Sixteenth.

Day 4

Day four found us all dug in with necessary improvements made to our position. Early in the morning, I was called up to the company command post, where a short meeting was held with our commanding officer, Lieutenant Fogarty, in which he informed us that he was sending our first sergeant, along with some ambulatory wounded, to the rear. The first sergeant was completely exhausted and on the brink of collapsing.

Lieutenant Fogarty asked me if I would move forward and see if I could get a triangulation on the artillery that was giving us so much trouble. I took a sergeant with me, and we moved to three different locations, plotting the area that seemed to be where the artillery was coming from. When you are in heavy woods, such as we were, the direction of sounds is distorted due to echoes and the density of the trees, so it was difficult to pinpoint the actual area from which they were firing. When I got back to the company command post, I found that a treeburst had taken Lieutenant Fogarty along with several others. Lieutenant Fogarty was an excellent combat officer and his loss was mourned by all who served under him. His radio man was spared, so we still had some contact to rely on.

We had been making very good progress by outflanking some of the log bunkers and confronting the German defenders from a different direction than where they had set up their defenses. It was apparent that the defenders were in the bunkers not first-class soldiers, but had been sent to delay us while the main forces pulled back, then the artillery and mortars would inflict heavy damage on our ranks. The Germans who surrendered seemed more than willing to give up. Their ages, uniforms, and equipment indicated they were inexperienced replacements sent in to be sacrificed.

When a prisoner was taken, there were not too many alternatives as to his disposition. I would send a runner to take him back to the rear, hoping that there could be contact with units where the prisoner could be taken care of. Usually, there would be some shots fired in the rear and the runner would again join us, no questions asked.

E Company had encountered some extensive resistance and the commanding officer of E Company had called for some artillery. Whether because of short rounds or the wrong coordinates, the bursts landed on or very near E Company resulting in casualties, including Captain Zell Smoot, commanding officer of E Company. Another officer lost in just two days.

As late afternoon approached, we were ordered to hold up, dig in, and set up a perimeter defense. Very shortly after we had set up, two German soldiers came walking toward us on the left of my platoon where I had set up a light machine gun. They were talking and carrying their weapons like they were hunting squirrels or

THE SUN ROSE CLEAR

rabbits. They were shot and lay wounded all night. The next morning, as we advanced again, I noticed they were both dead and had attempted to patch each other up with their first aid kits. In combat, you find yourself in a position where life is cheap and you see death all around you and your thoughts of protecting your men, as well as yourself, are paramount above all else. Your knowledge of the whole situation is so narrow that it obliterates all else except in your immediate vicinity, and you react accordingly.

C rations, K rations, and D bars were our only fare and, as we could start no fires. It was always a cold meal in a cold woods. It amazed me that the men, including myself, could keep going effectively on such rations. At one point, while going through some thick spruce, I ran across a pile of vomit that some German soldier had given up. It consisted of carrots, potatoes, and chunks of meat and I thought, how much more efficient their lines of supply were than ours if they could serve their troops a balanced meal. The pile was rather fresh, so it was quite evident that remaining alert was a top priority.

When we came out of the denser part of the forest we were in a more or less open area surrounding a castle. During an earlier shelling of the castle, a mortar shell had landed in the court yard inside the castle's perimeter, and there was a quite large hole, about ten yards across and eight to ten feet deep where there had been some sort of a basement. We had thrown all the resulting debris of the battle down this hole, among which were the ends of an iron bed. Several German bodies were thrown in this hole, and one of the bodies landed with its back draped over the bedstead. It was a rather gruesome site to behold.

I had selected a corner of the castle which at one time had been quarters for swine, as it had clean straw on the brick floor. It was warm, dry, and very comfortable in comparison to the forest. Among some of the items found were glass jars of meat and, after warming it up on our little gas stoves, we enjoyed real meat for the first time in a long time. The canned cherries were also excellent. That night, I enjoyed about six hours of warm sleep.

Just as it was breaking daylight the next morning, we observed some movement to our left front and, upon putting the glasses on it, found it to be a man coming in with his hands over his head. The only clothing he had on was GI underwear. It turned out to be one of the men who had been on outpost. Sometime during the night, he had been pulled out of his foxhole by the Germans and was being taken back toward their lines when their patrol ran into one of ours. There ensued a brief fire fight, during which he had time to escape back toward our lines. The Germans had made him take off all his clothes, including shoes and socks, no doubt to obtain GI clothing, as well as to prevent his escape. He was a tall, thin individual and as he came in, it reminded me of the way Ichabod Crane was supposed to have looked.

That day we received replacements and, as we lined them up to orient them to the situation, check their gear, and assign them to platoons, I was surprised to find they carried voluminous jungle packs. They must have been hurriedly sent to us just as soon as they got off a boat from the replacement depot. Upon questioning the men, I found that they had just had the minimum of basic training. My platoon received nine replacements, and I lined them up with their packs in front of them and told them to throw everything in the hole except a blanket, shelter half, extra socks, and toilet articles, which would constitute their combo pack. It was really sad to see them sort out all the personal things they were carrying.

As they approached the edge of the hole, the first thing they saw was the one German body draped over the bedstead, his face looking right up at them. The shock to a replacement seeing such a sight really had a sobering effect; it was rather difficult to imagine their feelings.

About two hundred yards from the castle there was a fork in the road, one branch going east to the village of Merode and the other continuing uphill to the castle. After the replacements had remade their packs and I had checked their weapons and ammunition, I took them to our dug-in positions across the road and assigned them to the squad leaders, instructing them to put one new replacement in with one of those who had experienced the trials of going through the Hurtgen.

The Germans had been shelling the junction where the two roads split, so we had moved away from that point as far as possible. A medium tank came up the road and the driver, not being familiar, had stopped north of the "Y," had gotten out of his tank, and was standing alongside. The Germans laid a shell at the intersection and down went the tank driver. I hollered to a medic and we went down in a hurry to where the tank driver was lying. He was very pale but conscious and, upon examination, was found to have a quite large hole through the upper part of his thigh just below the buttocks. The medic said, "Boy, that is a stateside hole if I ever saw one." He was removed to the rear on a stretcher-bearing jeep after being patched up in the field.

I started back to the castle along a path. The medic and a corporal were on the path ahead of me. As we approached the road, they stopped to let a jeep pulling a trailer pass. The road was muddy from the rain and snow, and the jeep's tires dug into the ruts. As the jeep and trailer passed, there was one hell of an explosion. The medic crumpled and the corporal went down; all I received were some holes through my jacket. The Germans had cleverly laid the mine deep enough, with the road being used extensively, the unit passing over it would eventually set it off. The medic was dead, and the corporal had many lacerations around the upper part of his body. It seemed that we were continually having casualties that we could ill afford. It was getting to the point where we were all expecting to get killed or wounded at any time.

Later on that evening, we received two replacement officers. Upon talking with them, I found out they had been stationed along the coast of Florida with an antiaircraft battery and had little or no infantry training. Although I oriented them with our past experience, it was difficult for them to comprehend. My impression was that they were perhaps ROTC graduates. After they had been assigned to the Second and Third platoons, I offered one of them, Lieutenant Senor, to share my temporary quarters in the swine facility. I really felt sorry for them, suspecting that they would not fare well once the action started again. The latter proved to be an accurate assessment.

The day before Thanksgiving we were still confined and not stirring out of our positions other than checking on equipment, ammunition, and field rations. The day after Thanksgiving remained status quo. Someone in the higher echelon had inquired if all the units had received the traditional dinner of turkey, dressing, mashed potatoes, cranberries, etc. F Company, Twenty-sixth Infantry was the lone unit not to have participated in that holiday event. Headquarters sent up a bunch of marmite insulated cans with warm food in them and I had to figure out how to feed those who were dug in their holes without encountering more casualties. I talked it over with my platoon sergeant, Sergeant Sheffield, and asked if he would go with me to help carry the cans. The plan was to stop at each hole and have the men put their mess kits out, and we would fill them. He agreed. We ran carrying the cans between us and established a record for fast food service in the Hurtgen Forest. Luck was with us. During this operation no rounds came in and, although a little late, the change in diet was really welcome.

Final Day

The final day of combat in the Hurtgen Forest for F Company of the Twenty-sixth Infantry actually began on the late afternoon of the twenty-eighth of November. The officers decided that E and F companies were to attack the village of Merode and Schlich. Jump-off was to be at 9:00 a.m. Sectors were assigned to each platoon of F Company, with the mission to take the castle of Merode. F Company was to initially provide covering fire for E Company, which would go around the right flank and proceed to the village of Schlich. Two tanks, one medium and one light, were to provide support for the operation. My platoon, the First, was to lay down covering fire across a field which was flanked by forest cover on the left and two rows of willow trees on the right.

Desiring some indication as to what we would encounter the next day, I crawled over the crest of the hill where we had dug in on the reverse slope and, just after getting over the crest, I noticed a camouflaged bunker right in front of me, with the opening facing toward the German lines. I heard some voices in English and called and identified myself, crawling around the edge of the small bunker. There were two young GIs in it, neither of whom looked older than nineteen or twenty. Their ammunition clips were lined up on the ground in front of them and, not too far in front on a down slope, were the bodies of three Germans who had evidently stumbled onto the two GI sharpshooters early that morning. The GIs told me there were still snipers around that they hadn't been able to locate. Looking down the slope, which was covered with ferns and a medium density of oak trees, I made note of where I could set up my two light machine guns to provide the covering fire.

I think it was a day prior to this that we had all received Christmas cards to send home with the First Division crest on them. We had all the men fill them out, and as I look back now, the greater majority of the men who filled out the cards were to become casualties the next day. How awfully sad it must have felt to the recipients of the cards when they found out later that the sender had become a casualty shortly after sending it.

That evening of November 28, 1944, a GI by the name of Dowd came up to me and stated that he had been assigned to my platoon. By the way he was dressed and his actions, he was not a recruit and he had seen combat. I inquired as to why he had been sent to us from the Third Battalion. He put it bluntly saying, "I am a f_ _k up." He definitely was not a garrison soldier, but he was wise to combat situations, one you would want beside you when the going got tough. As far as I was concerned, he was most welcome. I asked him what he would like to handle in the way of a weapon. He said, "I like the BAR (Browning Automatic Rifle) and I'm good with it." If there was ever anything I needed, it was a good BAR man, as none of the replacements could handle one and it was difficult for any of the older men to carry it due to its weight.

To say that I was apprehensive about the coming day's encounter would be putting it mildly. A new commanding officer, two new inexperienced platoon leaders, and a large number of new replacements did not appear to me to be the right combination for a cohesive fighting unit. It had all of the earmarks of a disaster, which it eventually turned out to be.

At the appointed time on the morning of the twenty-ninth, the squad leaders started their men out and, with an eye toward possible snipers, advanced carefully over the crest and proceeded down the slope. The Second and Third platoons were on my right, and E Company was to the right of them with two tanks. We had not proceeded too far before encountering small arms fire. The two new lieutenants, along with a number of others who had been advancing standing up, became casualties. The lack of training was quite evident on their part. My platoon sergeant,

THE SUN ROSE CLEAR

Tom Sheffield, and I tried to get the men moving forward, but many of them were dead. One of our aid men had taken off his bag and was about to apply gauze and tape to a downed man when the snipers shot him. There were so many wounded or dead that Tom went over to pick up the aid bag. As I approached him, his head snapped sideways and when he turned and looked at me, I could see he had been shot through the mouth. It looked like half his jawbone and teeth were gone where the bullet came out. I gave him two shots of morphine and motioned him to go back over the hill.

My radio man, Pee Wee Humphrey, motioned to me that the CO wanted me on the radio. We were on our stomachs in the tall ferns and, when I picked up the radio, the CO told me to take charge of the Second and Third platoons also. I asked the CO where he was, and he said on the right flank. After contacting the CO, I was able to locate and move to his position. The CO and two other officers were huddled in a small depression and I informed the CO that, as far as I was concerned, the Second and Third platoons did not exist. The men I had tried to get moving forward were all casualties.

I went back to see how my own platoon was doing. The din was terrific, as we were under heavy mortar and artillery fire. I crawled back to where my squad leaders had set up and motioned to Sergeant Cramer to come over. He had set up on the extreme left flank at the edge of the field, and I told him to get his men and follow me, as we could not stay there under the barrage. He and I had just separated and taken a few steps apart when a 120 mm mortar landed right where we had been standing. When my head cleared a little, I found I was laying in a depression in the ground with my lower body way back over my head. With some difficulty, I got untangled and sat up. My helmet was gone, as well as my M1 rifle. When I looked around, I noted that Sergeant Cramer had gotten up and was staggering around.

As I sat there trying to get the ringing out of my head and get my eyes focused again, another 120 mm came in about twenty yards to my right, but did not thoroughly explode. It ended up in a piece of metal resembling a wheel which tore through the brush, knocking down small trees. Knowing that the only way out of such a situation was to go forward into the more or less neutral area between the small arms fire and the mortar and artillery area, I picked up a helmet, motioned to Cramer to come, and started toward the village along the willow trees to our right.

When I got to the tree area, GIs were laying all along the bottom of the bank trying to take cover where there was none. Both Cramer and I tried to get them to move forward with us, but mortar bursts were dropping all around, and it seemed to freeze them right where they lay. There was so much noise that perhaps they couldn't hear.

As we ran down the ditch into the village, I looked back to see where Cramer was, and I saw our two tanks taking off back over the hill we had just come down. At the end of the ditch there was a medium-size house. We approached the back door. The usual procedure was to either kick the door in or shoot the lock out and then throw in a grenade. Why I didn't do it this time I'll never know, but I just pushed the door open and was looking down a stairway going into the basement. At the bottom of the stairway, there was a bed, and in the middle of the bed was a young woman with the bed clothes covering the lower half of her body. She had jet black hair and her hands were in a praying position. I shudder to think of what would have happened if I had thrown the grenade in, as she was evidently crippled.

I hollered for "soldaten," and I'll be darned if two well-dressed German soldiers in uniform didn't come up the stairs with their hands above their heads. Checking them for weapons revealed none. One was evidently a cavalry or motorized soldier, as he had on leather leggings and pegged pants with a clean tunic. The other was a plain *Wehrmacht* individual.

While trying to get information out of my German prisoners, the door opened and in came the CO and his executive officer. When the CO saw I had prisoners, he walked up to the one with the cavalry dress, grabbed him by the throat, and choked him until the guys eyes started to bulge. My thought was how in the hell am I going to get any information out of a dead German. The CO was irrational and kept hollering, "You son-of-a-bitch. You've killed all of my men." Using my hands locked together, I gave his arms an upward thrust and knocked his hands off the guy's neck. I told the CO that my mission was still to get to the castle, and I needed this guy for information. I grabbed the guy and went out the back door to where Cramer and two others were crouched along a brick wall.

I asked Cramer if he knew what the situation was beyond the wall. He said he didn't, so I told him to take one of the men and see if he could find an area opposite the castle where we could observe the area around it. He came back shortly, saying that, as he approached the back end of a building opposite the castle, he saw eight Germans run across the street and into the castle area. I took the prisoner with me. I had just jumped over the wall when the ground started heaving with mortar bursts in the area just behind us.

I, along with the prisoner, took refuge in a five-by-five shed that was made out of cement. The cupboards along the walls were lined with empty glass canning jars. The building shook and heaved, knocking the glass jars down. The breaking of glass plus the din from exploding shells made both of us start shaking. I had a pack of Lucky Strike cigarettes and, for something to do, I took one out and lit it. I noticed that the German was also shaking badly, so I offered him one, which he gratefully accepted. So here we both were, American and German, standing shoulder to shoulder, smoking a cigarette.

After the shelling had subsided, I looked out and found that Sergeant Cramer and the two other GIs had taken refuge in a small nearby shed, so we made a run for the building they had picked out. The building Sergeant Cramer had picked was a brick home that fronted the street; it had a big bay window with no glass in it. Looking out, we could see the castle across the street set back among trees and thick shrubbery. Our brick house had a stairway going down into a small basement that contained a potato bin about three-fourths full of potatoes. It was now late in the afternoon and starting to get dark. All of a sudden in through the back door came Dowd with his BAR. He was a welcome addition, except that he didn't have too much ammunition and the rest of us had a total of about ten clips for our M1s among us. The CO had his radio man with him, a guy named Miller, so he did have communications with the battalion CO and no doubt informed him of the situation we were in.

After we had settled down in the potato bin, it gave me a chance to think about our position. I was so utterly exhausted, both physically and mentally from the day's events that it was hard to think, especially with my ears ringing. As near as I could determine, myself, four GIs, and a German prisoner occupied a position in the village of Merode that was the farthest advance into Germany at that time.

Shortly after that encounter, we heard tanks on the street in front, and I thought that the tanks that had run off were finally coming back to give us some support. How wrong I was. All of a sudden, the BAR cut loose in the front of the house and, as I started up the steps, I met Dowd coming down. He said it was a Tiger tank that he had fired at and it was coming straight at the building we were in. The tank stopped, and then there was one hell of a blast that knocked down part of the floor above us. Dust and debris filled the basement. The Germans then started dropping concussion grenades through the hole.

I hollered to Cramer and wanted his thoughts on what we should do. We both agreed that we had to surrender, which was something that had never entered my mind until that moment. I shook the German prisoner and told him to holler "Kameraden." When he talked to them in German, they hollered back something like "come, come, schnell." The only thing that had saved us from the tank blast and grenades was a cement wall about two feet thick, behind which was the potato bin in which we had sought cover. One of the men lay with his feet beyond the cement wall; he had taken fragments in both feet. He was hollering and moaning, which didn't help the situation we were in. Part of the steps had been blown away, so we had to help each other up out of the hole.

The Germans lined us up along the outside of the building with our hands on our heads, and I thought for sure they were going to mow us down. I think they would have, had not the prisoner intervened on our behalf, as I had treated him fairly. The troops that captured us were paratroopers and had their jump helmets on. As we were lined up, I noticed that the building down the street that I had first entered was on fire. I found out later that when the CO had found his position untenable, he had ordered the radio man to destroy the radio, after ordering our own artillery to lay down a barrage, which was now landing in the wooded area surrounding our position and the castle. Our German captors and the rest of us lay down alongside the building, all of us equally shaking.

This was the final episode of F Company, Second Battalion, Twenty-sixth Infantry, First Cavalry Division, in the battle of the Hurtgen Forest.

11/29/89

Forty-five years ago today, I and the remnants of F Company were forced to surrender in the village of Merode after receiving very heavy casualties. We had nothing left except one BAR and three M1s, and were nearly out of ammunition. We had no supporting equipment, such as bazookas, mortars, machine guns, or tanks. The tanks had gone off and left us. One of my men was also wounded, which left only three of us capable of any resistance to the German Tiger tanks and the elite Paratroop Regiment.

I was transported to the prisoner of war camp in a boxcar that was so packed with prisoners that they had to sit or stand in alternate shifts. This trip took thirteen days. At this stage of the war the British and Americans were bombing German rail yards on a regular basis, and the prisoners were in constant fear of being killed by their own allies. One boxcar was hit and all of the prisoners killed.

We were taken initially by rail to Latvia and then marched to a prison camp. I and several others became very ill and subsequently were put on open gondolas and transported by train to Oflag 64, near Luckenwalde, Germany. Officers and enlisted men were segregated in the camps. The enlisted men were put on forced labor, whereas the officers were not. There were 1,500 officers at Oflag 64.

My illness was a severe mastoid ear infection. A Polish POW doctor treated it with the only thing he had, carbolic acid. It killed the infection and allowed me to recover, but I would never hear with that ear again.

The POW diet consisted mostly of soup made of beet tops, potato peelings and other vegetable waste. Although our diet was poor, we were not abused by our captors. The prisoners' thoughts while in camp were primarily about food, warmth, and home. We refused to accept our status as POWs.

Oflag 64 was "liberated" from the Germans by the Russians, but the Soviet military would not release the prisoners from their control. On the night of May 4,

THE SUN ROSE CLEAR

Sid Miller

1945, I and three others stole some bicycles and rode toward the American lines. The trip was hazardous, but we were able to make contact with a unit of the U.S. Ninth Infantry Division on the west bank of the Mulde River on May 5, 1945.

I was sent to a hospital in France for May and June 1945. I returned by ship to the United States arriving on July 4, 1945. My hearing deficit was permanent and, therefore, I was sent by the U.S. government to a hospital in Louisiana to learn lip reading before being discharged from the Army.

I eventually returned to my premilitary career with the Wisconsin Department of Natural Resources at fish hatcheries in Madison, Green Bay, and Hartman Creek outside Waupaca, Wisconsin. When Hartman Creek Hatchery became a state park, I transferred to the forestry service.

Sid Miller

> Sid's wife, Lillian, spent the war at her parents' farm home. She notes that Sid's letters were frequent and always upbeat and with a great sense of humor. His positive attitude and his combat instinct and a lot of luck probably accounted for his survival.
>
> Sid Miller went to a reunion of the Twenty-sixth Infantry once, but there was no one there he knew, so he never went back. When he surrendered, all but three of his comrades had been killed.
>
> Sid Miller died on October 19, 1995, at the age of eighty-one. Lillian noted recently, "The war and the POW experience had weakened his ability to fight any longer."

THE LONGEST YEAR

As told by
Bill Cook

The U.S. Army broke out of the hedgerow country of Normandy at the beginning of August 1944, moved on to liberate Paris, and began the advance across France and Belgium toward the Rhine River. The elite SS (Schutzstaffel-select military units of fanatical Nazis) and the conscripted Wehrmacht troops of the German Army withdrew to defensible positions, including the heavily fortified Seigfried Line in the north and the impregnable Fort Driant in the south.

The fighting became very fierce through September and October 1944. General George S. Patton's Third Army attacked Fort Driant and the city of Metz in the south, suffering enormous casualties, but achieving victory by the end of November 1944. On November 28, 1944, the Allies also broke out of the stalemate at Maastricht-Aachen in the north, breached the Siegfried line, and were on the attack. By early December 1944, the Allies were advancing everywhere, except from the Ardennes Forest, the Eifel Mountains, and the Hurtgen Forest, which occupied the center of the American line.

On December 16, 1944, the worst nightmare of the SHAEF (Supreme Headquarters Allied Expeditionary Forces) generals was realized. The Germans were attacking in force in the Ardennes! Hitler had withdrawn German troops from the Eastern front in Russia to complement his forces on the Western front in carrying out a surprise attack at the weakest point in the Allied lines. The military strategic purpose of the attack was to split the Allied Forces and seize the Port of Antwerp, Belgium,

Bill Cook

133

disrupting the Allies' major supply lines. Panzer armies attacked the Allied armies with a four-to-one advantage in tanks and an eight-to-one advantage in infantry. The Allied Forces were in full retreat, creating a huge bulge in the center of the Allied lines.

General Eisenhower determined that the key to the battle was the crossroads village of Bastogne. He quickly dispatched the Tenth Airborne, One hundred-first Airborne, and the Eighty-second Airborne divisions to Bastogne, and ordered General Patton to head north to attack the German left flank by no later than December 23.

The airborne units were sent to Bastogne under rapid deployment conditions and reached Bastogne before the Germans. The presence of the Allied forces at Bastogne forced the Germans to go around the town, significantly slowing their advance. The U.S. Sherman tanks inflicted three-to-one losses on the superior German Panzer tanks.

The Allies at Bastogne were quickly surrounded and outnumbered by the well-supplied Wehrmacht armies, but they refused to surrender. Christmas Eve and Christmas Day of 1944 were anything but silent nights around Bastogne.

The Battle of the Bulge continued on through January 1945. A pincer action on the German flanks by General Patton's Third Army from the south and the British forces of Field Marshall Montgomery from the north closed the bulge which had extended seventy miles into the American lines and gradually forced the Germans to retreat. American casualties in the Battle of the Bulge were 80,987.

I was born on September 13, 1925. On May 23, 1944, two weeks before the D-Day landings at Normandy, I was drafted into the U.S. Army and given an all-expense-paid trip to Camp Hood, Texas, for basic boot camp, followed by advanced combat infantry rifleman training. After a fifteen-day furlough at home, I was shipped overseas, embarking from Fort Kilmer, New Jersey, and arrived in Liverpool, England, fifteen days later. I traveled from there to Southampton by train and was transported across the English Channel to Le Havre, France, on a British ship. Aboard ship, our American troops were served mutton stew, which was not palatable to an American GI's taste. I arrived in Le Havre in November 1944. I had just turned nineteen years old.

My first glimpse of war in Le Havre harbor revealed buildings partially blown apart and rubble everywhere. We proceeded to Camp Lucky Strike, a misnomer if I ever heard one. It had been raining for a long time, and the camp was a sea of mud. I was assigned to the First Platoon of Company C, Tenth Infantry Regiment, Fifth Division. This was the Red Diamond Division, a part of General George Patton's Third Army. We were transported by truck from Camp Lucky Strike to Saarlautern, Germany, near Saarbruchen.

A fire occurred in a house we were staying in when my buddy kicked over a C-ration can with gasoline and a wick in it, which we were using for light. The whole room went up in flames, and we were lucky to get out. My raincoat was mostly burned up, so the next morning I went to the supply sergeant for a replacement. He handed it to me and, when I unfolded the coat, it was full of blood and had a bullet hole through the back! I washed it off in a stream and put it on. It was a gruesome welcome to the war.

The Battle of the Bulge started on December 16, 1944, and on December 20, General Patton's Third Army was diverted north from Metz to attack the German's left flank. We were loaded on trucks and driven to the area of Echternach, Luxemburg.

We were fighting in thick pine plantations, in hilly and rough terrain. There was a lot of snow, and it was very cold during this northern European winter. We were always shivering and never warm. I had taken a shower in early December. It was to be my last one for more than four months. We remained in front line combat positions for the next twenty-eight days.

General Patton was a daring, gutsy leader and occasionally seen right in the center of the battle. However, his ego drove him to achieve the objective, oftentimes at the expense of very high troop casualties. He told us that tanks cost $100,000 each and soldiers are worth $10,000; tanks are small in numbers and troops are numerous. The message was clear; we were expendable. We tried to stay clear of the tanks as much as possible, because tanks draw artillery fire.

On January 28, 1945, our platoons were due to rotate to the rear area for two weeks of R&R, but before we could leave, our company was assigned to secure a village. Patrols to the village during the night had not reported any German troops or expected resistance. We marched forward, strung out in combat formation on the side of a big hill advancing toward the village. About halfway up the hill was a road running parallel to our position. The Germans were dug in all along that road and had not been detected. We had walked into an ambush. They opened fire on us with small arms and machine guns. I lay in the snow for two hours because any movement on my part drew fire from the Germans. Finally, I heard somebody close to me say, "Komrade" and, to my surprise, saw my buddies with their hands up in the air. Our entire platoon had been surrounded and captured. Our platoon leader, Lieutenant Hopkins, had been shot in the hip. I offered my overcoat as an improvised stretcher.

The Germans lined us up along the side of a long white building and searched us. I thought this would be the end, because the Germans had expediently killed many prisoners during the Bulge campaign. However, there seemed to be a rapport between their troops and ours that I cannot explain. They marched us out of the village within an hour. The troops guarding us were not hostile, but as we marched through the countryside and villages, the civilians were hostile. I suppose you and I would feel the same if forced from our homes in the wake of war.

We were marched to Whittlich, Germany. It took us three days and three nights to get there, during which time we had nothing to eat and no water, except when we were allowed to eat snow off of the telephone poles along the road. The Germans would not allow us to drink from the streams, as they were known to be polluted.

In Whittlich, we were placed in a prison, and when the large steel doors slammed behind me, I knew I was really a prisoner. We sat on the floor for the night and were fed a chunk of bread and some watery soup, which was served in our helmets. These were the same helmets that we had used to urinate in while pinned down in our foxholes earlier before our capture. They had been rinsed with cold water before going back on our heads.

The next day, the Germans took us by truck to an Arbietz Command, or work camp in Ludweiler. There were about thirty privates and PFCs with me. We were billeted in an old amusement hall and slept on a bowling alley under our overcoats, as there were no blankets. Breakfast was some ersatz coffee made of burnt barley and a cup of watery soup made with some type of sugar beet. In the evening, we had two or three small boiled potatoes, about the size of golf balls, and one-fifth of a small loaf of bread. We had no soap or towels. We worked in the forests during the day cutting trees or in a sawmill making charcoal from the wood we had cut. This charcoal was used as a fuel to produce methane gas that could power some of their vehicles.

After forty days, we were marched to a train a day's march away and were taken to Stalag 12A, a prisoner of war camp, at Limburg, Germany. After one week, we were again loaded on boxcars and spent most of a day locked up in a rail yard. When the Germans finally obtained an engine to move us, an American P-47 strafed the train and blew up the engine, wounding several of the encased prisoners. Wounds were wrapped with paper bandages. A day or two later, we were again in boxcars, fifty men to a car, and again we were strafed by U.S. planes and the engine was blown up. We stayed in the boxcars for six days before we were taken off the rail line and marched again. We slept in barnyards and barns along the way. We could hear gunfire and tanks in the distance, and one night our guards, who were Eastern Europeans forced to fight for Germany, just disappeared and left us. On March 28, 1945, a U.S. tank regiment liberated us. We were somewhere near Giesen, Germany.

I was so relieved to know that our nightmare was over that I just put my head down and cried like a baby.

Most of us were suffering from malnutrition, frostbite, and dysentery. We were taken to an abandoned German Army barracks and given C-rations and white bread. This first taste of white bread was like tasting angel food cake! We were taken to a field hospital and then evacuated by C-47 cargo planes to Rheims General Hospital in Rheims, France. We arrived on the Saturday before Easter 1945. The first thing the hospital staff did was take all of our clothes and burn them, lice, fleas and all. We were given a hot shower, the first in four months, and then they doused us with DDT powder. That night, I had my first full night of sleep in a bed since I arrived in Europe more than four months earlier. When I awakened on Easter Sunday, I felt as if I had been reincarnated!

I was in the hospital for thirty days. A nurse took my picture because I looked so scrawny. On May 8, 1945, we were placed aboard a troop ship and transported from Le Havre to England, picked up more troops, and then took another fifteen-day cruise to the good old U.S.A. There were a lot of teary eyes as we passed the Statue of Liberty in New York Harbor.

I returned to Waupaca, Wisconsin, on May 23, 1945, one year to the day after I had left.

Bill Cook had initially been assigned to cook and baker's school when he entered the military, but the need for replacement infantry riflemen quickly changed the course of his military career. After the war, he went to work at Hartman's Bakery in Waupaca until 1951. He then became a fireman and later an electrician at the Wisconsin Veterans Home at King, Wisconsin. Bill met his future wife at the Indian Crossing Casino Dance Hall on the Chain O'Lakes, where many romances from the 1920s to the 1960s began. Bill and Leta were married on November 3, 1947. They have enjoyed fifty-four years together. Now, at age seventy-six, Bill remains very fit and active. Bill and his wife are deeply involved in the activities and the camaraderie of the local VFW post and auxiliary.

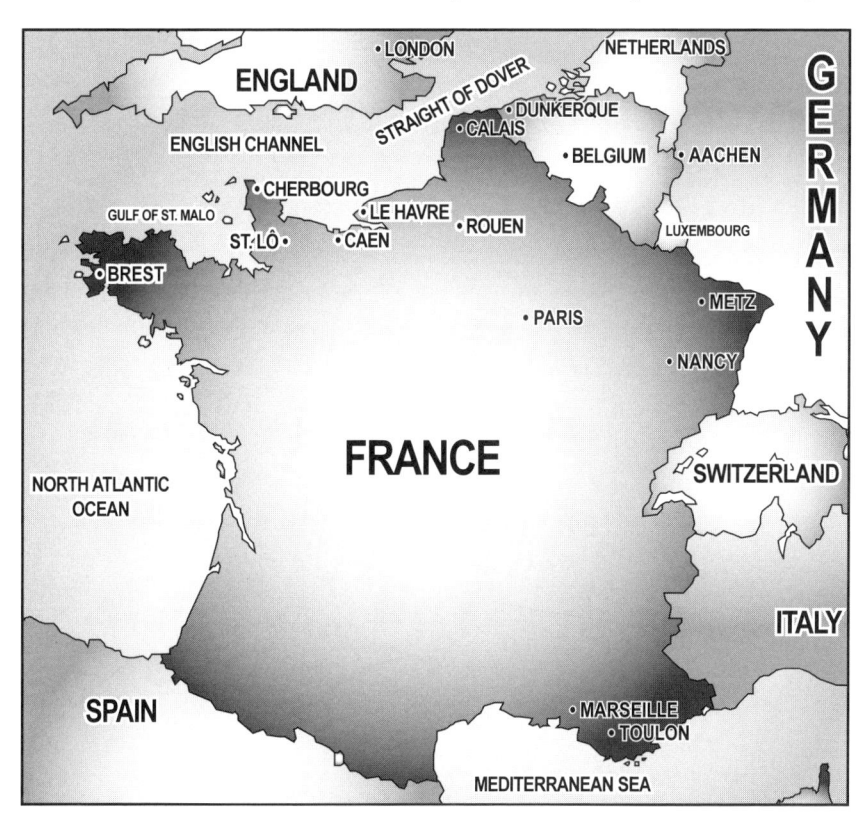

DARKNESS OVERHEAD

MONUMENTS: CHARLES GOTTSCHALK
As told by
Lowell Peterson

The air war in Europe was an ongoing daily reality throughout the early 1940s. Delivery of planes to Great Britain was critical to maintenance of the Allied effort against the Nazis and the German Luftwaffe. The American industrial war machine was fueling the viability of this fight for the preservation of freedom. Lieutenant Charles Gottschalk, high school class of '41, from a village of two-hundred people, would pay the supreme price in support of that effort. This is his story witnessed through the eyes of the author as a child.

The ageless, moss-covered, granite gravestones in the small country cemetery are aligned like soldiers in stark contrast to the casual, gently rolling hills and valleys that surround this hallowed place. This quiet sanctuary, with its freshly-mown grass, encompasses a serene elegance. There is nothing distinctive to separate one plot from the scores of others. I pause to read the inscription engraved in marble, as memories from my childhood come flooding back, overwhelming my mind.

The first tombstone reads: Irving Gottschalk, 1884-1962. The second: Hilda, 1887-1970. The third: Lieutenant Charles, 1923-1944.

Let me disturb the peace of this family for a few moments, as I take you back with me more than fifty years, so you, too, can capture in your mind the history that dwells here.

I was a young boy, eight years old in 1944, when I became aware of a special person in my hometown. He was just called "Gottschalk" (pronounced "Got-shock"). Although there were other Gottschalks, when you said Gottschalk, everybody knew who you were talking about. Irving Gottschalk was the blacksmith, the only blacksmith for miles around. He pounded the hot iron with his hammers, and made the plowshares and the horseshoes so important to the farming economy of the area. He shod the horses and trimmed their hooves at the farms, in the twilight, after closing the blacksmith shop, and he did it with master professionalism. Outside the horse barn on our farm, I watched Gottschalk,

THE SUN ROSE CLEAR

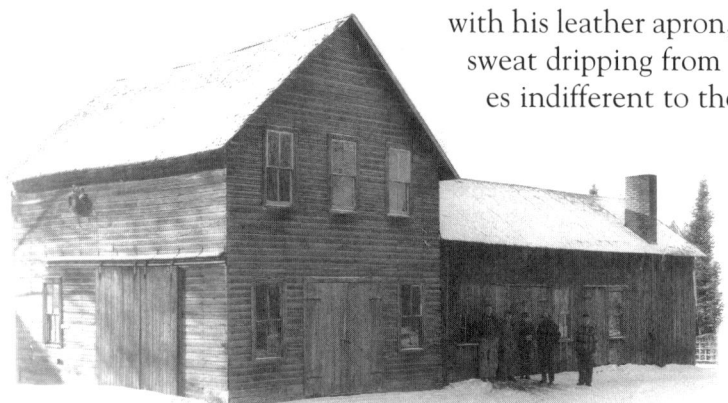

with his leather apron, trimming those hooves, the sweat dripping from his bald head, and the horses indifferent to the process, swatting flies with their tails. My dog, Pal, savored the chips of horse hoof like modern dogs savor the flavored horse or cowhide treats bought at the supermarket.

The blacksmith shop was a weathered, gray, clapboard structure, without the dignity of paint, residing about a block off Main Street in a quiet town, nestled in the glacial hills of central Wisconsin. The double doors provided entry and exit for horses and machinery in need of Gottschalk's expertise. The clapboards and single-glass-pane, wood-sashed windows provided very little protection against a harsh Wisconsin winter. The pot-bellied stove, the hearth, and Gottschalk's personality provided all the warmth that was necessary. The populace of this town was ethnic Scandinavian, opinionated, and politely tolerant of outside influences, like "city folks," other nationalities, and Catholics. Norwegian and Swedish were spoken on the street without apology, and everybody went to the Lutheran church on Sunday.

The retired men, whose social life consisted of frequenting the park benches in front of Jole's barbershop, playing cards at the local taverns, and picking up their mail at the post office, also almost daily, made their way to the blacksmith shop to listen to the day's "sermon" from Gottschalk.

I remember going there with my dad numerous times to get a broken piece of iron fixed and back in service on a farm implement. There was a certain chaos present in the building, with pieces of metal, plows, harnesses, and other implements scattered about, with ownership known only to God and Gottschalk. There he stood, bigger than life at the hearth, with the hot coals glowing and the bellows pumping air. He had his leather apron on over his bib overalls, and the obligate sweat flowed down his cheeks and arms, soaking his denim shirt. His powerful arms never quit moving, with the hammer held in one hand, pounding the hot metal that was held by tongs in the other hand. Several trips from the hot coals to the anvil, with the hammer shaping the metal into its final appearance, was an act of magic to behold. When Gottschalk got it just right, he would take it out of the coals, look at it briefly with pride, and thrust it into the water bucket to fix the shape of the metal forever, his humble work of art. The sizzle of that final thrust and the steam, as it rose from the bucket, was as impressive as an opera finale. I don't remember ever being anything but in awe as I watched the master work in his kingdom.

The most amazing thing during this performance—with muscles in constant motion, and steel twisting and turning and the heat, sweat, enterprise, and economy all being melded into one—was that the master craftsman never quit talking. He entertained his audience with stories, sometimes in Norwegian, sometimes in English, and sometimes half and half. There was a constant monologue about news, weather, crops, politics, and local gossip mixed with light-hearted stories, jokes, and laughter. The stories might be about Ole, who went fishing up north, drank too many beers, fell out of the boat into the lake, and came up out of the water with his fishing license gripped in his teeth as his billfold floated away. Priorities are priorities, after all. Or he might tell about Arden driving through town, going to the garbage dump, with the garbage can in the back of his truck spouting flames into the air. Everyone on the street was waving for him to stop. He thought everybody was friendly that day, and he waved back. Some hot coals,

THE SUN ROSE CLEAR

Gottschalk, the blacksmith (far right) entertaining gathered farmers with one of his "sermons".

discarded in the can, had come alive as the air rushed past the top of the can.

His audience of retirees and farmers sometimes would just get up and leave if the conversation turned political and did not please their philosophy. But don't worry, they'll be back tomorrow. I never left that shop without a smile, and even my dad, who was a very serious person, would always leave there uplifted, smiling, and laughing. The stress of a million problems was lifted from countless souls by the philosophy and sermons of Gottschalk.

I slowly became aware, however, of an inner feeling in my heart, that there was a sadness in Gottschalk that transcended the mirth, humor, and positiveness that he portrayed to his audience.

In the dark days of World War II, every community in the country watched its youth march off to war to fight the Nazis and the Japanese. There was a sense of pride among parents and elders in these young men and women, but there was also a solemn fear that was never spoken. The pride of the community and the parents was manifest in several ways. One was to have a satin red and white banner in your house window with a blue star on it, showing that you had a son or daughter serving in the military. Another was a large board, set up in a prominent place in the community, with all the names of the youth in military service on it. Our community's board, a monument to its youth, was on a slight knoll between the bank and the community hall. I remember that board as if it held the names of all the saints of the Lord. Why? I am not sure. We all became patriots in WWII, no matter what our age. Our heroes were the names on that board. As kids, we carried toy pistols in holsters with "U.S." branded on the side. We wore patches on our sleeves for military units. We bought savings bond stamps at twenty-five cents each, and collected scrap iron and milkweed pods, all for the war effort. Instead of cops and robbers, we played soldier games.

One day I realized that on that board with the names of our heroes, two names were written in gold which meant, they had been killed in action. One of them was Lieutenant Charles Gottschalk. I quickly and tearfully ran up Lake Street, and in the window of the Gottschalk house, one of the two blue stars on the satin red and white banner in the living room window had been replaced by a gold star. A tearful Hilda rocked in her living room behind that window.

I remember Lieutenant Charles Gottschalk only as a photograph of a curly-haired, blonde, fair-complexioned boy, with little or no beard, a sly smile, and a soft-brimmed Army Air Force officer's hat, tipped slightly and cockily to the left.

I began to understand, as I grew older, the sadness in old Gottschalk's eyes I had seen as a child. I also understood more fully how he handled the loss of his son, by beating the metals into beautiful, useful forms, while controlling his audience, and making his natural humor a positive force in his life, and in the lives of all of us. The image of Gottschalk on the farm, attending to the horses away from his "stage" in his shop, however, was even more telling. On these occasions, his eyes were sad, and he didn't talk much, as the sun waned in the west, and the shadows from the horsebarn covered all of us—Gottschalk, the horse, me, and my dog.

The blacksmith shop is gone now, a victim of time. I am sure that many people of a younger generation, who saw it standing there before its demise, thought of it only as an eyesore. Little did they realize the temple it had been.

It was fifty years later that I discussed this again with my dad, who was now more than ninety years old. He told me that Lieutenant Charles Gottschalk had died crossing the Atlantic. His Air Force duty was to ferry planes from the U.S. to Europe, to be used in the war against the Nazis. He apparently ran into a severe Atlantic storm while piloting a new bomber to England, and was lost at sea within one hundred miles of his destination, in Great Britain. Youth and future lost, as it would be for so many.

I recently was in to New York City and found that, at the tip of Manhattan

THE SUN ROSE CLEAR

with the Statue of Liberty looking on, there is a monument to all servicemen lost at sea in WWII. The name of Lieutenant Charles Gottschalk is forever engraved on that monument.

As the memory of WWII has faded, Lieutenant Gottschalk's name may go unnoticed in his hometown cemetery or in New York, but in the 1940s, men little more than boys, like Lieutenant Charles Gottschalk, volunteered their lives and the hopes of their parents, their communities, and their country to defend liberty, and eliminate evil from the world. I am forever grateful to these men. We loved you. (Please see photos in the color section.)

Editor's Note: All of the photos in this section (Monuments: Charles Gottschalk) are from the personal collection of Ila Gottschalk, Omaha, NE.

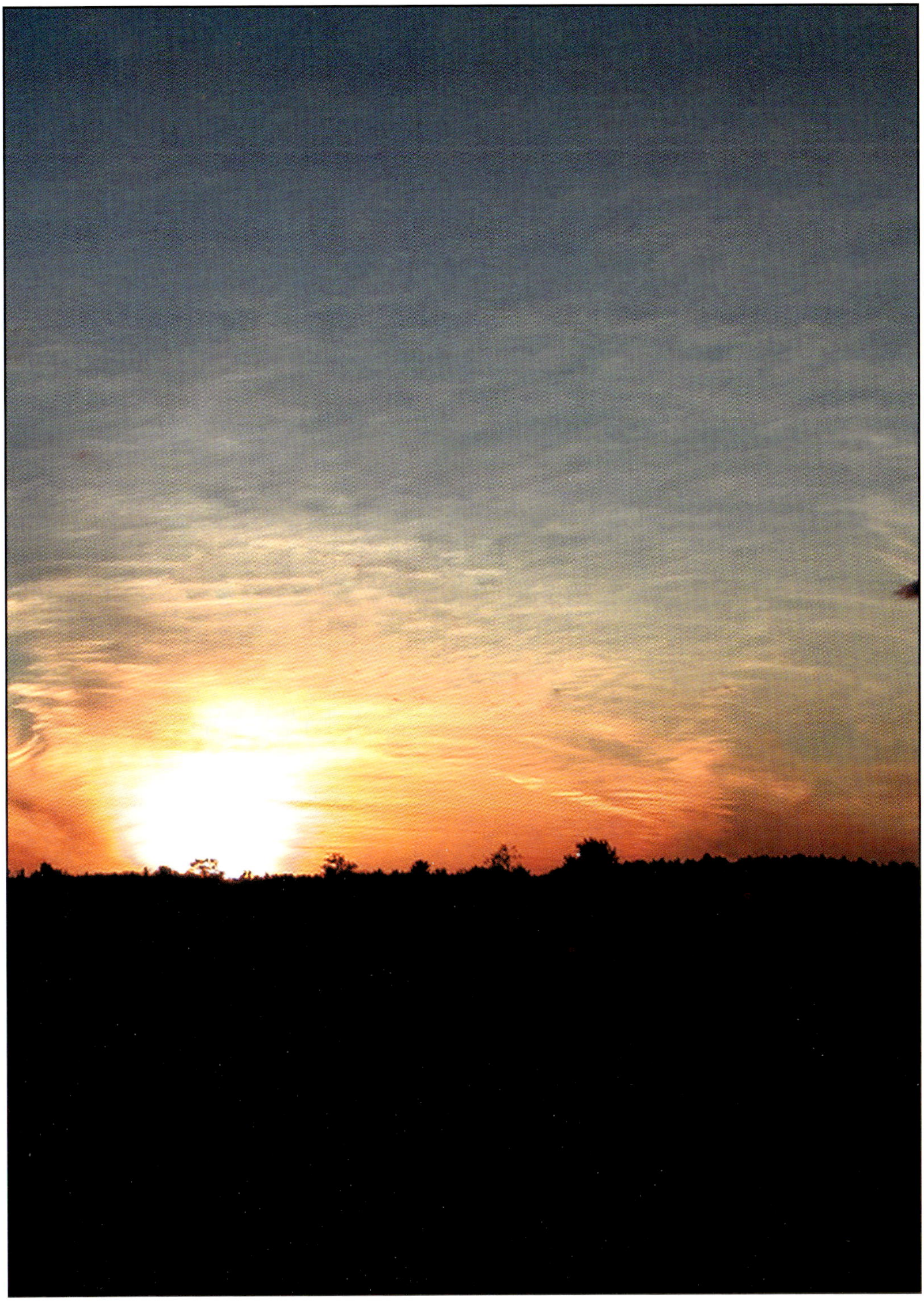

CHINA SERVICE *(page 69)*

Flag of Nationalist China with Chinese characters worn on flight jackets of the Flying Tigers. The patch was created by the Chinese so the civilians would recognize them easily and help whenever they could.

Translated the patch reads: "Coming to China to fight in the War of Resistance; A foreign man, in fact, an American. Soldiers and civilians, all together, protect and help him." (Signed by the Chinese Aeronautical Command.)

Editor's Note: The Chinese could already tell who were Americans. The patch only served as a target for Japanese spies and snipers. It was soon abandoned. (From the personal collection of Malcolm Rosholt.)

Malcolm Rosholt 2001, age 94, residing in the King, Wisconsin, Veterans Home.

MONUMENTS:
CHARLES GOTTSCHALK
(page 141)

Lieutenant Charles Gottschalk during pilot training.

10th MOUNTAIN DIVISION *(page 171)*

10th Mountain Division Memorial at Tennessee Pass, Colorado. (Courtesy of the Denver Public Library, Western Historical Collection.)

FREEDOM OF WORSHIP
(page 196)

*Farmington Lutheran Church,
Waupaca, Wisconsin.*

CORREGIDOR
(page 31)

Gunnery Sergeant Werner Jensen

THE UNLIKELY PATRIOT
(page 210)

*The grave sight of Sergeant Brownie
of the K-9 Corps.*

MOUNT SURIBACHI
(page 220)

Thomas H. O'Brien

CALL ME DIXIE
(page 205)

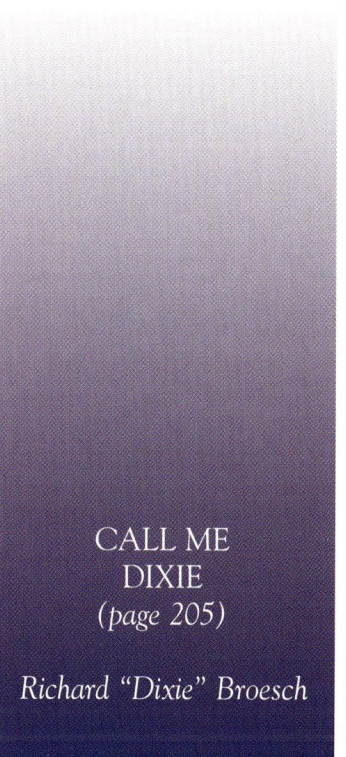

Richard "Dixie" Broesch

"Dixie" and his grandchild.

THE U.S. FLAG OVER TARAWA

THIS U.S. FLAG FLEW OVER TARAWA, A TINY ISLAND IN THE GILBERT GROUP. AFTER STRIKING DOWN THE JAPANESE FLAG, THIS FLAG WAS RAISED UP ON A PALM TREE, AND FLEW FOR THE 72 HOURS IT TOOK TO CAPTURE THE ISLAND. IT WAS RAISED BY SGT. HAROLD SHORT, WHO WAS IN THE FIRST WAVE TO HIT THE ISLAND, AND IT WAS LOWERED BY SGT. SHORT WHEN HE LEFT THE ISLAND FOUR DAYS LATER. AFTER RAISING THE FLAG, SGT. SHORT WAS ASSIGNED PILL BOXES TO DESTROY WITH HIS FLAME THROWER, AND WHEN THAT WAS ACCOMPLISHED, HE WAS GIVEN THE TASK OF CLEARING THE TREES OF SNIPERS, TIED TO THE TOP OF THE PALM TREES.

THE MARINES PAID A HIGH PRICE FOR THE ISLAND, LOSING 980 DEAD AND 2101 WOUNDED, WHILE KILLING ABOUT 4690 JAPANESE, MANY OF WHOM WERE FROM THE ELITE IMPERIAL JAPANESE MARINES.

DONATED BY SGT. HAROLD SHORT, U.S.M.C.
2nd. MARINE DIVISION
1942 – 1947 AND 1950 – 1951

A TATTERED OLD FLAG
(*page* 218)

THE 367ᵀᴴ FIGHTER GROUP
As told by
Arnold Abel

On D-day, June 6, 1944, the 367th Fighter Group provided an air umbrella over the invasion fleet followed in the ensuing days by missions against coastal targets around Cherbourg, France. The Allies desperately needed to gain control of the port of Cherbourg in order to land supplies in support of the invasion. Flak from antiaircraft batteries surrounding Cherbourg blanketed the sky. In the three weeks following D-day, the 367th lost fourteen pilots from antiaircraft fire. Cherbourg fell to the massive Allied land and air assault on June 26, 1944. On July 18, St. Lo fell to American troops, and the stage was set for "Operation Cobra," an enormous air-and-ground operation across France, toward Germany, ordered by General Omar Bradley. It began on the morning of July 25, 1944. The 367th provided close air support along the roads as the German Army positions were overtaken.

Out of the entire 392nd Squadron of the 367th Fighter Group pictured above the arrows identify Arnold Abel (left) and Lieutenant Diefendorf (right). In the background is the P-38 airplane. (France, 1945.)

THE SUN ROSE CLEAR

I entered the Army Air Force in February 1943 and went through intensive flight training in five different flight schools in California and at Luke Field and Williams Field in Arizona before I shipped out for Europe in August 1944 to join the 367th Fighter Group. Prior to my arrival, the 367th had moved its flight operations from England to France on July 19, 1944, about six weeks after D-day, and by July 28, all the squadrons were stationed at captured or newly-created airfields in Normandy. At St.-Mere-Eglise, pilots and ground crews lived in tents in cow pastures and flew their P-38 airplanes off dirt airstrips.

I flew a total of thirty-one combat missions in the P-38 Lightning, and forty-seven combat missions in the P-47 Thunderbolt, and was an assistant flight leader of the 392nd Squadron, nicknamed "The Dynamite Gang"! Our mission was to attack enemy controlled roads, convoys, railroads, boxcars, and airfields in support of the advance through Normandy, as the Germans retreated.

The 367th Fighter Group received its first Presidential Unit Citation, the highest combat unit award, for bombing three enemy airfields and engaging more than fifty enemy aircraft in aerial combat, destroying twenty-five and damaging seventeen, on August 25, 1944. By the end of August, the Allied armies, with our support, had moved three hundred miles eastward toward Germany.

I respected the German pilots. They were very good. Their bases were close by, and they would fly a mission, land, refuel, and come right back up at us again and again, flying many missions per day. I remember being so close to the German front lines that at times I would have 20 mm artillery shells shot at me from the ground as I took off from our airfield.

If we were shot down or had to bail out and were lucky enough to survive but were unable to evade and escape, we wanted the German military to capture us. The military, in most cases, would protect us and send us to a prisoner of war camp, but if civilians captured us, they would kill us. I witnessed a friend and fellow pilot, shot down over a village that we had been strafing, who was able to glide his plane to a landing near the village. We tried to drive the civilians away with further strafing, but as the pilot exited his airplane onto the wing, the civilians executed him, shooting him in front of our eyes. The other pilots, including myself, who witnessed this went back the next day and leveled the village, and from that time on, any bombs that had not been dropped at assigned targets were brought back and dropped on that village.

In October 1944, bombing, strafing, and air-to-air combat were unending over the city of Aachen. We were challenged on every mission by Messerschmidt ME-109s, and Fokker-Wolf 190s of the German Luftwaffe Airforce. The aerial combat or "dogfights" were awesome. On October 2, Aachen became the first German city to surrender to the allies. We continued to move forward from confiscated airfield to

Field Marshall Kesselring's headquarters after the attack by the 392nd "Dynamite Gang" fighter squadron.

THE SUN ROSE CLEAR

Lieutenant Arnold Abel in photo taken to commemorate awarding of the Silver Star, which he never received.

confiscated airfield, and were now stationed at Juvincourt, near Reims, France.

On December 16, 1944, German Field Marshall Von Rundstedt threw thirty-six German divisions and six hundred tanks into the center of the American lines, in what was to become known as the Battle of the Bulge. The clouds and low overcast prevented any help from our fighter and bomber airplanes, but when the weather cleared, the 367th escorted bombers and supply planes to the relief of the surrounded American units in the Bulge area and at Bastogne. On December 24, I was part of a "mass gaggle" of two thousand bombers and eight hundred fighter planes that attacked thirty-one major tactical targets in the Bulge area.

The 367th Fighter Group was a part of General George Patton's Third Army. General Patton liked pilots and the air support that would help him achieve his goals. I remember that he often sent the 367th, 6 ft. x 6 ft. trucks loaded with cases of whiskey, labeled, "for pilots only". Our Fighter Group was able to lay napalm "eggs" right on top of the German Panzer Tiger and Panther tanks, which would destroy the tanks and their crews, even though artillery shells could not pierce the tanks' heavy armor. We moved on to St. Dizier, France, in February 1945, and began flying the P-47 Thunderbolt in support of General Patton's advance toward Germany. By March 1945, the 367th Fighter Group was stationed near Metz as the Third Army, and the allied front was advancing rapidly.

Forty-eight pilots of the 367th Group were assigned to attack and destroy a castle at Ziegenburg near Bad Nauheim and Frankfurt on March 19, 1945. Field Marshall Albert Kesselring, German Commander-in-Chief West, and Albert Speer, Germany's Minister of Armaments and War Production, were meeting at the castle on that date. Von Rundstedt had been replaced by Kesselring on orders of Adolf Hitler. Lieutenant Diefendorf, leading the 392nd "Dynamite Gang" squadron, put his one-thousand-pound bombs right in the front door of the castle! We later learned that Field Marshall Kesselring and Minister Speer hurried to the bunkers below and survived, but the first four bombs from Diefendorf's squad killed thirty German soldiers. We made eleven direct hits on the castle. The 367th Fighter Group received its second Presidential Distinguished Unit Citation for this action.

We moved again, but this time to plush hotels in Eischborn, Germany, as the war neared its end. The 367th flew its final combat mission on May 8, 1945.

> *First Lieutenant Arnold Abel won the Distinguished Flying Cross for leading a mission protecting a group of U.S. bombers from attack by three German jet airplanes that had just been introduced to combat by the Luftwaffe. He also holds the EAME Ribbon with four Bronze Stars and the Tenth Oak Leaf Cluster to the Air Medal. He was proposed for a Silver Star at one time, but for some reason never received it.*

Lieutenant Abel notes, "The camaraderie with my fellow pilots is the most important thing in my life, next to my family." This camaraderie continues to this day through reunions and by exchanging cards at Christmas. Pearl, his wife of fifty-seven years, notes at the reunions, Arnold and his buddies can be seen off by themselves in small groups, making movements with their arms and outstretched hands, slanting first one way and then the other, reliving their combat days.

> *The 367th Fighter Group was activated at Hamilton Field, California, in July 1943, and consisted of the 392nd, 393rd, and 394th squadrons. The 367th embarked for England by ship in early 1944, planning to fly the single engine P-51 Mustang fighter plane upon arrival, but when the group arrived at Stoney Cross in England, they were profoundly disappointed. Waiting for them were P-38s! Learning to fly the twin engine P-38 was painful, but the pilots developed confidence in the airplane as they witnessed its superior aerobatic maneuverability. The 367th flew its first combat missions out of Stoney Cross on May 9, 1944, crossing the English Channel and entering France over Cherbourg. Sorties deep into northern France, provided fighter protection for B-17s and B-24s, as they bombed strategic targets.*
>
> *At the end of the war, the 367th Fighter Group had been in combat for exactly one year and had flown 14,175 combat sorties. They had destroyed 432 enemy aircraft, 384 locomotives, 4,672 motor vehicles and 8,288 railroad rolling stock. Of 350 pilots assigned to the 367th Group, 80 had become fatalities of war in the European campaign.*
>
> *Editor's Note: All of the photos in this section (367th Fighter Group) are from the personal collection of Arnold Abel.*

"SWEDE"
As told by
Lloyd "Swede" Nelson

Following Swede's death, his wife, Nathalie, received a letter from her husband's aircraft commander, Robert B. Bieck. It states, in part:

Looking back, I have known Swede for fifty-seven years. It has been a privilege. I am sure you are aware I took over a crew that was thoroughly disorganized, even dysfunctional. I found that I had only two people upon whom I could rely, Ralph Nieland and, most importantly, Swede. Gradually, we began to assemble an outstanding team. If I achieved even a modicum of success, I must give unswerving credit to people like Swede. We developed from a rather unprepossessing crew to a lead crew, and then we became Pathfinders, the ultimate achievement. Subsequently, I thought I might get a B-29 crew and go to the Pacific Theater. I contacted Swede and was thrilled that he volunteered once again to join me. Alas, it was not to be. The war ended. We then went our separate ways. Swede was outstanding in his field. He was intensely loyal to me. There have not been many like him. What else can one say?

I enlisted in the Navy after the attack on Pearl Harbor, but they discharged me in March 1942, due to a leg injury I had received playing football. I was drafted back into the Army Air Corps in November 1942, and was assigned to the aerial gunnery and armament school. After graduation, I became a top turret gunner on a B-24 bomber as part of a ten-man air crew.

The bomber crews consisted of a pilot, copilot, navigator, radio operator, bombardier, and five gunners. There was a gunner in the tail, nose, and turret, and also waist gunners at each side of the fuselage, operating twin 50-caliber guns controlled by electric push buttons. We wore a receiving headset and used an intercom to talk to one another.

Our crews were referred to by the last name of their pilot. My crew was called "Bieck Crew" and our B-24 was named "Partial Payment". Its nose was painted to look like a hungry, open-mouthed shark, with jagged teeth and a mean eye. We were part of the 453rd Bomb Group, Second Air Division, Eighth Airforce. Each bomb group was made up of four squadrons, with eighteen crews per squadron. One of our group operations officers was actor, Jimmy Stewart. He was just another one of the guys at our briefings. Walter Mathau was also in the division in the headquarters department.

Our Bomb Group was sent to Old Buckenham, England, and quartered in huts with two crews to a building. We did not fraternize much, except for the occasional crap game or blackjack game.

Old Buckenham was a small town, and the local children used to come to the airfield where the airmen would give the kids special treats and try to cajole their mothers into doing our laundry. Since the dollar was much more valuable than the English pound in those days, the women were paid handsomely for taking in the washing.

One guy in our hut got some popcorn sent to him from home, and as he was popping it on the stove, in came the English kids. They had never seen anything like this. Their eyes were as big as half dollars. The relationship between the servicemen and the children was so warm that many of the former youngsters, now adults, fly to the U.S. each year to attend reunions of the Second Division.

When our crews needed rest and recuperation, the airmen were given leave and sent to resorts along the English coast. We went to Southport and stayed in a resort run by the American Red Cross. It was just total relaxation away from the base and away from the war. Our hosts did everything they could to make things comfortable for us.

Our bombing missions out of England into Germany were always a scary adventure, as we never knew what to expect. Every mission was different. The early part of 1944 was a rough time, and the air battles that were going on were terrific. We were penetrating deep into Germany, trying to knock out their airplane production factories and oil refineries. However, anything related to the Nazi war effort was a bombing target. High priority targets were well defended by German antiaircraft artillery, and their fighter planes were up in force, also trying to protect these areas. During these missions, there were lots and lots of planes in the air. On the first mission over Berlin, March 6, 1944, around 650 bombers took part.

When we became airborne, it took a couple of hours to get all the planes into formation. We called it "assembly". First, you formed up as a squadron, then as a group, and then as a division. When enemy planes attacked us, there was a lot of confusion, and you never knew if you had hit the German fighter planes or not. Everything happened very fast. As a turret gunner, you had to have 360-degree vision. On the Berlin raid, sixty-nine U.S. planes were lost. The worst air battle that my group took part in was over Brunswick, Germany. Out of twenty-eight

THE SUN ROSE CLEAR

bombers in our group that day, we lost twelve.

If your plane was hit in the gas tank, you were immediately on fire and your worst fear was that the ship might blow up before you could get out. This happened often. One time, I witnessed a bomber right behind us get shot down and it dropped on top of another bomber, taking it down also. We were never quite sure how many of our planes had been downed, so we had to wait until we got back to our base before finding out who didn't come back. Occasionally, when planes were shot down, the airmen would manage to parachute to safety, evade capture, and return to their unit. They called it "walking back". Some made it back, but not many. We carried snapshots hidden in different parts of our flying suits, so that if we were shot down, these pictures could be used by the underground to make false passports. We also carried escape kits, maps, pills, and even tiny compasses, which we hid in our ears.

My closest call came when an enemy fighter hit our plane and we lost an engine and had to limp back to England alone. Was I scared? You bet I was scared. I think everybody was scared. Under combat conditions, your mind is not what it should be; you're involved in something that's not real.

Sometimes the worst part of war was waiting on the ground. You never knew from one day to the next if your crew would be called on to fly a mission. You had to keep your mind occupied with other things, otherwise you'd go crazy wondering if the next mission was going to be the last one.

Initially, the bomber crews flew a total of twenty-five missions before being sent home. Then D-day came along and short runs over the channel protecting the ground forces were needed, so they raised the quota to thirty. Seven of the ten original members of my crew stayed together through all thirty missions. This was rare. I don't think there were more than four or five of the eighteen crews in our squadron that finished as they originally started.

After our thirty missions were completed, we were sent back to the states. My last raid was to Munich, and it was a long haul. I completed my flying on July 12, 1944, but I waited for the other crew members to finish their quota, and we went home together. We were shipped back to the United States on the ocean liner *The Queen Mary* in September 1944.

I'm pretty proud of my service. We were all volunteers. We didn't have to fly—not the enlisted men. We had the privilege of quitting anytime we wanted to, but I never did.

Swede Nelson returned to Weyauwega, Wisconsin, after the war and was reunited with his wife, Nathalie, whom he had married prior to going overseas. He operated "Swede's Bar" for many years. Being a great outdoorsman, he continued to do a lot of fishing on the Wolf River, as well as hunting and trapping in the woods and swamps near the river. In his later years, Swede required open heart surgery for a coronary bypass and was recovering when he suffered a cerebral hemorrhage, which led to his death.

Swede frequently attended reunions of the Second Division and kept in telephone contact with several members of his original aircrew. His daughter and son-in-law, Diane and Thomas Sweet, donated Swede's flight jacket to the Experimental Aircraft Association, in Oshkosh, Wisconsin, and it remains on display in the EAA Museum.

Swede's decorations included an Air Medal with three Oak Leaf Clusters, an ETO (European Theater of Operations) Ribbon with two Major Battle Stars, and the Airforce's highest award, the Distinguished Flying Cross.

PILGRIMAGE OF A COMBAT GLIDER PILOT

As told by
Harold "Bud" Menzel

Bud Menzel, combat ready in England.

Operation Market Garden was conceived by British Field Marshall Bernard L. Montgomery and reluctantly approved by U.S. General Dwight D. Eisenhower. On September 17, 1944, one British and two American divisions parachuted into Holland to conquer the bridges and roads of the lower Rhine. Control of the road to Arnhem from Eindhoven through Nijmegan and capture of the canal bridges was critical to the success of the operation. Hundreds of C-47 aircraft transported paratroopers and towed gliders loaded with men and equipment across the heavily defended coast of northern Europe. The operation was destined to fail due to heavy German resistance and the inability of the allies to secure and hold the roads and bridges. The bridge at Arnhem would prove to be, as the movie based on the book by Cornelius Ryan exclaimed, "A bridge too far".

Jack, a dentist in Nijmegan, who had witnessed the airborne invasion of Holland on September 17, 1944, asked, "Why did you come back?" My wife and family had joined me on this nostalgic trip in the 1970s. I told him that the magnificence of the Dutch people had something to do with it. I knew that, after all these years, I could relate to them because they understood the circumstances of our WWII operation. I now, on the basis of this nostalgic trip, feel compelled to reveal in a detailed fashion what gliders were used for in WWII and to relate my experience as a combat glider pilot in operation Market Garden.

The combat glider in general use was the CG4A, nicknamed the "cracker box". The main wing strut of the fabric-covered CG4A was buried in a few inches of plywood. The CG4A would burn up completely in eleven seconds. A big bump into the turbulent slipstream behind another aircraft might cause the wing struts to pull loose, in which case the wing would fall off. If a wing came off, you could not get out, as the only exit from the glider was twenty feet to the rear. No one ever escaped through the Plexiglas window of the cockpit.

The glider carried various loads. It could carry fourteen men and a pilot, or it could carry five men, a pilot, and a Jeep. It also could carry seven men and a 75 mm Howitzer, or seven men and a trailer loaded with ammunition. When we flew into Holland, a buddy of mine flew alone, without a copilot, with a full load of Composition C, a highly volatile and powerful explosive.

There was a slide rule type of gadget which was supposed to assist us in appropriate loading, but no one, to my knowledge, was ever taught how to use it. The way gliders were tossed around in the slipstreams, the load would not remain stabilized anyway. If we were carrying men, we could shift them around, but if you had a load of equipment, all you could do was fight the wheel and the trim tab control to keep the craft level. In a practice mission, if the load shifted, you would just cut off and land, but on a combat mission, you stayed on rather than be called a coward.

Gliders and glider pilots were expendable. The glider, made of tubular aluminum, plywood, glue, and fabric, was designed to complete a single combat mission and be abandoned. The pilot sat just back of a window of Plexiglas, and if he was tall, he had to lean forward to keep from hitting his head on an aluminum bar. Tall glider pilots could always be recognized by the scab they carried on top of their heads.

We were towed at airspeeds up to one-hundred eighty-five miles per hour (MPH). The gliders actually were "redlined" (maximum safe speed) at one-hundred forty-seven MPH airspeed. In heavy flak and small arms fire, the tow pilots tended to put their noses down and open the throttle with little regard for the glider. Sometimes the wings came off. We were not allowed parachutes on a combat mission, so any chance of escape was ruled out. If you lost a wing or a tail, you just tried to calmly accept your fate in the few seconds that were left. Anyway, we all were sure it would not happen to us.

THE SUN ROSE CLEAR

Gliders were mainly used to carry troops and weapons to specified points behind enemy lines. Usually, we preceded a mass invasion as the most efficient way of delivering a striking power behind enemy lines. Our duties were to secure bridges and roads and create havoc upon the enemy and his communications, hopefully preventing a counterattack in force by the enemy before our main invading armies had gained a foothold.

The landing in Holland carried the official name of "Market Garden". It was an endeavor to gain a foothold across and north of the Rhine River, to better enable a pincer movement to develop against the German industrial complex in the Ruhr Valley. At that time, General George S. Patton had penetrated to Metz, south of the Ruhr. If our mission was successful, the British Second Army, made up mostly of Canadians under General Dempsey, was to proceed north of the Rhine, and then push south and east. Patton was to push north and east, and the grand plan was to close off the Ruhr. If we were successful, no doubt it would shorten the war. The U.S., Polish, Canadian, and British airborne troops were involved in the invasion. The Polish Brigade and the British First Army drew what turned out to be the toughest assignment. They were to attack Arnhem, north of the Rhine. On the morning of September 17, 1944, Dempsey was poised at the Albert Canal on the Dutch-Belgium border, while Patton at Metz was chewing his nails and cussing. I was being briefed at Cottesmore, an airfield in England.

I was a member of the Forty-fifth Squadron, 316th Troop Carrier Group. We were to make up an eighty glider formation, of which I was number seventy-nine. The tail end of the formation is not desirable because the antiaircraft flak has time to zero in on the end. Combat briefings for glider pilots are rather comical. Our briefing officers really did not know what to tell us. They would say, "You will probably run into flak." This always drew a big guffaw. They would tell us what our route would be, but this really did not make much difference, because we were going to go wherever the tow pilots pulled us. We were given combat kits that contained aspirin, sulfa powder, sulfa tablets, morphine, and "invasion money", for the country we were going to invade. As I remember, we got about five dollars; however, we all knew that the real money was cigarettes.

Normally, tow pilots did not like to pull gliders. It slowed them down considerably. At ten minutes out from our target, the tow plane would flash a red light on the top of the C47 Dakota. At five minutes out from the target, we would get an amber light and then, at thirty seconds out, we would get a green light. This was supposed to give us time to pick a likely landing spot. Some tow pilots were not that generous. They would flash the green light and then, in five or ten seconds, release the glider themselves. This action was deplorable to us because the stretched nylon tow rope would snap back and often take off an elevator control on the tail or an aileron control on the wing that stabilized the flight of our glider. It could also entangle itself and not get dislodged from its latch to the glider. If this happened, the rope would catch a tree or power line, causing the glider to crash. Knowing this possibility, glider pilots would pop the release as soon as the green light flashed and find a spot to land. Usually, our landings were "controlled crashes". Plowed fields were best because the gliders would come to a stop faster. We had a wood skid under the nose, and the trick was to force the glider landing onto the skid without nosing over. We had to discipline ourselves to ignore the enemy action and the admonishments of our troopers on board in order to make a safe landing.

My tow pilot for Mission Market Garden was Lieutenant Brown. I did not know him well, but I liked what I knew. My crew was an "old" sergeant of twenty-four and six eighteen-year-old troopers. I was twenty-five years old. They were conditioned, trained, and brave. I still think that combat volunteers are the "cream of the crop". There was a little extra apprehension at takeoff time because we had heard a rumor, which turned out to be true, that Hitler had ordered the immediate execution of any captured airborne soldier. Another last-minute bit of intelligence was that the Jerries were going to initiate the use of poison gas so at the last minute we were issued gas

Bud Menzel (right) and friend next to his glider.

masks. I reasoned that in the confusion of an airborne assault, the enemy could not possibly risk poisoned gas for the fear of killing their own troops. I tore the gas mask out of the kit and filled it with B-ration chocolate bars.

Takeoff was scheduled at noon, but we were at the flight line by eight a.m., checking our loads and getting acquainted with our troopers. There was always laughing and joking to bolster spirits. We named our gliders for girlfriends or for states we came from, and covered them with lewd paintings and with insults to the Germans. I read recently that Walter Cronkite made the Holland Mission with the 456th Parachute Artillery. If he did, he left with us, because that is who we carried. I would guess from watching him on television over the years that he would have the guts to do it. Eighty gliders, with the tow planes in place and the tow ropes stretched out and connected, is an unusual and impressive sight.

We took off at noon and had a rather routine flight over England and the North Sea. When we approached Walchern Island off the coast of Holland, the flak barrages came at us. They took a toll of several gliders and tow planes. The flak was intermittent the rest of the way, but through the cockpit windshield, I could see flak bursts and smoking tow planes constantly. About a half hour out from our target, I was looking to my left side and saw Number 78 catch a burst of black flak directly in the nose. The glider disintegrated. The pilot was Reese Hill. A fine quarterback at the University of New Mexico, he had named his glider "Flak Bait". Then I looked to my right and Number 80 had disappeared as well. Next, 77 went down, and meanwhile, several others were going down in front of me. The tow planes were horrible to watch, because when they were hit, they usually exploded immediately.

When we got to our landing zone, there was a huge gap between my glider and the balance of the formation. The gap had been caused by gliders and tow planes being shot down, and I was separated from the others by at least a mile. The sky was a mass of fire. We found out later that the mission had been fully anticipated by the Germans. A Dutch underground captain, who helped plan the mission, was a double agent. He was eventually executed in the Tower of London.

Planes were exploding and gliders, missing wings and tails, were careening crazily through the air. I saw three parachutes come out of a burning tow plane. Then after what seemed like a minute, a fourth chute popped, just before the plane exploded. I think at this time I had forgotten that I had to land in that mess. Gliders had a telephone line strung along the tow rope for communication between the glider and the tow plane. My lack of concentration was put to a halt by the calm voice of Lieutenant Brown. "Menzel, we're quite a ways

U.S. Airforce glider in flight.

behind the others, and it looks like they're starting to release. If you'd like, I'll keep you on until we reach the rest of the formation."

"What a guy," I thought. "No," I replied, "I'll just get off right here. Thanks for the ride and I hope you get back safely."

"Same to you," were his last words. He flashed the green light and I banged the tow release at the top of the windshield in front of me and started looking for a place to land.

I saw what I was looking for, forced the nose down hard, banked sharply, and headed for what looked like a good field beyond a haystack. It was about a mile away, and we were approaching at three thousand feet. Small arms fire from the ground was beating a steady tattoo against the fabric of my glider. As bullets ripped through the fabric, they made a "pop," like a gun firing. Tracer bullets are an amazing illusion. They seem to float at you very slowly. You have a desire to reach out and catch them. It does not dawn on you at the time that there are five other bullets between each set of tracer bullets. The troopers in my glider were yelling a few words of encouragement, and a few admonishments about crashing as well.

As we slowed down from 160 to 85 miles per hour, the glider no longer roared from the vibration. It became a delightful whisper in free flight, similar to a pine forest in a breeze. "You're going to hit that haystack," one of the troopers shouted, as I raised the nose into a stall position, getting ready to "squash in". We were taught, told, and yelled at that our best chance of survival was to land as slow as the glider would fly. It was true. More glider pilots were killed landing than from enemy fire. In spite of the appropriate procedure, there is a terrible urge to get out of the sky in a hurry when it is full of bullets and flak. My glider started to flutter and stall just fifty feet past the haystack. I got it into a full stall and squashed in hard. I slammed on the brakes to force the glider onto the nose skids and kept it there by keeping just enough pressure on the brakes to prevent nosing over. We skidded to a stop just ten feet in front of a ten-foot-deep ditch.

Seconds before the full stop, the troopers crashed right through the fabric sides of the glider. I started to jump out of my seat. As I looked down to find the latch, I noticed that the sand from a large sandbag under my seat was all over the floor. I had placed the sandbag there at the advice of the squadron leader, who said that we should have that extra protection. Obviously, a bullet had come right up underneath me and had broken the sandbag. I gave that squadron leader silent thanks.

I grabbed my rifle and dove out of a hole made by one of the troopers and joined them in the ditch. We heard a low-flying plane approaching at great speed and thought it was a Spitfire there to blast the Germans in a section of the Black Forest just a few hundred yards away. We stood up to cheer him, but soon realized that "our" Spitfire was a German ME 109, as we saw the crosses under his wings. His strafing fire landed well ahead of us, but we had been taught a lesson. We settled down to figure out where we were. The dark forest was just a short distance to our north, indicating that we were about twelve miles from our target, which was the lovely little town of Grosbeak in Holland. We were about to be among the first Allied troops to cross into Germany. The German city of Kleve was about ten miles to our north and Goch about eight miles to our east.

It didn't seem real. All I knew about Holland was wooden shoes, cute little hats, skating on the canals in the winter, and the story of the boy who stuck his finger in the dike. There was none of that here now.

It was getting dark fast and we decided to make for the forest. We went back to the glider and loaded up with bazookas, ammunition, and medical supplies. We moved up the ditch toward a road and came upon a large culvert. There we found a little Dutch boy comforting his sister, and as we came close, we heard him repeat over and over, "Amerikana." We gave them chocolate, pats on the head, smiles, and then moved on. We came upon another group of troopers who had obtained a boy of about fourteen for a guide. We joined them and soon others joined us.

Among the troops that joined us was a pilot, clothed in flying coveralls, a pilot hat, and a leather jacket. He was walking as nonchalantly as if he was going after groceries, and he had a .45-pistol in his hand. His face was puffed up to almost twice normal size, his hands were blistered, and his jacket was baked. He gave no facial or vocal indication of his obvious misery. "Hi, Menzel," he greeted me matter-of-factly. My face must have appeared as blank as my mind. Then I realized his had been the fourth chute to come out of that burning tow plane. He had stayed back to help the wounded radio operator get out. He informed us that he was capable and willing to do anything the rest of us would be called on to do. This was the fifth time that he had been shot down. He said that he kept coming back for more because it was the only way he could know for sure that he still had the courage to do it. He actually was shot down one more time at Wesel, the last airborne operation of the war.

We began to draw enemy fire. We started running in a zigzag pattern twenty feet apart toward the forest. We would run thirty feet and then hit the dirt. The Jerries were firing at us consistently now. I wished, on the way across the farm field, that I was in better shape. We got into the woods and felt safe as darkness set in rapidly and a drizzle started. We moved through the forest, reached Grosbeak in the middle of the night, and awaited further orders. The weather had turned bad all over Europe and England, which meant the second- and third-day reinforcements were not going to arrive. The entire mission was now shorthanded and in danger of collapsing.

That first morning was an unforgettable experience. Little girls came out in their cute hats and orange costumes. The Dutch people had saved coffee and orange drink so that they could serve us when we liberated them. Jack, the dentist from Nijmegen, told me upon my return years later, that his father had compelled him to hoard film so that he could take pictures of their liberation by the Americans. They were always certain it would be the Americans. Orange color was everywhere, a color that had been forbidden during the German occupation. The Dutch absolutely insisted on helping us. They would brave withering enemy fire to go out and pick up resupply para-packs. They gave directions and donated their vehicles. They offered the only food they had. They set up first aid stations, guided, and informed us. To say that the Dutch cooperated with us, would be a gross understatement. I still come close to tears when I recall that first day in Grosbeak.

Jack, the dentist, also told me that his father, a doctor, had had a long talk with him shortly before he died. The crux of the conversation was this: "Even though we lost our wealth in the invasion and liberation, and never got it back, I want you to know, Jack, that it was worth it, and I would gladly give it all up

THE SUN ROSE CLEAR

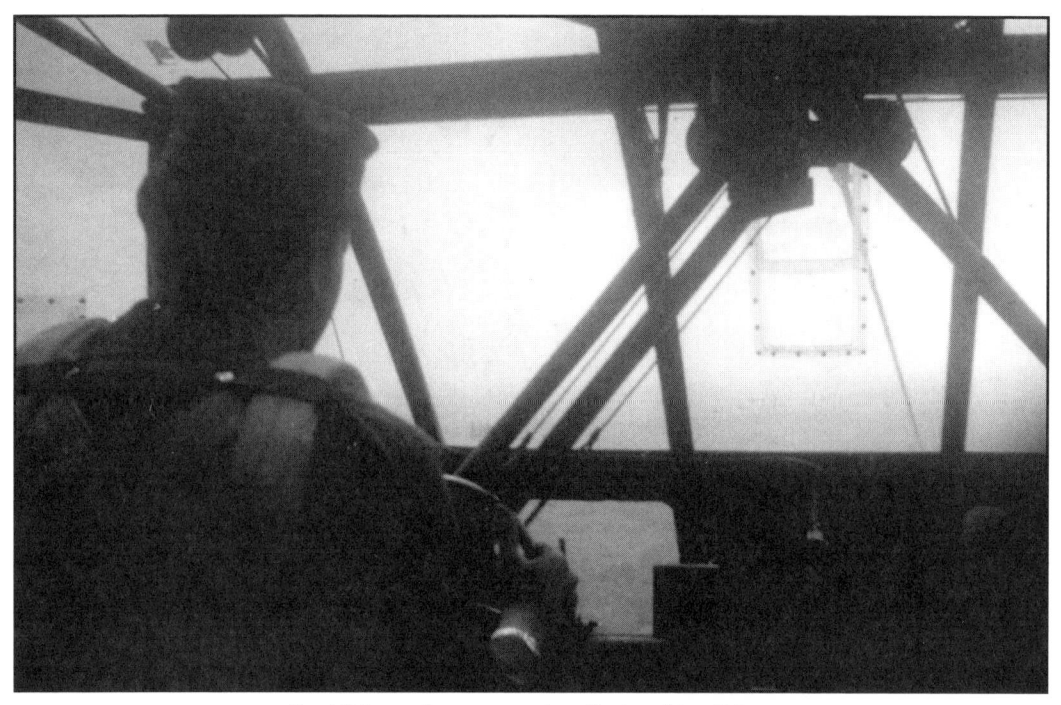

Bud Menzel at controls piloting his glider.

again, for the thrill of regaining our freedom." Jack, who was fourteen years old at the time, feels the same way.

We were ordered to the bridge at Nijmegen. As we started out of Grosbeak, a little blonde boy grabbed me by the leg. He seemed to be about five years of age. Our captain observed the situation and called a five-minute break. I hugged and played with the little boy, and when we had to leave, he had to be torn from my arms. It was love at first sight. I think of that moment often.

When we reached the top of a little hill at the north end of Grosbeak, some strafing ME 109s caused us to take cover. It became apparent that they were not after us, but were firing at a Howitzer battery to the east of our position. They were pulling up from their dives just over our heads. We opened fire with our M-1 rifles. It seemed silly, but on the third pass, someone scored a hit. Smoke began to curl out from the rear of one of the planes. It pulled up sharply and the pilot bailed out. We set out to capture him, and as we approached, we noticed that he was eating some paper. A sergeant hit him in the mouth with a gun butt. That created quite a bloody mess. As hard as war makes one feel, that bothered me a lot. The guy was just being ridiculously heroic. The papers were routine flight instructions and meant nothing to us. Mueller, a glider pilot who got killed later on, could read and speak German, and questioned the guy for several minutes; then a trooper was dispatched to take the German to the Control Point.

We moved on. A short distance up the road to Nijmegen, we came across a field where a number of gliders had landed. It was a comic sight. The Jerries were strafing those useless gliders. They made a dozen or more passes and destroyed every glider in the field. Coming to another clearing, we spotted a group of Jerries sneaking into a vegetable cellar. We rooted them out with hand grenades. We sent the survivors back to Grosbeak with two more troopers. Taking prisoners when troops are short handed is a handicap in war. I, for one though, never would have killed one. I would rather disarm him and let him go rather than kill him.

We made it to Nijmegen, but the enemy pressure increased, and we soon got the word to fall back. We had been in Holland for eight days. On the morning that we got back to Grosbeak, we had a real exhilarating shock. We heard a high-pitched scream in the mist over our heads. Out of the clouds in front of us came an airplane flying faster than anything I had ever seen. Jets were now in the war for Germany, and soon they would be attacking our bombers.

As we passed back through Grosbeak, the same little boy darted out and grabbed me by the leg again. I wanted to take him with me. We had another tearful parting, as he was torn away from me for the last time. I told my wife and children about the little boy many times. A few years ago an old buddy dragged out his picture album, and in it were a half dozen pictures of the little boy and me.

Communication was not very good, and we were in danger of being cut off. Several of us found a German ambulance in the backyard of a hotel. We took it, along with the last two bottles of gin that the hotel owner possessed. Naturally, he insisted on us having it. After all, he was Dutch. We drank the gin, laughed, joked, and headed south. When we ran out of gas, we started walking again. The Belgium border was our target. We soon began to see evidence of the difficulty that Dempsey's army had in reaching us. Destruction was everywhere. Destroyed trucks littered the countryside. Tanks, half-track armored vehicles, and guns lay in every position conceivable except upright. We had walked a short distance when we drew fire from a windmill that pinned us down. Two of us crawled down the road a ways, and then, while the rest of the guys were shooting at the windows of the windmill, keeping the Jerries busy, we each tossed two grenades into two different windows and the shooting stopped. It was quiet except for one guy moaning. We moved on. The Jerries were peppering gunfire at us from the trees along the road, constantly cutting off the road in front of us. A truck came along loaded with other U.S. glider pilots and troopers. We piled on and headed south. I don't think any of us thought we would make it to our lines.

However, late that afternoon, we spotted some strange men in black tams and shirts. They were Belgian and we were in Belgium. Brussels had only been liberated a week previously, but the British bank was already in business. I had an account in England and, to my almost total disbelief, they cashed a check for me. I headed for a big fancy hotel, intent on having a shower and a shave. There was no hot water. I left and started looking for an airfield. I finally found one and hooked a ride with a resupply plane heading for England. The pilot, feeling sorry for me, landed me at Cottesmore. It was evening when I got there, and I was the first one back. The tow pilots had reported the mess in our landing zone and had predicted that we would all be killed. Lieutenant Brown spotted me. He knocked over a table, as he came right over the top of it to greet me. Needless to say, Lieutenant Brown is another one of the many remembrances that I shall always treasure about the Holland invasion. It isn't everyone who has the opportunity to experience mankind at its best, right in the middle of the horribleness of war, but I did, and I shall always cherish that experience.

> *Harold H. "Bud" Menzel was born in October 1919, in Park Falls, Wisconsin. When World War II started, Bud left college and volunteered for military service. He met and married Annette Edwards before going overseas. When Menzel was missing in action in Holland, fortunately, he returned safely to England before his family was notified.*
>
> *When Bud returned from the war, he was extremely tense and nervous, and slept on the floor for months. Adjustment to a civilian, noncombat life was difficult. He eventually entered the University of Wisconsin in Madison, followed by the University of Colorado at Boulder, receiving a law degree. He was active in the Republican Party and met General Dwight D. Eisenhower four times, the last three times at fundraiser events during the Eisenhower presidency. Menzel, in November 1993, wrote in a letter to his sister, Vera:*

> The first time I saw Ike was late in July of 1944, at Greenham Commons Air Base in England. The U.S. Airborne 17th, 82nd, and 101st Divisions; the British Red Devil First Airborne Division; General Sosabowski's Polish Brigade; British Glider Pilots; U.S. Glider Pilots; and a least fifteen Troop Carrier Air Corps groups had gathered at Greenham Commons Airfield. There were seventy-five thousand troops in attendance. We were all called to attention. Ike was introduced. His first words in his "crisp" way of speaking were, "Why don't you all stand at ease, or sit down if you'd like." Then, he announced the formation of the First Allied Airborne Army. When he was

finished, I turned to my buddy, Walter "Tombstone" Menneg and said, "Someday, that man will be President."

Bud Menzel died in 1993 at the age of 74.

Editor's Note: All of the photos in this section (Pilgrimmage of a Combat Pilot) are from the personal collection of Vera Eichstaedt (Bud Menzel's sister).

WINTER SKY

THE TENTH MOUNTAIN DIVISION
As told by
Lavern Trinrud

10th Mountain Division History, by Thomas R. Brooks, Turner Publishing, 1998, describes this elite unit in detail, from concept until the conclusion of World War II.

The threat of U.S. involvement in the war in Europe seemed increasingly evident in 1940. Charles Minot "Minnie" Dole, who had initiated the National Ski Patrol in 1936, developed the idea for a warfare mountain unit, trained in winter conditions and supplied with appropriate clothing and equipment. He was able to convince President Franklin D. Roosevelt, Secretary of War Henry L. Stimson, and General George C. Marshall Jr. to evaluate his idea; on October 22, 1941, General Marshall and Secretary Stimson informed Minnie Dole that a mountain division would be activated at Fort Lewis, Washington.

Brooks notes that it soon became obvious that "it was best to turn skiers into soldiers rather than soldiers into skiers." To join this unit, recruits needed to make an official application accompanied by letters of recommendation, as well as passing rigid physical and written exams.

In 1942, a permanent training base was built for the Tenth at Camp Hale, Colorado, which the troops called "Camp Hell" because of its altitude, weather, terrain, and remote location. The morale of the unit deteriorated when the Tenth was sent to Camp Swift, Texas, for infantry training but eventually, the Tenth reestablished its identity as a mountain division and on November 6, 1944, was reorganized under Major General George P. Hays, who became its commanding officer.

Several Allied divisions had been pulled out of Italy in August 1944 to aid the invasion of southern France, so the Tenth Mountain Division was sent to Italy in December 1944 as a replacement unit. General Mark Clark, Commander of the Fifth Army in Italy, stated, "I was happy to get any division at that time and, of course, the Tenth Mountain was ideally suited for the high Appenines" (mountain range).

Over the next four months, the Tenth Mountain troops distinguished themselves in combat from Monte Belvedere-Monte della Torraccia to Riva Ridge. They were the first American soldiers to break through the German lines into the Po Valley at San Benedetto on April 20, 1945. On May 2, 1945, the German Army in Italy surrendered. After 114 days of combat, the Tenth Mountain Division had suffered 992 mountaineers killed, 4,154 wounded. Lieutenant Robert Dole, a future U.S. senator and presidential candidate, was seriously wounded in the fight for hill 913.

THE SUN ROSE CLEAR

I was born on July 26, 1922, lived on my family's farm, attended a one-room grade school, and graduated from high school at Scandinavia, Wisconsin, in 1941. When World War II erupted later that year, I wanted to enter the military because I felt deeply patriotic. All of my friends were going, and all that you'd heard about was the war. My father was dead set against my desire to join the Armed Forces, for reasons probably only parents of the World War I era can understand. Therefore, I stayed at home on a farm worker deferment until 1944.

I had heard about the ski troops of the elite Tenth Mountain Division and knew that many of the fellows I had competed against in major ski jumping tournaments across the Midwest were with this unit. I wanted to join and I wanted to ski! It was a matter of pride. I finally was so frustrated that I felt compelled to go against the wishes of my father. I obtained the three letters of recommendation that I needed to become a part of this unit from a neighbor and ski jumping judge, Frank Carlson, high school professor, A. O. Lee, and an uncle, Oscar Knutson.

I was sent from Fort Sheridan, Illinois, to basic training at Fort Hood, Texas, in May 1944. I was accepted into the Tenth Mountain Division at Camp Swift, Texas, in the fall of 1944, but unfortunately, by this time, the ski troops had become primarily an infantry unit. I was now Private Lavern Trinrud, infantry soldier, assigned to Company E of the Eighty-sixth Regiment.

At the end of November 1944, the various regiments of the Tenth Mountain Division were transported to Camp Patrick Henry, Virginia, to await embarkation for Europe. On December 4, 1944, my unit left the United States on the SS *Argentina*, and arrived near Naples, Italy, two days before Christmas. We were moved further north along the coast by ship and sent into battle as a replacement task force unit. I remained at the front lines from January 9, 1945, until February 2, 1945. After their arrival later in January, the Eighty-fifth and Eighty-seventh Regiments relieved additional combat task force units.

> *Thomas R. Brooks' history of the Tenth Mountain Division notes that on February 15, 1945, a field order was given that the "Tenth Mountain Division will attack on D-day to seize, occupy, organize, and defend the Mt. Belvedere-Mt. della Torraccia ridge, and prepare for action to the northeast." The mountains of the Apennine range were from three thousand to five thousand feet high and ran in a ridge, several peaks of which were called Riva Ridge.*

We often stayed in villages as we advanced, and would go out from there on patrols as a squad or platoon. The further north we advanced, the heavier the fighting became. By the time we reached Riva Ridge on February 18, 1945, I began to realize that, "Hey, I might not get out of here alive!" The fighting was fierce and the casualties were high. We found out later that only thirty percent of the division regiments made it to the top of the ridge. The others became casualties.

> *Torger Tokle, one of the Tenth Mountain Division's members, had entered the U.S. in 1939 from Norway, became an American citizen in 1943, and was killed in action on March 3, 1945. The* New York Times, *March 19, 1945, eulogized Sergeant Tokle in the following way. "Sgt. Torger Tokle, one of the greatest ski jumpers the world has ever known, has been killed leading his infantry platoon during an attack by the Tenth Mountain Division across the rugged Apennine peaks in Italy ... In four winters of campaigning in this country before entering the Army Ski Troops, Tokle had broken 24 hill standards while winning 42 of 48 competitions. At one time or another, Tokle held every major championship this nation had to offer ... .*
>
> In his history, Brooks describes what followed. *The Eighth Army and the Fifth Army continued to move relentlessly north, as the German Army made a last stand in the Apennines to defend their control of the Po River Valley. The Eighty-fifth, Eighty-sixth, and Eighty-seventh regiments of the Tenth Mountain Division infantry were part of the advance against stiff German resistance. The German Wehrmacht had twenty-seven divisions opposing twenty divisions for the Allies, but the Allied fighter bombers controlled the air. In three days, the Tenth Mountain Division took 1,200 prisoners and occupied 35 square miles of enemy territory at a cost of 203 killed, 686 wounded, and 12 missing.*

Private Lavern Trinrud notes: On March 3, 1945, the same day that Torger Tokle was killed, my platoon was on patrol and started to draw small arms fire from the rear. This resulted in a quick realization that we had advanced beyond our lines into an area between German positions. At about the same time, I suddenly felt like someone had just kicked me real hard in the back of my thigh, and I knew I had been hit. The rest of the platoon had no choice but to leave me there and head for cover, but they promised to send a medic back for me. I lay by a stone fence alone for hours while the battle became more intense and the mortars dropped everywhere around me. I was sure I wasn't going to survive; I prayed to God like never before. We lost more than half of our squad that day.

Finally, after many hours, an Army engineer happened to go past my position. He picked me up and, with fighting still going on around us, carried me on his back to safety.

I was evacuated to a field hospital in Bologna and then to Naples to another hospital, leaving Italy as WWII in Europe ended. I was transported to the Fitzsimmons Army Hospital, Denver, Colorado, for further medical care and rehabilitation, eventually being discharged from the hospital and from the U.S. Army in September 1945. I was awarded the Purple Heart.

THE SUN ROSE CLEAR

After the war, I returned to civilian life and farming. I became reacquainted with a high school friend, Geraldine Huffcut, who was in nurse's training in Chicago. We ended our long-distance courtship by getting married. Gerry and I have spent the last fifty-three years together and have four children, Cynthia, Carl, Keith, and Valerie. Needless to say, my boys were avid ski jumpers, and the children all grew to adulthood respecting country and flag and possessing a firm dedication to a God that had his protective hand on their father so long ago.

The Tenth Mountain Division was deactivated at the end of World War II, but was reactivated in 1948, initially as a training division. On February 13, 1985, the Tenth Mountain Division (Light Infantry) was officially reinstalled as a combat-ready unit at Fort Drum, New York. The Tenth would serve in Germany, Somalia, Haiti, and Bosnia. As this is being written, the Tenth Mountain Division is combating the war on terrorism in the mountains of Afghanistan.

Lowell Peterson

(Please see photo in color section.)

483rd BOMB GROUP
As told by
Harlin G. "Noggin" Neuman

Top row left to right: Lt. H. G. Neuman, Pilot; Lt. Don T. Carney, Co-Pilot; Sgt. Watt. Second row left to right: Herbert S. Ginoza, AG; Horace M. Rogers, APMG; Lt. Marvin W. Stoner, B; James Tappen, CG. Bottom left to right: Samuel H. Schooley, CG; Walter H. Bozeman, ROMG. (Photo from 483rd Bomb Group (H), courtesy Turner Publishing Company, Paducah, KY.)

THE SUN ROSE CLEAR

> *General Arnold ... sent Eisenhower a directive for the establishment of a new air force in Italy with a primary mission of strategic bombing ... The new force, to be called the Fifteenth Air Force, would be commanded by General Nathan Twining ... To prepare for the coming of the heavy bombers, engineers began the construction of heavy bomber fields around Foggia ... And they laid pipelines for aviation gasoline from Bari to Foggia.*
>
> *Thus was the Fifteenth Air Force born ... By April 1944, it had twenty-one heavy bombers and seven fighter groups.*
>
> *The airmen suffered greatly, from the intensive scale of operations and from high operational losses, it was not until December 1944 that the Fifteenth Air Force attained the ratio of two crews per bomber.*
>
> The Wild Blue
Stephen E. Ambrose
Chapter Four, p. 123

I was born in Waupaca, Wisconsin, on June 16, 1924. When I was seventeen years old, three other fellows and I traveled to Wausau, Wisconsin, and wrote a test to qualify for officer's training in the Army Air Corp. We were allowed to write the test at age seventeen and then be inducted into the army at age eighteen. I was the only one of the four that passed. After induction, at age eighteen, I went through rigorous training at Jackson, Mississippi; Greenville, Mississippi; George Field in Illinois; and MacDill Field in Tampa, Florida. Believe me, it was hard work, but I had a goal in mind to be an aircraft commander, so I put my nose to the grindstone. We flew all kinds of training planes and graduated from single-engine to twin-engine to four-engine craft. I found out that there is a proper technique and skill required to fly each of these aircraft. I studied hard and listened to my instructors, realizing that they were the teachers and I was the pupil.

The day finally came and I was designated as an aircraft commander in the B-17 "Flying Fortress" bomber. The left-seat pilot was designated the aircraft commander and the right–seat co-pilot was referred to as the pilot. I guess it made the co-pilots feel good to have this designation. The crew also included eight other men: the upper-turret gunner, lower ball-turret gunner, bombardier, tailgunner, two waist gunners, engineer, and a radioman. Ground crew specialists for refueling, instruments, engines, electrical, and propellers were also essential. We would find out during the combat situation that the sheet-metal specialists were also very important. They patched up the bullet holes and flak damage encountered on our missions.

The 483rd bomb group was a part of the 15th Air Force, 5th wing. I was assigned to the 815th squadron of this bomb group. There were four squadrons in each bomb group. Before we left the states for our overseas' assignment in Italy, we received new

B-17Gs. Our overseas destination was Sterparone, Italy, near Foggia.

I was fortunate enough to be able to fly my own airplane to Italy, but when I arrived I found that our six thousand-foot runway was still under construction. The flight across the Atlantic Ocean and Mediterranean Sea was very tiring but we were young and had a lot of energy and it was one hell of a thrill for a small-town boy. I was twenty years old.

Our combat flight preparations usually began with a five a.m. wakeup call, dressing warmly for the low temperatures at altitude, putting on our dog tags, and then strapping on a combat knife, and a .45 Colt pistol. Breakfast of powdered eggs, fried Spam, and coffee preceded our pre-flight briefings, which consisted of target, weather, and intelligence information. We carried survival kits with everything from gold currency to toilet paper.

All of our planes had a color painted around the cowling so it was easier to identify your squadron and get into formation once you were airborne. The color of the 815th squadron was blue. We carried six 1,000-pound or twelve 500-pound bombs and ammunition for all of our machine guns. We were happy to get the airplane off the ground at the end of the runway with that big load. After check-firing all of our guns we would then climb to 18,000 to 32,000 feet in formation. Our missions would last five to seven hours and were mostly over the Baltic and eastern Europe. We flew missions to Romania, Bulgaria, Austria, Hungary, Yugoslavia, and southern Germany.

Each bomb group consisted of fifty-six aircraft, twenty-eight flying and twenty-eight in reserve. Those flying were divided among four squadrons. Each of the four flights of the squadron would have three planes high, three lower, and one in the hole behind the others.

I flew my first combat mission in November 1944. It would prove to be a memorable event. This mission is described in detail in the *483rd Bomb Group (H)*, published by Turner Publishing Company, page 24 entitled: "Accident Report of B-17 #029."

Before take-off everything checked properly. When guns were checked over the Adriatic, the guns of the ball turret would not fire. Three men worked on it up to 15,000 feet, and without oxygen, at which time it was considered completely inoperative. About this time we developed a bad oxygen leak in the radio room filler hose. This was stopped to some extent by plugging in a walk-around bottle. Everything else functioned properly and we continued on course.

As we entered Austria we lost our #4 engine due to loss of oil pressure. Due to the general condition of the plane, we found it impossible to hold formation on three engines, so we turned back. Upon reaching the Adriatic I ordered the bombs to be dropped by the toggelier at his own discretion. He proceeded to drop the eight bombs by toggling them out. All bombs released except the one at #28 station. The three bombs above this one bounced off this bomb, breaking the bomb loose from the rear hook of that shackle, twisting the front hook, and breaking the arming wire, allowing the rear vane to unscrew and arming the bomb. Every attempt was made to get rid of the bomb but with no success. The armor gunner and toggelier strongly advised not to try and kick it, or jar it in any way, fearing it would explode, due to the plunger being openly exposed and the bomb swinging freely. Due to our altitude of 27,000 feet no attempt could be made to disarm the bomb.

Because of three good engines and sufficient fuel we returned to our home base in hopes of receiving instructions as to how to disarm the bomb before attempting a landing. Upon arriving over the field we received instructions and the pilot and tail gunner proceeded to remove both front and rear fuses. This was done by the tail gunner, Harold Schooley, hanging upside down from the open bomb bay with the pilot (Neuman) holding onto his legs. Had he twisted the fuses the wrong direction, the bomb would have exploded. (Schooley later received a Distinguished Flying Cross for this act.)

While this was being done the co-pilot was left alone to fly the aircraft. It was during this time that #3 engine failed. From the right seat one cannot reach the trim tabs to balance the pressure on the controls. It took all of his strength to keep the aircraft from flipping over. The pilot returned as his (co-pilot's) strength was just about gone. Altitude could no longer be maintained, so it was necessary to land immediately. The bomb (was) still below the bomb bays so the doors had to remain open.

The normal landing procedure was made while also considering our two feathered engines on the same side. All trim was taken off before chopping the throttles. As we started leveling off for the landing, the combined efforts of the pilot and co-pilot were not enough to keep the ship straight. At this time fire was noticed in the #2 nacelle. The ship hit the runway while still swinging to the right.

The ship then hit a roll of runway matting taking the landing gear with it. The ship bounced off another roll and stopped against the third. When the ship stopped, the bomb bays and pilot's compartment were engulfed in smoke and flame. Three men got out through the nose hatch and the remaining seven through a break in the waist. The only casualty was the navigator who received flash burns on his face and hands while going through the bomb bay.

As we exited the aircraft, the firefighters approached and were waved off because of the 500-pound bomb that would soon explode in the fire. The exploding bomb threw aircraft parts, whole machine guns, and shrapnel 200 yards. The next day we all were sent to the Isle of Capri for a week.

I flew a total of 24 missions before the war ended. Each aircraft commander named his airplane. In the 815th, we had Chief Wahoo, Sweet Irene, Rapid Rabbit, etc. My plane was named "Miss Treated".

Most missions were the same—fly, get shot at by flak or German fighters, drop the bombs on the target, and get the hell out of there. It was tough watching other ships get shot up or shot down with casualties of various crewmembers. Fortunately, some were able to bailout and either reach safety, or become prisoners of war and survive.

The second catastrophe for my crew and ship occurred during a mission to hit a railroad marshalling yard in Florsdorfer, Austria, a suburb of Vienna. Heavy anti-air-

B-17 releasing its bombs. (Photo from 483rd Bomb Group (H) courtesy Turner Publishing Company, Paducah, KY.)

THE SUN ROSE CLEAR

craft fire shot us all to pieces. We were able to fly into Northern Hungary near Lake Balaton before I rang the bell indicating everybody should bail out.

The Turner book describes this event in the *483rd Bomb Group* history and the description is written by Donald T. Carney.

> *The 483rd Bomb Group target for February 20, 1945, was an oil refinery on the outskirts of Vienna, Austria. Bombs were dropped at 1310 hours from 26,000 feet. Over the target there was no flak or fighter activity, which was unusual for one of the most heavily defended targets in Europe. The only defenses observed were numerous surface smoke screens stretching like ribbons across the group.*
>
> *After "bombs away" we were in our rally turn when the tail gunner reported flak at 8 o'clock, low and coming up. We were instantly hit by about seven shells and the ship felt like it was falling to pieces. One shell tore half of the ball turret away and cut 11 of our 16 control cables, plus (blowing) large holes in the waist section. It also wounded the right waist gunner. Another shell shattered the right side of the radio room and damaged #3 engine, which later caught fire. Still another shell destroyed all of our radio equipment on the left side and wounded the radio operator. Two more shells failed to explode, but went right through both wings. Again, we were hit and #1 and #2 spilled oil over the wing and the cockpit windshield. Both engines failed. And still again, we were hit from above, penetrating the hydraulic oxygen lines behind the co-pilot. The resulting fires were quickly extinguished by the engineer. All of this happened within ten seconds and the aircraft shuddered so badly it was impossible to read the instruments.*
>
> *The engine damage threw us up on the left wing and we started almost straight down. We started to gain some control at about 14,000 feet and were able to temporarily hold altitude at 10,000 feet. As we gained control, #1 engine was feathered, #2 engine was a runaway, but finally the prop shaft broke loose and the prop just windmilled. It was a miracle, but the interphones were still working so we could execute our emergency procedures and minimize the panic. Reducing weight to hold altitude was the first priority. The entire ball turret was jettisoned. Except for the tail guns, everything loose went out. We headed East to reach the Russian lines, but continued to lose altitude slowly. The Austrian countryside and the Germans became clearly visible below. Our charts showed the Russian line was at Lake Balaton, Hungary. We overflew our estimate of their lines by ten minutes. By then #3 engine was on fire and failing. Bailouts started at about 3,000 feet. Neuman and I hit the silk under 1,500 feet, exactly one hour after being hit.*
>
> *Unfortunately, the charts were not correct and all of us were not safely behind Russian lines. Ginoza landed in German territory and was captured; one or two others landed in "no man's land" and were pinned down between enemy fire, but*

eventually reached the Russian side. Rogers broke his right leg on landing but was picked up safely. The navigator's chute did not open and he was killed. Neuman landed safely, but then spent some time on his knees with a Russian machine gun pointed at his head. I landed safely in a tree with two Russians shooting at me all the way to the ground. For the next month, under Russian supervision, we walked, sat, rode in model-A trucks; sat, rode seven days in a freight train car to Bucharest. We were finally flown out by New Zealanders on March 20, 1945.

The navigator whose chute didn't open was a fellow by the name of Neumandahl from Preston, Minnesota. When we had had our crew picture taken, he took the picture and therefore was not included in the picture. My tail gunner, Herbert Ginoza, was captured by the Germans and received some significant injuries when he was cut down from a tree where his chute had entangled. Ginoza had been the water boy for the University of Wisconsin football team in 1936 and I really liked that kid. He was from a wealthy family from Hawaii.

After the war was over, I flew my airplane back to the United States. I was discharged on April 20, 1946. I wasn't quite 22 years old.

Lieutenant Harlin "Noggin" Neuman was awarded:
* The Distinguished Flying Cross.
* The Air Medal with two Oak Leaf clusters.
* The American Theater Ribbon.
* The Victory Ribbon.
* The European-African-Middle Eastern Theater Ribbon with five Bronze Stars.
* The Presidential Unit Citation.

"Noggin" Neuman resides at the Wisconsin Veterans Home, King, Wisconsin, at the age of 78. He spent his post-war career in the retail lumber business. His wife and one daughter have passed away. A second daughter survives. His interest in flying was pursued privately throughout most of the past fifty-five years.

"In the little less than a year-and-a-half that the Fifteenth was in operation, it had 3,544 B-24s and 1,407 B-17s. Of these, 1,756 B-24s and 624 B-17s were shot down in combat."

The Wild Blue
Stephen E. Ambrose
Chapter 4, p. 126

COMBAT FROM AFRICA TO ITALY AND FRANCE: MY STORY

As told by
Leo Lang

Operation Anvil, the invasion of the South of France, began on August 15, 1944. Three U.S. and three French divisions were withdrawn from the Fifth Army in Italy, rendezvoused near Provence, and then landed between Toulon and Cannes on the French Riviera. The French captured Toulon and Marseilles as the U.S. Seventh Army units pursued the retreating German divisions up the Rhone Valley, joining General Patton's Third Army at Dijon on September 11, 1944. Meanwhile, the Allied forces in Italy continued to pursue the German divisions northward toward Bologna. Lieutenant Leo Lang fought in both the Italian and Southern France campaigns. This is his story.

I was born on June 8, 1915, and grew up on a large dairy farm in Wisconsin. We milked cows, hatched thirty-six hundred chicks every year, sold eggs to Milwaukee hotels, and ran a cheese factory. We also had a blacksmith shop and ran a sawmill and a well-drilling machine. Dad insisted, however, that we never use "the work at home" for an excuse to miss school.

I graduated as valedictorian from high school in 1933 and attended college, graduating with a bachelor's degree in 1939. I enrolled in graduate school at the University of Wisconsin and in 1941 completed work for a master's degree in education. The university required that graduates be present to receive their degree, but it was impossible for me to be at graduation on June 21, as I had been drafted into the

Army and ordered to report for induction on June 18. My brother acted as an impostor and went through the graduation exercises for me, wearing my cap and gown, shaking hands with the governor, and bringing home my diploma. I was already at Camp Wolters near Mineral Wells, Texas, making twenty-one dollars a month.

Following my basic training, I was assigned to the infantry communications school where I learned Morse Code and how to set up telephone and telegraph networks, as well as taking part in advanced combat infantry training. I was selected to remain as an instructor and later promoted to staff sergeant and chief instructor.

LaNore and I were married in December 1941, immediately after the Pearl Harbor attack and we remained at Camp Wolters until September 1942. My son, Merlin, was born there. I was then sent, unaccompanied by family, to Camp Davis officers training school near Wilmington, North Carolina. I was commissioned as a second lieutenant in AA (Anti-Aircraft) artillery on December 31, 1942, and was transferred to Camp Hulen, Texas, where I was assigned to the 439th AAAW Artillery Battalion. This Battalion had 850 men and was completely mobile.

Our unit left Texas for Camp Shelby, Mississippi, to undergo combined maneuvers with some infantry outfits before being shipped to Fort Dix, New Jersey, for overseas assignment. LaNore and my new son, Merlin, came down for a short stay while we were at Shelby. This was to be the last time I would see them until my return in the fall of 1945.

We sailed out of New York harbor in a convoy past the Statue of Liberty and proceeded in a zigzag course across the Atlantic Ocean, escorted by destroyers. We entered the Mediterranean Sea and landed at Oran, Algeria. At this time, the American Army was fighting in Morocco and heading east through Algeria toward Tunisia, as the British moved west from Egypt through Libya. Finally, after the vicious, intensive battles of the Africa campaign, the Germans surrendered. We ended up processing a lot of cocky, young, German prisoners.

Our outfit sat out the invasion and conquest of Sicily by the American and British armies under General George S. Patton and Field Marshall Bernard L. Montgomery. We were in the port of Bizerti, Tunisia.

As our unit crossed the turbulent Mediterranean Sea to Italy in landing crafts, everybody was seasick. After our amphibious landing on the shores of Italy, we experienced the continuous cold, rainy, and windy winter weather. The constant rain caused the rivers and streams to overflow, and the terrain soon turned into a muddy quagmire under the wheels of the army tanks and trucks. The pontoon bridges that our engineers had constructed across the Volturno River and its tributaries were always threatening to wash out. We moved our troops and equipment

THE SUN ROSE CLEAR

to the front line north of Naples, where the Germans had established a defensive perimeter.

Winter was a miserable time. Cold, rain, and snow were constant. There was no place to hide from the elements. Our clothing was the same clothing we had worn in Africa. We had no rubber boots and only leather ankle-top shoes, which were always wet and stiff. The mud was unbelievable. The Germans were dug in on the high ground, so our winter existence became a matter of personal survival against the elements until the weather improved in the spring.

We were assigned to join a British division of Indians from India and our mission was to take the famous monastery at Cassino. The monastery, on top of the mountain, overlooked the entire battlefield and from this high ground the Germans were directing artillery fire on our positions. We moved out and attacked the monastery garrison but finally were forced to pull back because of heavy casualties. Army headquarters then decided to bomb the monastery, a decision that has remained controversial to this day. I went up on a little hill to watch as the airplanes flew three abreast, dropping bombs on the city of Cassino and on the monastery for what seemed to be an endless period. Three of the planes became confused and ended up bombing Fifth Army headquarters. The bombing was a good morale booster but did nothing to shorten the war.

While we were trying to take Cassino and the monastery, an American and British force made a landing at Anzio, on the west coast of Italy south of Rome, with the idea of drawing the Germans away from Cassino. It did not work. Everything bogged down, and we settled in for a long, cold, wet winter. The whole front was then reorganized, and we joined American troops for the rest of the war. While we were with the British, we wore British helmets. This was meant to imply that Americans were not yet in Italy in force, but it did not confuse the Germans. "Axis Sally" announced on her propaganda radio program from Rome, "What's the matter with you Americans that you have to borrow British helmets?"

In early May 1943, when the weather suddenly turned very nice, our American forces opened up with the biggest artillery barrage I could imagine. Shells were flying over our heads in both directions. The Germans used delaying tactics by blowing up the bridges and retreating to Grosetto, where they dug in. The Allied infantry took off on the drive to Rome where there was no fighting. The American Army marched right through the city in spite of the mobs cheering the liberation. From then on, the terrain and the German resistance were both very rough, and our task became a matter of taking one hill only to find another valley with a small town pretty much destroyed, a bridge out, and another defended hill.

We had just started to set up camp near Rome when we received an order to come up to LaVarno immediately. The infantry units were under heavy pressure, and we were told to park our artillery guns and much of our gear and support personnel a distance behind the line. We had forty-eight hours to convert our artillery men into infantry men and move into the line to support the troops who were there so they could regroup. Our unit was to man a line that included all of the city of Pisa, south of the Arno River. The infantry had about three thousand men in this sector. We replaced five hundred men. Asking artillery men to become infantry men in forty-eight hours was not easy. I happened to be the only field officer in our outfit with infantry training, which made me rather popular.

I took my communications section of about seventeen men, some telephones, wire, a switchboard, and a radio, and went into the south side of Pisa three or four blocks from the river. There was a two-story building there with two-feet-thick stone walls that would withstand a lot of shelling. We placed the switchboard there and then laid twenty-seven telephone lines to the points we expected to occupy and hold, as well as to all our support units.

The Tower of Pisa was right across the river, next to the cathedral and Baptistery. The Germans were using the tower to watch us, direct artillery fire, and also direct snipers to harass us. Our army was not allowed to shell the area for a quarter of a mile around the Tower of Pisa. The Germans brought mobile artillery units into this quarter-mile area and fired at us down the road, but we could not fire back.

One day, I received a telephone call saying, "I'm Senator _____ from Washington, D.C., and I have it from good authority that the Tower of Pisa was shot down last night." I assured him that I was looking at it and that it was still there. He asked me my name and rank. I told him my name and rank and that I would like to invite the fool who made the "no fire" rule to get his butt over here and watch the German observers on the tower direct fire with no chance for us to shoot back. He interrupted me by saying, "I don't want to talk to any damn lieutenant; I want to talk to the commanding general," and hung up. I had his name and carried it around for a long time, but finally lost it. I had made a firm commitment to visit that guy if I ever got back.

There were no civilians in Pisa. Except for periodic shelling and sniper fire, the front was deadly quiet, which was hard to deal with. You could hear a rabbit hop from a block away. It sounded like a person sneaking up on you.

Mortar shells were forever breaking our telephone lines. We would repair them as quickly as possible, because these lines were our men's only means of communication. It also assured them that we were still there to give them artillery and mortar fire support.

We were in the line for five weeks before we were relieved to go back and get a hot meal. We had lived on individual field rations, which consisted of one can of beans, hash, or stew, and one can of crackers with a few pieces of candy and maybe a few cigarettes. Sometimes we had K rations packed in a box that looked like a Crackerjack box containing one small can of ham or cheese or scrambled eggs, with a chocolate bar, a few cigarettes, and some crackers. After five weeks, these rations got pretty monotonous. I lost over twenty-five pounds.

Dr. Daley, our physician, and I were given a three-day pass to go to an army rest and recuperation hotel in Sorento, Italy, south of Naples on the Coast. The hotel had nice beds, but I could not sleep because the bed was too soft, so I slept on the floor. We visited the Isle of Capri before we returned to Pisa. When we arrived, the men were packing up to go to Naples and embark to join the invasion force of Southern France.

We loaded all our troops and equipment on an LST and set out across the Mediterranean, which this time was reasonably smooth. The Jeep driver assigned to me developed appendicitis at sea and had his appendix removed on the captain's dining table aboard ship.

We landed on the French Riviera and moved inland rapidly past Toulon and St. Tropez, before going on to Marseilles and north along the Rhone River, through Lyons to Dijon, and then to Epinol. We were now members of the Seventh Army and joined up with General Patton's Third Army before turning east toward Germany.

The Germans put up token resistance, but the effectiveness of our troops, our Air Force, the French Underground, and the rather flat terrain made our advance pretty rapid. There was increasing evidence along the way that the French were "getting even" with citizens who had collaborated with the Germans. There was an increasing number of women with their heads shaved, and in one small village there was an arch in a small park where two people had been hung.

We were assigned to support a mission to place two pontoon bridges across the Mosel River near St. Die. It was raining and muddy. The engineers constructed the two bridges, and after their completion, the Germans started shelling and knocked out both spans. The infantry pulled back, but our large mobile artillery guns were covered in mud, so our artillery units could not move.

After extracting our units from the mud, we received orders to immediately report to a point further north. About four hours later, I was stopped by a military policeman, who told me not to go over the next hill because there were German tanks on the other side. I turned the convoy of 183 vehicles around, took them back to an open field, and saw to it that the men were fed and got some rest. I met with a group of Seventh Army officers at a briefing at three o'clock in the morning. They told us that our Forty-fourth and Seventy-ninth American infantry divisions had broken through the Siegfried Line and that a reconnaissance unit was needed to go through the breech. We were to proceed through the line about eight to nine miles to the small city of Hohfelden, dropping a gun battery section every half mile or so, and send two remaining batteries to a neighboring village of Hagenau. We were to secure the road, hold the villages, and protect against enemy strafing planes.

We crossed through the Siegfried line, which was a broad field of dragon teeth barriers, gun turrets, and hidden underground fortifications. After about a week or two, when the infantry had not arrived at Hohfelden, I took my Jeep and driver and went back to see what happened. We found the infantry, but they were not advancing. General Patton had refused to protect our flanks and, since he did not move his troops, our troops could not move. It confirmed my observations that Patton was only interested in his own troops and his own ego. It was very personal. My troops were out there with no infantry or armored protection behind us. The Germans were observed building up a force behind my troops, and it appeared they were getting ready to attack and cut us off. Headquarters radioed us to pull back immediately to a small town in France. When we arrived, it was December 24, 1944. The following morning, there was two feet of new snow on the ground as the chaplain led us in a Christmas service. At noon, the kitchen crew served us a hot turkey dinner.

After our stay in France, we went back to the front, passing through many badly damaged German villages and cities. The front moved on rapidly. Villages were ordered not to resist our troops or they would be destroyed. Our infantry would move through. If they received fire, they would withdraw and the village was destroyed. As we went along, some villages were completely intact and some were laid waste.

As the end of the war drew near in the spring of 1945, there was a report that German troops were moving south toward Hitler's hideout in the Alps. Our forces were ordered south to Stuttgart and then east to cut them off before they could get into the mountains. We were about fifteen to twenty miles east of Stuttgart when Germany surrendered. The war in Europe was over. Our troops ended up in the small village of Neckargamuende, about ten miles south of Heidelberg, on the Neckar River.

Of the six hundred men in my command, less than twenty had ever entered high school. Sixty-four could not read a *Dick and Jane* primer. These men were the core of the men who had fought and won the war. I had nothing but the highest regard for all of them. Our men, who had taught the troops how to fight, were now establishing schools to teach them how to enter life at home, make a living, and be good citizens.

There was a "nonfraternization regulation," meaning our troops were not to mingle or talk with the Germans. However, two of our laundry girls, sisters about fifteen to sixteen years old, came to the school I was teaching at one day and told me that they had been taken from their home in Poland and were sent into Germany as laborers when the Germans conquered their country. They had not heard from their parents or any of their countrymen. One of them wanted to marry our chaplain's Jeep driver. The Army did not permit this. The sisters kept hounding me, and I felt sorry for them. One day, they came and asked if I would get them into France. They could not get to France by themselves because all the roads out of Germany had road blocks. I told them that they should make themselves a set of Women's Army Corps uniforms, but to tell no one. About a week later, they came in looking for the world like a pair of sharp U.S. Army WACs. I prepared travel orders and passes and told the driver to take them across the border to a little French village. They used a camouflage-painted combat vehicle and passed through the roadblocks without any trouble. About forty-five years later at a reunion of the men of our outfit, there was a man and a woman whom I failed to recognize. It was the older sister and her husband, the chaplain's driver. She told us her younger sister had also made it to the States. They were now living in Pennsylvania. After all this time, I finally felt that maybe I had done something worthwhile, even though it was contrary to Army regulations.

As time went on, men received orders to return home, selected by a point system based on the number of months served. Officers with fewer points than I were going home, while I was passed over. It was finally determined that I had been declared "essential" and that I was to report to a new outfit in northern Germany in two weeks. Our commander told me to take my driver and get lost for ten days. We visited in the Alps, including Oberammergau. A group of nurses who had just come from Chicago were there, but I quickly discovered that I had nothing in common with them. They had absolutely no knowledge of what our life had been like for three years. It seemed as though they were from another nation. I then realized that going home might be a problem. Home had not changed, but I had.

When I got to my new assignment along with thirty men, we were told that we were being shipped to the Pacific War Theater. As we prepared to leave for the Pacific, the atomic bomb was dropped on Japan, after which Japan surrendered a few days later.

We received orders to report to LeHarve, France, for shipment home, sailing on the USS *West Point* to Hampton Roads, Maryland. I then went by rail to Camp Grant, Illinois, and on to Wausau, Wisconsin. LaNore and Merlin met me at the Wausau depot. It was wonderful to see them and to be home for good.

I had lived so long in an environment of artillery shells, mortar shells, sniper fire, booby traps, and land mines that it took months to separate the war from my person. This was the most difficult readjustment I had.

I have nothing but respect for the "common man" in the ranks who fought and won the war. It would be impossible for me to list the many times my life was totally dependent on them. I will never forget them.

After returning home, Leo Lang stayed with the Army Reserve, organizing battalions of artillery, and was promoted to lieutenant colonel. He served two years as inspector general for the Eighty-fourth Division in Milwaukee and was then transferred to the inactive reserve in September 1968. In civilian life, he became the district administrator for various school districts and served as teacher, principal, and administrator for the Campbellsport, Wisconsin, school district for thirty-two years before retiring in June 1980.

Leo Lang was awarded the Bronze Star medal for his service at Pisa, Italy. The citation read, "For meritorious achievement in action from 28 July 1944, to 26 August 1944, in Pisa, Italy. First Lieutenant Lang was assigned the responsibility of establishing and maintaining communications between elements of a newly converted infantry battalion and antiaircraft unit serving as infantry for the first time. First Lieutenant Lang established the necessary communications in a most expeditious and thorough manner. In maintaining the channels, First Lieutenant Lang personally supervised the repair of broken lines during heavy concentrations of hostile shell, mortar, and machine-gun fire. On the mornings of 3-4 August 1944, he personally checked and mended broken lines at an advanced outpost under sniper observation and harassing fire, approximately one hundred yards from the enemy positions. First Lieutenant Lang's leadership and disregard for his personal safety were an inspiration to the men of his command. His courage and initiative in the face of danger reflect great credit upon himself and are in keeping with the highest traditions of the Armed Forces of the United States." In addition to his Bronze Star medal, Leo Lang had received four overseas service bars, the American Defense Service ribbon, and the EAME Theater ribbon with one silver battle star, in addition to Letters of Commendation.

At age eighty-five, Leo Lang lives in quiet retirement in Campbellsport, Wisconsin. His son, Merlin, recently retired as the Department of Natural Resources Park Supervisor at Hartman Creek State Park at Waupaca, Wisconsin.

Lieutenant Leo Lang with his son Merlin, taken prior to going overseas. He would not see his son again for three-and-one-half-years.

DAYLIGHT OF HOPE

FROM DEPRESSION TO WAR
As told by
Lowell Peterson

It is only in retrospective contemplation that I can comprehend what devastation the decade of the 1930s had laid on the doorstep of the 1940s. Many of the once-proud and stately Victorian farmhouses of rural Wisconsin communities were a shocking sight to behold in the spring of 1941. Gray-black clapboard siding had lost most of its paint, and the front porch swings, where young people had daydreamed about their futures and adults had contemplated their past, now creaked in the wind from disrepair. Barns and machinery suffered no less a fate. Aging equipment, dehinged doors, and rusted steel roofs proclaimed evidence of material decay from which recovery appeared questionable. Food, clothes, heat, and crop seeds took priority.

The neglect was unintended. The Great Depression and the drought of the 1930s had devastated once-productive farms. Airborne dust from as far away as Oklahoma filtered the sun's rays through a pinkish-tan cloud. A wicked curse had descended upon what had been the land of milk and honey.

Poverty, hunger, hopelessness, and apathy exacted an emotional and psychological toll, as the unkind and unjust acts of nature killed the spirit of the hardworking farmers. The 1930s were, as my mother noted, "Hard Times"! Children accepted the state of affairs as the status quo because they had never known a different lifestyle. Banks extended credit to the limit while treading water themselves in an uncertain financial sea.

Brucellosis ravaged many productive herds of cattle; blight, locusts, heat, and drought withered crops. Year after year, a peck of potatoes was produced where bushels had once grown. Corn, clover, and grain never reached maturity. Fortunately, Wisconsin and the upper midwest did not suffer as severely as the plains states and the southwest.

Nevertheless, the vultures began to circle the prey. Men of money bought up farm after farm at sheriff's bankruptcy foreclosure auctions for a penny on the dollar in anticipation of economic recovery and enormous profit. These poachers' purchases were thinly disguised as humanitarian service to the farmers. The families' subsequent eviction was an affront to their human dignity. It must have seemed like a death spiral to them. They contemplated their misfortune, the unkind acts of nature and their fellow man, and then went on with their lives. Pride, hard-earned equity, and sense of responsibility drove the bedraggled farm families to fight harder to keep what they had, but sometimes they were forced to taste the "grapes of wrath".

Low-interest federal loans from President Roosevelt's New Deal agencies, as well as loan extensions from lenders and trusting neighbors, allowed the death gasps to be slowly replaced by hopeful sighs.

Nature thankfully responded to the wailing despair of the earth by bestowing rain and moderate temperatures conducive to the germination, growth, and maturation of crops. Markets slowly opened up as people around the world regained a sense of confidence and were able to restore their purchasing power. The agricultural machine sputtered to life.

As prosperity increased in the 1940s, houses and barns were painted, and roofs were repaired. Rural electrification brought electricity, power, and refrigeration to the farm. Cows were milked by machine and not by hand, and herds enlarged. Commercial fertilizers quadrupled crop production. The land once again responded to the power of the horse and to the hands of the farmer and his hired men. It was back breaking daylight-to-dark labor. The era of the horse began to fade, as the advent of the tractor and mechanization provided the key to success. The decision to buy a tractor, in 1941, instead of another team of horses was one of the most critical decisions my father ever made.

As the economy slowly recovered, war clouds were rapidly forming, and World War II would soon sweep around the globe. A war mentality consumed the country as the farmers' sons and hired hands marched off to war or to higher-paying jobs in the urban industrial complex, creating a vacuum in the rural communities.

Our hired man, Oscar Hansen, was drafted into the Army infantry. After basic training in Texas, he returned to our house on furlough for a visit. I was so proud and happy to see him in his uniform. During the time he had been our hired man, Oscar had teased me, joked with me, and often played games with me as the friend and "big brother" I didn't have. I had hated to see him leave, but I understood. Farmers sometimes received deferments for their sons and hired help but most of the young men felt in their hearts the "need to go". Older men and young children became the hired hands. Women left their farmhouses to help with the work.

My dad, reluctantly in desperation, hired a newly deferred eighteen-year-old as a farm laborer to replace the departed Oscar. The young man's ignoble interest was in getting enough money to put gas in his car and entertain his stable of girlfriends. He wasn't much help when he was working and was no help at all when he failed to show up on Mondays. His work ethic was tolerated once or twice, but the next time he showed up on a Tuesday after a weekend of levity, my dad asked him what his excuse was. His lame response was not convincing. My dad bellowed out, "Bullshit!" I was so stunned that I couldn't move. If that guy wasn't scared, I sure enough was. I had never heard my dad swear before and almost never since. That draft-dodging piker was sent off the property and down the road as my dad calmly climbed down from the straw wagon in the horse barn and went to the house to telephone the draft board.

Somehow the work got done. My high-school-aged cousins from La Crosse spent the summers with us on the farm. We worked hard in the fields and haymows throughout those summers of the war years. We would reward ourselves each evening with trips across the east field and over Jensen's Hill for a cool dip in Sand Lake's clear, refreshing water. It was a perpetual daily summer baptism that rejuvenated the body and the spirit.

After the war was over in 1945, Oscar Hansen stopped at our farm one day for a visit. I listened intently as he related to my parents the tragic story of war at the front lines. He told of being in a close-up, face-to-face confrontation with the Nazis while lying in a foxhole on a hill, exposed and pinned down under fire when his gun jammed. How much more alone and mortal could anyone possibly feel?

Oscar drove away from the farm that day and I never saw or heard from him again. I was sad and disappointed that my friend didn't want to be there with me any more. My mother and dad comforted me and explained compassionately that the war had changed Oscar, as it had so many others. He was just not the same person that we had known. Dad said he was thankful that Oscar had made it home alive, and Mom hoped that, as time passed, his inner wounds would begin to heal.

Although these years of my life had been difficult because of the hard work, they had been fun filled and happy. Adversity, natural and political, had attempted to destroy my country, my friend, and my beloved farm. Poverty and war had tested the American spirit, but a nation of committed people had survived.

These years were character building for young and old. I cherish the memories.

FREEDOM OF WORSHIP
As told by
Lowell Peterson

The stately, orange-brick church, proudly astride a grassy knoll, stands framed against the backdrop of a stony glacial ridge, as its majestic steeple reaches toward the blue heavens above. The stained glass windows bestow an artistic elegance to the comforting sanctuary within. Cattle grazing on the hillside nearby entrust a calm, pastoral serenity to the scene. Each Sunday in thousands of similar churches across the land, the faith of the worshippers presents itself for renewal.

The Sunday morning services in this, my country church in the 1940s, demanded a respectful attendance by the loyal congregation. No matter! The faithful came voluntarily from every direction in a steady stream of Fords, Chevrolets, Buicks, and Dodges, often arriving minutes before the bell tolled. The farm chores had been done early, and after a quick breakfast, the wives dressed up in their "Sunday" dresses, stockings, and (without question) hats. The children were also attired in their Sunday best, and the men wore two-or three-piece suits, white shirts, neckties, and hats, which were tipped in respect to the ladies outside the church.

The service was not only a faith-renewing experience, it was also the social event of the week. One would only be obvious by his or her absence. Each family was ushered to its usual familiar pew. To sit elsewhere would have created untold anxiety and confusion.

In the late 1930s, the teenage boys liked to sit together in the back row, and this was tolerated as long as they maintained respectful, quiet decorum. During the war years of the early 1940s, the back row still contained many of the same boys, now young adults in uniform, home on leave from basic training prior to "shipping out" to the war.

The Sunday worship service began with the entry of the choir, accompanied by organist Margarette Nelson, marching with their majestic, flowing, maroon robes through the center aisle, leading the congregation in the singing of:

Holy, holy, holy! Lord God Almighty!
  Early in the morning our song shall rise to Thee;

Holy, holy, holy! Merciful and mighty!
  God in three persons, blessed Trinity.

Holy, holy, holy! All the saints adore Thee,
  casting down their golden crowns ...

The songs, readings, and prayers soon were followed by the sermon, an elegant oration prepared and delivered by Rev. Larson, a revered and learned man. This declamation was meant to reassure, motivate, and solidify the faith. Rev. Larson inevitably quoted famous or classical literary works, told jokes to lighten the mood and capture the congregation's attention, or recited a poem to make a point. The message gave hope and courage at a time when the black clouds of war hovered overhead.

Each Sunday during the war years, the final recessional hymn following the benediction was a prayer in song written by E. Sparrow of Cardiff, England, entitled "God Bless Our Lads," sung to the tune of "Abide With Me."

God Bless our Lads in air, on earth and sea!
  Full well we know how dear they are to Thee!
Where're they go, whatever they may dare
  God, ever keep them in Thy gracious care.

God Guard Our Lads by night as well as day,
  For we, at home, for them will ever pray.
That war and strife and enmity may cease,
  And Thou wilt send us Everlasting Peace.

God Guard Our Lads. Oh, keep them ever near!
  Make strong their faith and drive out all their fear;
Give them a vision of Thy saving love,
  That nothing in this world can ever move.

God Guard Our Lads and though just now they roam,
  Grant us our prayers and bring them safely home!
God Bless Our Foes and cause their eyes to see
  that peace, alone, can come from Thee.

THE SUN ROSE CLEAR

After services, the children went directly to Sunday school, which always began with a loud rousing rendition of "Onward Christian Soldiers," accompanied by Margarette Nelson on the piano.

The men retreated to the furnace room to smoke, talk, and exchange news and the conversation inevitably turned to the war. The news of battles, the concern for the nation's freedom, and the welfare of the fighting men and women was on everyone's mind. Each family had contributed their sons and daughters, their energies, and their hard work to support the patriotic war effort. The justifiable defeat of evil deserved pursuit.

After Sunday school the families reunited to disperse as they had come. The whistle of the Soo Line steam engine gave life to the departure scene as the freight train approached nearby. Box cars and flat cars loaded with cargo to be used in the war effort proceeded with a clickety-clack, clickety-clack, clickety-clack along the rails to an unknown destination.

The families went home happier, motivated, relaxed, and confident that good would triumph over evil, and faith and freedom would prevail, with the help of God. As they drove away, they recalled the pastor's message and his sermon poem of that Sunday composed by their very own poet laureate of the congregation, entitled *For a Son in Service*.

For a Son in Service

Go with him, God, this boy of man's estate
so young yet old enough to learn the art
of this new world of weapons and of hate.

His hands will do their bidding. Guard his heart,
that it will never shirk what it must do
within the line of duty, yet still keep
a place reserved for all the love he knew,
the dreams of youth, the laughter and the hope.

Go with him, God, so many roads confuse,
mirages beckon and temptations come,
give him, through faith, the strength that he may choose
the road with You that brings him safely home.

Go with him, God, and keep him in Your care.
Then I will rest assured.
This is my prayer.

—Inga Gilson Caldwell

SUNDAY DINNER
As told by
Lowell Peterson

In the 1940s, social life consisted of church-related activities, trips to the movies, ballroom dancing, radio programs, books, magazines, and visiting neighbors. Televisions, video games, computers, and the multiple entertainment venues that currently compete for our attention did not exist.

An invitation to a Sunday dinner at Bill and Stella's was always welcome and eagerly anticipated. The thought of a beef roast, wafting its aroma throughout the house while it cooked in a covered, cast-iron frying pan on top of a wood burning kitchen stove, was heavenly. The boiled mashed potatoes, soon to be smothered in deep amber beef gravy, accompanied by fresh baked bread and vegetables dripping with sweet cream butter, created a mouth-watering dream.

Stella's effortless preparation of the meal revealed instinctual plus acquired skills, skills inherited from a loving mother, now senile, deaf, and feeble, but still supervising from a chair in the corner of the small farmhouse kitchen. Apple pies that had been baked early in the morning before church services now stood cooling slowly near the window sill, eyed longingly by Happy, the family's pet dog.

The atmosphere in the kitchen was alive with laughter and conversation as my mother pitched in to help where she could. The bond of friendship, respect, camaraderie, and just plain fun was evident as Stella and Gladys worked their culinary magic.

In the living room, still dressed in suit and tie from church services, Dad and Bill reviewed the crop situation, the weather, church issues, politics, and the war. Roosevelt was often praised and damned in the same sentence. I had been warned by my parents not to argue politics with Bill. His face and bald head would get pretty red during controversial political discussions.

The news of military servicemen was passed on from family to family, over party-line telephones. The often-unsaid, but clearly present, emotion was the concern for the safety of sons and daughters of friends and neighbors who had chosen to join the war effort.

I usually entertained myself by playing croquet in the yard, looking at magazines and old photo albums, or listening to mystery stories on the radio. "The Shadow" and "The Thin Man" were Sunday afternoon favorites. *Life* magazine, *Colliers*, and *The Saturday Evening Post* made the vast world around me come alive through word and picture. The vivid black-and-white photos in *Life* and the Norman Rockwell portraits on the cover of *The Post* told a story of the struggle and hopes of a nation at war.

Dinner was always announced with a smiling, cheerful, "Var sa göd," which literally translated from the Norwegian meant simply, "Come and get it." You never had to hear it twice!

The meal started with reverently reciting the table prayer. Our joined families were, without question, grateful for their ability to share their meager fortunes with each other. Bill, Stella, and my parents worried little about what they didn't have.

The conversation about the war and local issues continued throughout the meal. I was relegated to the role of listener, as children in those days were taught to "be seen and not heard." We had shared a meal, fulfilled social needs, and intermingled thoughts and ideas. When the dinner came to an end with apple pie, washed down with fresh whole milk, and topped off with coffee from the ever-present metal coffeepot on the wood stove, the conversation slowed. Everyone was too stuffed to talk very much.

As the ladies cleared and washed the dishes, the men lounged in big, soft chairs before taking a walk to the fields as they discussed crops, cattle, and milk prices.

After a few hours of visiting and relaxing, it was time to return home and resume the daily farm and barn chores activity that, for a few hours, had been put out of sight and out of mind. The body and soul of the friends, however, had been restored, renewed, and refreshed by spending this Sunday together. The laughter and conversation echoed in their hearts and minds for days to come.

In the same house, in the same kitchen, on a gray, dreary, wintry day three years earlier, December 7, 1941, the satisfaction of the meal and the camaraderie was dampened, seemingly forever, by the radio boldly and sadly announcing, "We interrupt this program to bring you the following special bulletin … ."

Now, in the fall of 1944, as the troops marched slowly across France toward Germany, and by sea, island-hopping ever closer to the mainland of Japan, there was reason to be optimistic, but the end was not clearly in sight.

Would it ever end? Would sanity and reality be restored? Would the boys ever return to their families, friends, and neighbors for Sunday dinner?

COMES THE SUN

CALL ME DIXIE
As told by
Richard Broesch

The tragedy of war is veiled in many forms. This story speaks to one of the unfortunate turns of fate that changes the course of a lifetime.

"What do you think, Dutch?"
"Not bad, Dusty, not bad; the kid can run and he fields cleanly. Not bad with the stick either. Singles hitter. Hits behind the runner well. Good bunter with speed out of the box. Ya, I'd say he is a potential pro prospect."
"I agree. Why do they have him pitching? I think he's a natural shortstop. He's not a bad pitcher for high school baseball, but pro hitters will eat him alive. You can't get by in the minors or big leagues on a fast ball and a curve. Well, Dutch, maybe he'll continue to develop. He's just a kid. I'll give you this, he's a hell of a good athlete! He probably can make it as an infielder."
"Let's keep an eye on this kid, Dusty. When he gets out of high school, he'll only be seventeen. I think we can sign him to play for one of our farm teams. He's got a good chance of moving on up toward the majors. Not sure he'll make it. Depends on whether his arm holds out and whether he can hit double A or triple A pitching. Let's give our report to the front office and see if they're willing to flash some of that Yankee pinstripe mystique and hard cash in front of the kid."

My name is Richard Broesch and I was born on September 16, 1925, in Kenosha, Wisconsin. I love baseball, and I can't really remember a day since I was six years old, when the temperature was above freezing, that I wasn't playing. It may have been stickball in the alley, bouncing a tennis ball off a garage door, or throwing a ball into the air to camp under, but it was baseball one way or another. I was totally consumed by my love for the game. The milk delivery man, with his horse-drawn cart, would come down the street and see me playing ball every morning and he would shout out, "Say Charlie, how's the game going?" (Charlie Grimm was player-manager of the Chicago Cubs). When I wasn't playing ball, I was listening to the Cubs games on the radio. The Cubs' players were my heroes, but I also liked the Brooklyn Dodgers, and loved it when the two teams played each other. When I finally became old enough to play on organized teams, I learned the thrill of competition. Of course, I had my paper routes and odd jobs in the neighborhood, but when the jobs were over, I grabbed my glove and my Louisville Slugger bat, which was mended with friction tape, and headed for the ball field.

By the time I got to high school, I had picked up a nickname. Everybody called me "Dixie." I guess it was because I bragged about my favorite Brooklyn Dodger player, Dixie Walker, and because I thought every good baseball player had to have a groovy nickname.

I don't like to brag, but I guess I was just as cocky and confident about my abilities as any kid who ever played the game. I was very versatile and could play center field or shortstop or pitch with equal skill. I favored shortstop, however, because more balls are hit at you at that position than when you are in center field. I also wanted to play nine innings of *every* game, and no pitcher gets to do that. I was also a pretty good hitter. I usually could count on getting on base about three times per game by hitting singles, bunting, or drawing a walk. During my senior year in high school, I became aware that I was being scouted by professional baseball. I felt like I was in heaven and all my hopes were being realized.

December 7, 1941. Well, you know what happened then. The world changed. Everybody started going off to war. Ballplayers left for the war from the major and minor leagues. All of a sudden, baseball, and anything not directly related to the war, was put on hold. When I was seventeen, I graduated from high school, and, with my parents' consent, I joined the Marine Corps in 1943. I didn't know it then, but I was "in for the duration" of the war, spending the next thirty-four months as a Marine. I was in the Second Marine Division which embarked with three thousand troops for the Mariana Islands on a large liberty troop transport ship in June 1944. En route, we had practice alerts, but one time we did go to general quarters alert and watched our destroyer escorts throw depth-charge cans at a enemy submarine that had been spotted in the area. War was becoming a reality.

We arrived on Saipan right after the "Marianas Turkey Shoot," in which our carrier pilots shot down almost five hundred Japanese aircraft in an air battle. On Saipan, the monsoon rains hit, and it was impossible to keep the water out of our tents, no matter how deeply we dug the trenches around them. We were always wet and shivering. There were a lot of cases of malaria and dengue fever, which is better known as "break bone fever," because of the severe aching that occurs. Saipan was not a tropical paradise.

The Second Marine Division was on standby for the Battle of Iwo Jima, but remained in reserve. Our division was involved in the Battle of Okinawa, acting as decoys, feigning landings on the east coast of the island to draw the Japanese away from the true landing sites on the west coast. The kamikaze suicide plane air attacks of the Japanese on our fleet were scary, because the fanatical attacks by these planes were indiscriminate. They came in out of the sun and dove at landing craft as well as at larger ships. I saw an LST (landing ship-tank) loaded with troops get hit. It exploded in flames and disappeared. I assume all aboard were killed. I had wanted to be in combat, but after that experience, I wasn't so sure.

The Second Division was sent back to Saipan and I was assigned to the Eighth Regimental Combat Infantry team to prepare for the landing on the mainland of Japan. We were to be in the first wave spearheading an amphibious assault at Kagoshima on the island of Kyushu.

During the period of preparation for the invasion, the brass somehow heard that I was a baseball player. One evening they picked up some of the fellows and me in a truck and took us to the special service barracks. From then on, we played a lot of baseball, but if the invasion of Japan became imminent, all the other ballplayers and I were to resume our normal combat assignments. I worked a switchboard at night to justify my military existence.

In Saipan, we had a beautiful baseball field in a valley shaped like a natural amphitheater with hills all around. One day, the fleet ships docked to replenish supplies and refurbish before moving on. Each fleet carried "special services" people wherever they went, and this particular fleet had sixty professional baseball players, many of them major leaguers. While on Saipan, these players divided into two teams of thirty each and played baseball games against each other, changing the participants every few innings. Some of our Marine baseball players were asked to join each of the teams. Luckily, I was one of them. I played shortstop and even got to play ahead of some of the Triple A players that the fleet had brought. I was playing with major leaguers Johnny Mize, Johnny Vandermeer and Pee Wee Reese. I was able to hit a double just past the outstretched hands of left fielder Barney McCoskey.

Pee Wee Reese, shortstop for the Brooklyn Dodgers before the war, watched me like a hawk, commenting on my fielding techniques during the game. Pee Wee told me, "You have to get into professional baseball when you get back home." His encouragement was all I needed to set my course for the future. I can't think of a time in my whole life when I was any happier. What a thrill!!

After the Japanese surrender, I was sent with occupation troops to Nagasaki, and eventually to Sasebo, Japan, for the next six months. In Japan, we played a lot of baseball and basketball. The Japanese loved baseball, and I remember playing a lot of catch with the little Japanese kids. The Marines offered me the opportunity to attend Officers Candidate School (OCS) and continue a military career, but I turned it down. I said, "No, I want to go home and play baseball."

> "Dutch, the kid's back. Remember? Dixie Broesch. We scouted him before the war. He's twenty or twenty-one now. Let's find out if he still has the talent to make it in the big time."
>
> "Okay, Dusty. Arrange a workout for him with our farm club up at Fond du Lac. I'm curious to see what the Marines did for this kid and whether he still has some of that talent we saw a few years ago."

In the spring of 1946, I was invited to a tryout with the New York Yankees farm club at Fond du Lac, Wisconsin, with hopes of a minor league assignment. My friends encouraged me, saying, "Everybody knows about you. You'll make it, we know you will." Finally, I had a chance to realize my dream. My strong throwing arm and slick fielding better not fail me now.

Before the tryout camp was to start, I became ill. At first I just didn't feel well; then I began to run a fever, and my muscles began to ache. My neck felt stiff, and I was as weak as a pussycat. I thought I had the flu, but one morning I awoke and found that I could not move my left leg. It was paralyzed. I had polio. I didn't know it then, but when I failed to improve, the doctor told me that I would never walk again. There apparently was a polio epidemic in Kenosha spreading through the community, and soon all the public beaches and public parks, including the baseball fields, were declared closed and off limits to try to stop the disease.

I was mortified by my bad luck. After an initial period of anger, I became deeply depressed. I cried like a baby for days. It was so ironic. I had been at war for almost three years with the potential to risk major injury or death at any time, but it was not the war that ended my career. It was an illness. It was devastating to see my baseball career, the love of my life, snatched from my grasp. My dream had been so close. After many months, I was able to come back to reality and deal with my illness in the only way possible, and that was to accept it. Franklin D. Roosevelt had been afflicted with polio, and lost most of the motor function of his legs, similar to how this horrible disease had affected me. I figured that if he could be president and lead the nation through the war with his disability, I, too, could survive.

With the help of the Veterans Affairs Office, I obtained jobs, and eventually a scholarship to Marquette University. I graduated in 1951 and worked for the Master Lock Corporation for thirty-one years. I was married for forty-eight years and have three fine children. I am now seventy-six years old and live at the

Wisconsin Veterans Home at King, Wisconsin. I get around well with a motorized wheelchair and with arm canes and braces on my legs.

When I lived in Milwaukee, many of the Milwaukee Braves and Milwaukee Brewers players became my friends. It was a camaraderie born on a ninety-foot square diamond. Milwaukee Brewer shortstop Robin Yount's picture is on the wall of my room, to remind me of the shortstop I might have been.

Everybody still calls me Dixie.

"The Marine Corp taught me confidence through discipline."

Richard Broesch

(Please see photos in color section.)

THE UNLIKELY PATRIOT
As told by
Lowell Peterson

Patriots come in many disguises. I would like you to meet one of these shrouded warriors, whom, I am sure, you would be happy to have as a friend.

I lived with the Kendly family. Orrin Kendly, son of Mr. and Mrs. Palmer Kendly of King, Wisconsin, was the master of this family, and was my guardian as well.

I grew to adulthood in King, Wisconsin, which is the location of the Grand Army Home for Veterans. This location was established by the State of Wisconsin after the Civil War as a domiciliary to care for the wounded, maimed, sick, and homeless veterans who had left the cities, farms, and villages of Wisconsin, to serve on the North-South battlefields, including Gettysburg. Many Wisconsin veterans of the Spanish-American War, World War I, World War II, the Korean War, the Vietnam War, and the Gulf War would subsequently call the Veterans Home, on the banks of beautiful Rainbow Lake, their home.

Because of their daily association with the veterans, the Kendlys developed a sense of patriotism, respect for the American flag, and a knowledge of the wartime sacrifices necessary to protect the nation and the Constitution. They clearly remember the deaths and military funerals of civil war veterans, Spanish-American war veterans, and World War I veterans who lived here. It is not too surprising, therefore, that when World War II came along, my family decided that I, too, should serve my country. On May 29, 1943, they accompanied me to my induction into the U.S. Armed Forces. It was a sad farewell for both of us. By August 1943, I had completed my basic and specialized training and was sent into the thick of battle on the islands of the South Pacific. After Pearl Harbor, there was a desperate need for special forces troops. I was trained to do a unique job, but due to prewar isolationism, the U.S. was way behind in this training program. The Germans had highly trained two hundred thousand troops just like me, and the Japanese had trained almost as many.

THE UNLIKELY PATRIOT

There were four major training camps established in the U.S. for our special mission. Our forces would serve in Sicily, Italy, France, the Aleutians, the South Pacific, and the China-India-Burma Theater. During my combat time, I experienced the courage, companionship, deep loyalty, friendship, and above all, mutual love and respect from and for my fellow soldiers. I became a part of a team that advanced into battle, fully trusting every trooper on my right and my left. Our military education was an education in death. We were taught to be killers and to protect our compatriots to the death. We learned a dozen ways to quickly, silently, or slowly kill, but with precision.

Our platoon of troops would advance ahead of the main body of troops and point out the enemy, so that artillery could be called in. Then our Marine infantry could engage the enemy from a point of advantage. I was shot and wounded by a sniper during one of these South Pacific island battles, blinding my right eye. The United States military decided that I had done my duty. I was going home. I received a citation for my service and an honorable discharge on October 13, 1944.

I returned to my home at King, Wisconsin, and developed a friendship with all the other vets at the veterans home. I was a pal and a friend to everyone in this elite community. I loved the Vets home. The veterans were my comrades in arms. The veterans understood what I had been through, and I understood what they had been through. I had been there. We had a common bond.

On May 18, 1949, I was killed by a hit-and-run driver in the King area. I was buried in the Grand Army Home Cemetery for Veterans of all Wars on May 19, 1949. I received full military honors at my funeral, and my grave marker was erected by the King, Wisconsin, Post of the American Legion. Reverend Ralph R. Holliday, chaplain of the Grand Army Home for Veterans, officiated at my funeral service. He read a poem that he had written which said in part, "How fitting it is that he should be returned to King to mingle with comrades. We commend him to The Creator on High, who will continue his comradeship in the sky."

I guess I forgot to tell you my name early in this story. All my friends called me "Brownie." I loved that name, and my ears perked up when I heard it. You see, I was Sergeant Brownie of the K-9 Corps, a German Shepherd dog, who because of my family's patriotism and their desire to serve their country in time of need during World War II, volunteered my services to the United States military. I am forever grateful to my family and to my comrades in arms. (Please see photo in color section.)

HEAT OF THE DAY

IWO JIMA: OPERATION DETACHMENT
As told by
Lowell Peterson

This story will serve as an introduction to the three stories that follow. You are about to be introduced to the most incredible battle of all time and three men who lived it, fought it, smelled it, tasted it, and were lucky enough to survive.

"This will be the bloodiest fight in Marine Corps history."

Lieutenant General Holland M. Smith
Commander, Fleet Marine Force

The author's note, pages XIII-XV, of *Iwo Jima, Legacy of Valor* by Bill D. Ross (Vintage Books, 1985), describes succinctly the bloody cost of the battle of Iwo.

The island of Iwo Jima, a fly speck in the vast Pacific Ocean, became the most expensive real estate in the world for a period of thirty-six days in 1945. U.S. Marine amphibious forces and the U.S. Navy committed 75,000 troops to the battle for this diminutive island, suffering 25,851 casualties, of which 6,821 were killed in action. Of 22,000 Japanese soldiers, only 1,083 would survive. Twenty-seven United States Marines would receive the Medal of Honor on the volcanic sands of Iwo Jima, one-third of all such awards given to Marines in World War II.

Iwo Jima, Legacy of Valor, describes in detail the battle for this Pacific isle. The following narrative summarizes the story.

Iwo Jima, eight and one-half square miles of mountainous terrain, achieved this costly importance because it was large enough for an air field, was only 650 miles due south of Tokyo, and effectively blocked B-29 Superfortress bombers attack routes to Japanese mainland targets. B-29s that were disabled by antiaircraft fire or by fighter attacks were unable to limp back to the Marianas and often had to ditch at sea. A recovery base close to the mainland targets was desperately needed.

Lieutenant General Tadamichi Kuribayashi, who had received part of his military training and education at the U.S. Army Cavalry School at Fort Bliss, Texas, vowed to the Emperor to defend Iwo Jima to the death.

The Fourth and Fifth Marine Divisions, and a fraction of the Third Marine Division, were the designated invasion force under the command of Lieutenant General Holland M. "Howlin' Mad" Smith, the Senior Marine Commander in the Pacific. "Operation Detachments", the Iwo Jima invasion plan, commenced on February 19, 1945. In the next thirty-six days, sixty percent of the Marine assault troops, and thirty percent of all troops involved, would become casualties. Naval and air bombardment began in earnest on D-day, at 6:30 a.m. from eight battleships, nineteen cruisers, and forty-four destroyers. Six waves of 1,360 Marines per wave, were then amphibiously landed on the beach by Amtracs and Higgins boat landing craft. At 9:02 a.m., the message was flashed to the flagship, "Boats on the beach!" Before noon of D-day on Iwo Jima, the Navy and Marines would lose more men and ships than were lost on D-day at Normandy, in Europe.

At the end of D-day, only a few hundred yards inland had been secured. It would take six days to accomplish the advance that had been the D-Day objective of the invasion (i.e., the control of the southern one-half of the island and the conquest of the 556-foot high Mt. Suribachi).

At 10:31 a.m., on February 23, 1945, the Stars and Stripes were raised for the first time on the peak of Mt. Suribachi. The following day, a larger flag, 8 ft. x 4 ft. 8 in., was brought ashore, attached to a large metal water pipe, and raised ceremoniously as the smaller flag was lowered. The second flag-raising was carried out by members of the Second Battalion, Twenty-eighth Regiment, Fifth Marine Division, as Associated Press photographer Joe Rosenthal captured the moment of glory on film. It was to be the most famous picture of World War II and of the century. After the war, the three-dimensional reproduction of this photo was cast in one hundred tons of bronze for all Americans to honor in Arlington, Virginia. Following the jubilation of the flag-raising, it would take another thirty-two days of vicious combat, and major number of casualties, to secure the island called Iwo.

The Japanese had fortified the island with deep bunkers and caves, heavily protected by large artillery guns and mortars, stretching hundreds of feet into the hillsides, where they had garrisoned supplies, ammunition, food, water, and hospitals, as well as their troops, in ventilated, lighted tunnels. The final encirclement of General Kuribayashi's headquarters cave at Kitano Point, and the final battle for Iwo Jima, was consummated on March 26, 1945. The general was never captured, and his body was never found.

IWO JIMA: OPERATION DETACHMENT

"Victory was never in doubt. Its cost was. What was in doubt, in all our minds, was whether there would be any of us left to dedicate our cemetery at the end, or whether the last Marine would die knocking out the last Japanese gun and gunner."

Major General Graves B. Erskine
Commander, Third Marine Division

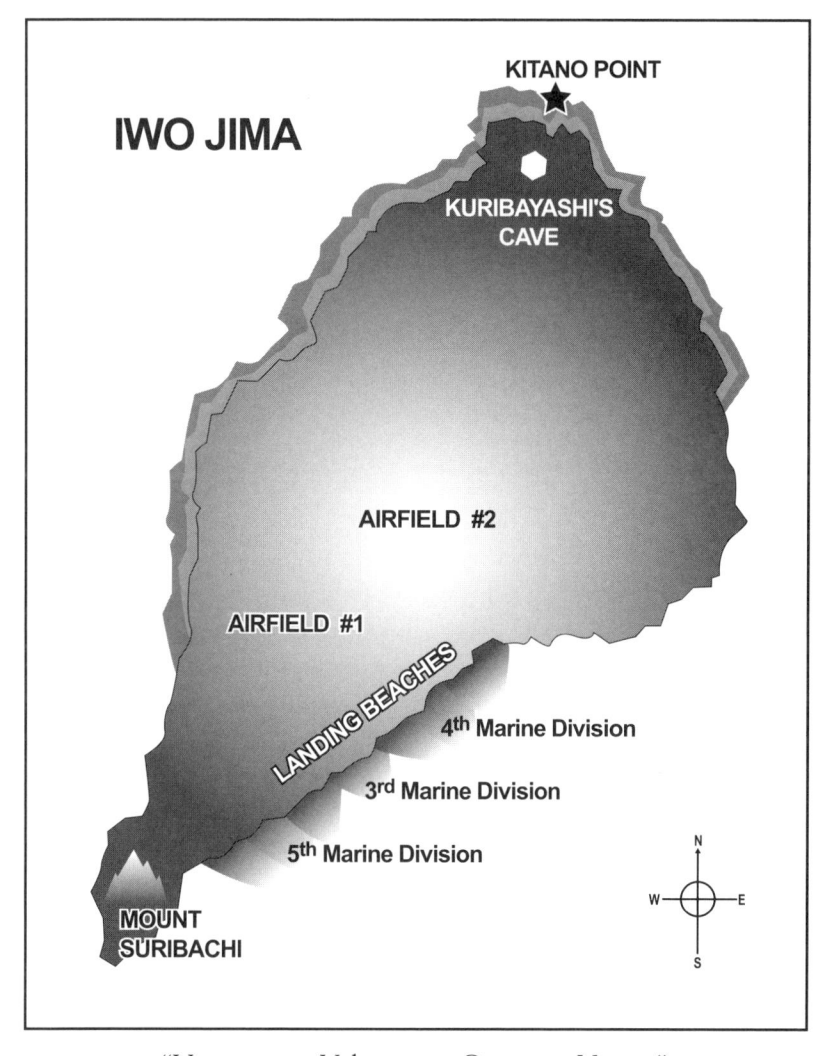

"Uncommon Valor was a Common Virtue."

Fleet Admiral Chester A. Nimitz
Commander-in-Chief, Pacific Fleet

A TATTERED OLD FLAG
As told by
Harold Short

Harold Short served in the Marine Corps from 1942 to 1947, but was called back to active duty at Camp Pendleton, California, from 1950 to 1951 to teach demolition to Marines bound for the Korean War. Short recently donated the battle-worn, forty-eight-star American flag that he carried throughout the Pacific War to the Rose-Harms American Legion post in his adopted hometown of Grafton, Wisconsin. He lives in Stordock Hall at the Veterans Home at King, Wisconsin.

I joined the Marine Corps in Clearwater, Texas, in January 1942 at the age of sixteen. I was 6 ft. 4 in. and the recruiters believed me when I told them I was eighteen. I was sent to Parris Island, South Carolina, for basic training and then was selected for Airborne training at Fort Bragg, North Carolina, before embarking for Auckland, New Zealand. There I joined the Marine Second Raider Battalion, "Carlson's Raiders" (Colonel Evans F. Carlson, commander).

Guadalcanal with its jungle heat, humidity, disease, and the enemy was frightening. Jap snipers tied themselves in treetops that formed canopies high above the thick jungle grasses below, waited until our Marines passed by, and then shot them in the back. We learned to clear the treetops with flamethrowers before advancing. We called the flamethrowers "the devil's breath". When the guy right next to you gets killed, all you can do is pause a moment, say, "Better him than me," and go on. In battle, there is no time for remorse.

Following the Battle of Guadalcanal, I was reassigned to a special weapons unit as part of the Third Marine Division and became a Marine demolition expert skilled in blowing up enemy gun emplacements located in fortified "pillboxes", and "bunkers". In 1943 and 1944, I was involved in the landings on Tarawa, Saipan, Tinian, Eniwetok, and Kwajelein in the South and Central Pacific areas. Tarawa Atoll is a part of the Gilbert Islands, and in World War II, it was part of a defense perimeter protecting approach from the south to the Japanese-controlled islands in the Marianas, the Carolines, and the Philippines.

The American conquest of Tarawa was critical to advancement northward. At Tarawa, the temperature was over one hundred degrees, and we never had enough water to drink. You can only carry so much in a canteen.

Coming ashore at Tarawa was a real challenge. The coral reefs cut our clothes to shreds and slashed our legs. In addition, there were underwater barbed wire castanets placed by the Japanese at lower leg height and also at waist height. The Japanese 40, 50, and 70 mm artillery guns fired at our landing craft. I saw LCPs (landing craft personnel) blown right out of the water. Once we got ashore and took control, I blew up those guns with two packs of thermite satchel explosives down the barrels. When I arrived ashore, I struck down a Japanese flag and hoisted the American flag on a palm tree.

The Battle at Tarawa only lasted three-and-one-half days, but in that time one thousand Marines and four thousand-eight hundred Japanese lost their lives. Two thousand Marines were wounded. It became known as the "Battle of Bloody Tarawa". On Tarawa, I was hit by sniper fire in my left forearm, and the scar from this sniper's bullet eliminated the upper part of my favorite tattoo. When I left Tarawa, I lowered the American flag and placed it in my backpack, where it traveled with me throughout the rest of the war.

At 9:00 a.m. on February 19, 1945, as a member of the Twenty-seventh Regiment, Fifth Marine Division, I accompanied the first wave of troops to land at "Red Beach I" on Iwo Jima. The island smelled of sulfur and was covered with black volcanic sand. The heavy artillery fire made the landing a slow and deadly undertaking. My platoon used flamethrowers to clear the Japanese out of the caves and tunnels so that I could blow up the gun emplacements.

I was on Iwo Jima four days before being wounded in the flank by a sniper's automatic weapon. I was evacuated to a hospital ship offshore and then to a hospital in Pearl Harbor, Hawaii. I missed the flag-raising on Mt. Suribachi by one day. (Please see photos in color section.)

MT. SURIBACHI
As told by
Thomas H. O'Brien

"Semper Fidelis" (always faithful) is the Marine Corp motto. I cannot imagine anyone who epitomizes this motto more than Tom O'Brien. The hours I have spent with him have been holy hours spent in the presence of a true American hero. It is beyond comprehension to believe that this man or any could endure such hardship and adversity and survive. He did it because it was expected of him. His four-room apartment is decorated with mementos of his service and pictures of his commanding officers, and his chairside table holds at least three Marine Corps publications. For more than sixty years, Tom O'Brien has lived, breathed, and almost died many times for the United States Marine Corps.

Lowell Peterson

I was born in New York City in 1925. My father was an immigrant from Ireland, where he had been very active in the Separatist Movement, living "underground" as a fugitive until he was lucky enough to get a sponsor to come to the U.S. He entered the States through Ellis Island and, with the help of the New York Irish community, went to work as a New York City cop. I grew up around Seventy-sixth Street and First Avenue, and remember a lot of fights in the streets and in the pubs, most of which were started by my older brother, when someone would slander our Irish heritage or call us "shanty Irish".

I entered the Marine Corps on March 17, 1942, at the age of seventeen. Basic training at Parris Island, South Carolina, was followed by amphibious training at Camp Pendleton, California, prior to embarking for the South Pacific, stopping at Pearl Harbor en route. I was a member of Able Co., First Platoon, First Battalion, Seventh Marines (Regiment) of the First Marine Division. I arrived off the coast of Guadalcanal on August 15, 1942. Prior to going ashore, we were told in our briefings that casualties would approach ninety percent. On the radio from Japan, "Tokyo Rose" was broadcasting a similar grim fate for us. It always amazed me how she knew the names of our units, right down to the platoon level, and also what our destination was. The depressing thought of possibly becoming a casualty in the upcoming battle weighed heavily on our minds as we entered our landing craft to go ashore. Because of the high waves and rough seas, some Marines were killed, injured, crushed, or drowned while attempting to enter the landing crafts.

The first wave of amphibious landings at Guadalcanal had commenced on August 7, 1942. I was in the fourth wave to go ashore. I remained in combat in the jungle of Guadalcanal until November 1942. We were to seek out the Japanese defenders, eliminate them, or drive them off the island while at the same time defending Henderson Field from Japanese counterattack. The trees in the jungle formed a canopy above our heads, fifty feet in the air. The Japanese would "shinny" up the trees and tie themselves there, waiting for our patrols to pass, and then the snipers would shoot the last troops in the back. We would rake the treetops with rifle fire, machine-gun fire, and flame throwers, killing the snipers who would then dangle in death from their ropes. We also discovered that the Japanese did not have pins to pull on their hand grenades to activate them. They had to hit the grenades on rocks or on their helmets to activate them. We learned to listen for this sound, take cover, and fire in that direction.

I remember that at Guadalcanal, after our very difficult amphibious landing against stiff Japanese resistance, we then moved inland through the jungle, clearing out pockets of enemy concentrations. We had been in the jungle for weeks under conditions of extreme hardship, constantly battling snipers, and armed confrontation. Guadalcanal is not the end of the world, but as they say, you could see it from there! One day I was sent back to the beach to pick up more ammunition. The closer I got to the beach, the more I could smell coffee. I thought I was hallucinating.

When I got to the beach, I found out the Army had arrived and set up camp with tents, kitchens, and showers. We had secured that beach with great losses. I went to the mess sergeant and asked him if I could fill up five canteens with coffee to take back to my troops. We called coffee, "hot joe". He had a large bucket, about three feet in diameter and three feet high, full of steaming coffee. My Marines had not smelled or tasted coffee in two or three months. He said, "You can't have that coffee; that's Army coffee."

I went insane! I unshouldered my carbine, locked and loaded a round of ammunition, pointed it at him, and demanded my five canteens of coffee! Needless to say, I got as much as I could carry. My troops felt like they were in heaven with that fresh coffee. It was the morale boost they needed. In retrospect, I probably would not have shot that mess sergeant, but I sure thought about it for a minute.

The Battle of Guadalcanal was the first of five major Pacific campaigns of WWII that I would take part in. I, like many of my fellow Marines, contracted malaria, and after I left Guadalcanal, I was given six months of R&R (rest and

THE SUN ROSE CLEAR

recovery) in Australia and New Zealand; some of this was hospital time to get over my malaria. I was then sent back to Pearl Harbor for reassignment.

At Pearl Harbor, I joined the Twenty-second Brigade, which had just returned from Samoa; we were assembled and prepared for further amphibious attacks on islands of the Pacific. The next landing that I took part in was at Guam, where I received some shrapnel wounds.

After Guam, I again returned to Pearl Harbor and was assigned to Baker Co., Second Platoon, Eighth Marines, Second Marine Division in preparation for the amphibious assault on Tarawa. Tarawa was horrible. I was in the first wave of troops to go ashore, but the beaches had been poorly scouted by the Navy, and, as a result, the Higgins landing craft could not get close to the beach because of a large, shallow coral reef. They dropped us off far from shore, under heavy enemy fire coming from the island. The coral is razor-blade sharp and ripped our clothes, legs, and torsos. We lay on the coral, in the water, for three days before we could get to shore. We stacked the dead bodies of our fellow Marines in front of us to act as barriers to the fire coming at us from shore. Finally, the Navy bombarded the shore enough and put down enough smoke screens, that we could establish our beachhead and move inland.

It was bloody in the water, but even bloodier on shore. The Japs hit us with several "banzai" attacks. We could hear them chanting and screaming, working themselves into a frenzy before they attacked. Then they would charge our positions in great numbers. We had two men to a foxhole, sitting back to back and returning fire and grenades at short range. Much of the fighting, however, was hand-to-hand with knife and bayonet. I was bayoneted during one of these attacks. When the battle was over, the ground was covered with Marines and Japanese, locked in death, just as they had been locked in battle. Bodies lay everywhere. The battle for Tarawa continued until we secured the island and killed or drove off all of the Japanese. After it was over, I was again sent back to Pearl Harbor.

While I was lying on a stretcher, waiting to get on a hospital ship at Pearl, a Red Cross worker gave me a cigarette and lit it. When I told her I was a Marine, she slapped the cigarette out of my mouth, hitting me hard enough to daze me. I thought, "What's your problem, lady?" She'd probably been frustrated or jilted by a Marine somewhere along the way. The Red Cross also made us pay for our coffee and donuts. Needless to say, I have never had much to do with that organization since.

The Battle for Saipan was just as rugged as all the others. Again, I was in the first amphibious landing wave. During one of our confrontations with the Japanese, I had my canteen and cartridge belt ripped right off my body by a riddling burst from a Japanese machine gun. The Japanese had a lot of Russian weapons, which surprised me, as I thought Russia was our ally. I also was shot by a sniper on

Saipan. As we drove ahead, the Japanese chose to jump off Suicide Cliff rather than surrender to us. When we got to the end of the island, we observed that the bay below was filled with floating bodies. The amphibious landings at Tarawa and Guam were in 1943 and Saipan was in 1944.

I was now twenty years old and a sergeant with Charlie Co., Second Battalion, Twenty-seventh Regiment, First Platoon, Fifth Marine Division, commanded by Major General Keller E. Rockey. I had already served in four major campaigns and been with three different Marine divisions. We again left Pearl Harbor and spent several days at sea. At 0900 on February 19, 1945, I landed with the first wave at Red Beach on the island of Iwo Jima, near the base of Mt. Suribachi. We stayed pinned down on the beach under heavy Japanese gunfire for three days and three nights. On our first day ashore, we lost our first lieutenant, our captain, our major, and most of our regiment. I was the only noncom (noncommissioned officer) left in the regiment and, therefore, I assumed command.

On the morning of the fourth day, we were ordered to make an all-out assault on Mt. Suribachi and take it at all costs. Marines were assembled from surviving remnants of various regiments to spearhead the attack. My Twenty-seventh Marines joined what was left of the Twenty-eighth Marines, and we started up the mountain. We were under continuous enemy gunfire and engaged in hand-to-hand combat with knives and bayonets. Night was upon us, so we dug in, got a little rest, and waited for morning to make the final assault to the top. Three hundred Japanese troops inside the caves of Mt. Suribachi awaited our advance. In the early afternoon of the fifth day, I was hit twice by small arms fire and was also bayoneted, but I still fought on with everything I had left in me.

I was able to make it to the top of Mt. Suribachi with my men, and even though I was seriously wounded, I felt an overpowering sense of accomplishment. At the top of the mountain, I was able to man a machine gun and help protect the six men who raised the *first* American flag on the volcanic crest of Mt. Suribachi. The frenzied Japanese made suicide charges against our position with swords, grenades, and small arms fire, trying to prevent us from raising the stars and stripes. They died there; I saw to that. One of the flag raisers at the famous *second* flag-raising a day later, after Mt. Suribachi was secured, was PFC Ira H. Hays, a Navajo Indian, who was a member of my platoon. After the initial flag-raising, I collapsed from blood-loss and was carried down Mt. Suribachi on a litter to the beach and taken out to sea to the USS *Mercy* hospital ship. I did not witness the second flag-raising but was very proud to have been present at the first. Of the six "leathernecks" that I helped protect as they raised the first flag, only one survived the Battle of Iwo Jima. I had convinced my best friend from high school to join the marines and, after three South Pacific campaigns together, he was killed at Iwo

Jima, fighting side-by-side with me. This emotional wound was deeper than any of my combat wounds.

On the hospital ship, they just took a scissors, cut all my clothes off, and threw them away. I could not remember my last bath, and I had not shaved. My socks were rotted to my feet. I was bloody, dirty, and muddy; I just plain stunk!

After treatment at the Army hospital on Saipan and at Balboa Navy Hospital in San Diego, I recovered satisfactorily from my wounds. I was then sent to Guam, where I joined Easy Co., Twenty-second Marines, Second Platoon, Sixth Marine Division to prepare for the invasion of mainland Japan. After the bomb was dropped and the war was over, I was sent with the Sixth Marine Division to Tsingtao, China, to help supervise the postwar Japanese disarmament. I spent the next three years in China.

Following my China service, I returned to the United States, where I served as a Marine drill instructor for a period of time and put two platoons through training. It was pretty easy duty, but I just did not like it. I asked for a transfer and was assigned to Able Co., Seventh Marines, First Platoon, First Marine Division. I had gone full circle. This was the same exact unit I had entered right out of Camp Pendleton in 1942. In 1950, I was sent to Korea and fought for the next eighteen months from the Inchon landing to the Chosin Reservoir, where my regiment became encircled and trapped. The enemy was on top of the hills all around us and could have attacked and wiped us out. They were blowing bugles and whistles, yelling and screaming for hours on end. Our general told us that we were going to fight our way out and take our dead and wounded with us. The regiment was going to leave together. We fought our way out, but only a few survived. We were referred to as "The Frozen Chosen Few", because we all suffered from severe frostbite. The ravages of battle, wounds, frostbite, and combat fatigue had taken their toll. I spent a good deal of hospital time before being discharged from the Marines, on August 17, 1954.

After discharge from the Marine Corps, I worked as a physical therapist in Kenosha, Wisconsin, prior to retirement. I then purchased property north of Iola, Wisconsin, and lived there for several years prior to moving to the Village of Iola.

Tom O'Brien wrote recently: "… A monument stands tall, flying the stars and stripes, in Arlington National Cemetery, Washington, D.C., commemorating the historic moment in history when the flag was raised by the marines on Mt. Suribachi, Iwo Jima. I beg you, please give respect to our flag that we gave our blood and lives for, in so many battles, in order that our nation could remain free. I am proud to be an American, to have been a United States Marine, and to have served my flag and country in the time of need."

Gunnery Sergeant Thomas O'Brien received the following decorations:

- ★ Good Conduct Ribbon.
- ★ Asiatic Pacific Ribbon with five bronze battle stars.
- ★ Presidential Unit Citation Ribbon with two bronze stars.
- ★ Purple Heart Ribbon with three bronze oak leaf clusters and medals.
- ★ The Bronze Star Ribbon and Medal - 1943.
- ★ The Navy Cross Ribbon and Medal - 1945.
- ★ China Service Ribbon and Medal - 1946 to 1948.
- ★ World War II Victory Ribbon and Medal.
- ★ Korea Ribbon with one bronze battle star.

The Navy Cross (Distinguished Service Cross) is the second highest military honor, next to the Medal of Honor. It was awarded to O'Brien "For conspicuous gallantry and intrepidity in action at the risk of life beyond the call of duty."

Membership in the Legion of Valor is limited to persons previously recognized with the Medal of Honor or a Distinguished Service Cross. On February 18, 1993, Gunnery Sergeant Thomas O'Brien became a member of the Legion of Valor.

O'Brien notes that he does not consider himself a hero. He feels strongly that those who gave their lives in the service of their country and did not come home are the real heroes of war.

Lowell Peterson

(Please see photos in color section.)

TOWARD KITANO POINT
As told by
Courtney L. Coffing

The sun finally broke out as I looked back at Mt. Suribachi and saw the American flag waving. I turned to a buddy and said, "I see they got the flag up," and he replied, "You're right," and that was all we made of it at the time.

Courtney L. Coffing (taken in Guam prior to the attack on Iwo Jima).

I entered the Marine Corps on December 22, 1943, becoming a member of Charlie Company, Twenty-first Marines, Third Marine Division, under the command of Major General Graves B. Erskine. Charlie Company was composed of three rifle squads and a mortar section.

I left Camp Pendleton and landed at Guam two days after the island was declared secure. After eight months on Guam, a twelve-mile hike with packs and rifles led to our departure on the USS *President Coolidge*, destination unknown. By February 19, 1945, we had our answer. We were off the coast of Iwo Jima. We entered our Amtrac landing craft to go ashore, but high seas and twenty-foot waves made the transfers difficult, and everybody was seasick. On D+2, February 21, 1945, I landed on the warm, volcanic ash beaches of Iwo Jima. The day was cold, cloudy, windy, and rainy. Walking was difficult and tracked vehicles had difficulty maneuvering in the soft soil. Our regiment fought across the island, captured Motoyama Airfield Number 1 and on D+4 captured Motoyama Airfield Number 2.

Intense fighting occurred from D+5 until D+16, as we advanced through the central section toward the northern part of the island. Japanese soldiers would spring out of caves like ants, and retreat to safety after firing their weapons. Nighttime was a restless affair. I felt much better after the dog handlers arrived.

The dogs helped us avoid surprises. We used our mortars to shoot illuminating flares into the night sky to discourage the enemy, as well as to provide light for our tanks to see their targets. In combat, the days and nights meld together in perpetual terror. On one afternoon, our unit was pinned down for several hours under fire from a 20-mm antitank gun. It was finally silenced. The Baptist chaplain, armed with a .45 pistol, won a Bronze Star for retrieving wounded from the front line. On D+16, March 6th, after a particularly frightening night attack, Able Company's mortar squad was almost completely wiped out. I became the new squad leader for Able Company. It was a long and scary night for us.

When the Twenty-first Marines reached the ocean on the side of the island opposite the landing sites on D+18, a canteen was filled with ocean water and sent back to General Erskine with the message, "For inspection, not consumption," a token that indicated to him that the island had been sliced in two. It would take another eighteen days to eliminate all Japanese resistance.

On D+35, Sunday, March 25, 1945, a deep trench was dug in the volcanic sand near Kitano Point, on the northernmost coast of Iwo Jima, which allowed water to seep in and then be pumped into a tower to provide us with an American luxury, a shower. Due to the volcanic heat, cold water from the sea had to be mixed with the water to make it usable. It was my first shower in a month.

After the island had been secured, a memorial service was held at the Marine Memorial Cemetery, a sacred place that had not existed thirty-six days earlier. It was now the resting place for 6,821 Marines. A dozen small graves formed an arc around the flagpole, the burial site of dogs who had also died in combat.

On D+36, I left Iwo Jima and arrived on Guam, April 1, 1945, the day that Marines were again landing on another Pacific beach for the last great battle of the war, the Battle of Okinawa.

Courtney Coffing now lives in retirement with his wife, Wanda, on North Main Street in Scandinavia, Wisconsin. He is an active member of the Local VFW Post 9748. His postwar years took him on a circuitous route through New Orleans, San Antonio, and Europe before settling in Ohio, where he was employed by Coin World *magazine prior to moving to a similar position at Krause Publications in Iola, Wisconsin.*

THE LAST STORM

SUGAR LOAF HILL: THE BATTLE OF OKINAWA

As told by
Raymond Moe

    The Battle of Okinawa left 110,000 Japanese military dead and 150,000 Okinawan civilians dead (one-third of the island's population), at the expense of 20,195 American dead and 55,162 wounded.
    During the Battle of Okinawa, kamikaze suicide air attacks by 1,915 Japanese airplanes sank 38 United States ships and damaged 368 others. Fortunately, this loss did not include any battleships or carriers.
    The Sixth Marine Division, between May 12 and May 18, 1945, suffered 2,662 casualties, killed and wounded, and 1,289 had to be removed from battle because of combat fatigue in capturing the hill called "Sugar Loaf". The Tenth Army commander, Major General Simon Bolivar Buckner, was killed during the advance. Although many Japanese prisoners were taken, flushed out of deep and extensive cave networks, Japanese soldiers and civilians also chose death by suicide rather than capture by the Americans. Some chose the sword, bullets, or hand grenades, but large numbers threw themselves off the cliffs into the sea, as their last ritualistic, ceremonious, dedication to their god, the emperor. Formal, unconditional surrender of Okinawa and all the Ryukyu Islands by the Japanese occurred on September 7, 1945, but official U.S. control had been established on June 22, 1945.

Sugar Loaf Hill. (From the collection of Gardner N. Soule, Shelburne, Vermont.)

THE SUN ROSE CLEAR

Raymond Moe

My name is Raymond Moe. During World War II, I was a corporal in the Fifteenth Marine Artillery Regiment, activated on Guadalcanal in October 1944, formed from the Fourth, Twenty-second, and Twenty-ninth artillery regiments, to be a part of the Sixth Marine Division.

After graduating from high school in 1940, I worked in a steel mill near Chicago, but in 1943, when my brother joined the navy, I returned home to Wisconsin to help on the family farm. Because I had registered for the draft in Chicago, I was called back to Illinois to be drafted. Much to the chagrin of my father when I returned home, he learned that I had been diverted to the marines rather than the army. My father had heard about the high casualties the Marines were suffering on the islands of the South Pacific and surmised that the army would be a lot safer. I was standing in line for my physical when a Marine sergeant came up to me and asked if I had a strong preference for the army. I said no, so he said, "Why don't you go over there in that line and sign up for the Marines?" I thought about it for a minute and then did what he said. I realize now that the sergeant was on orders to "cherry-pick" the fittest recruits out of the line, and I guess, being fresh out of the steel mill and off the farm, that I fit his criteria. Troops were being recruited to support the massive Marine amphibious force buildup in the Pacific and to supply replacement troops for casualties.

Boot camp at San Diego and artillery training at Camp Pendleton preceded being shipped out to New Caledonia and later to Guadalcanal in early 1944. The training at all of these sites was extremely intensive, to the point where it was a relief to quit practicing and finally ship out to battle. As the convoy of men, machines, and supplies was gathered for its several-thousand-mile advance to Okinawa, my unit remained aboard an LST (landing ships, troops) for two weeks off the shore of Guadalcanal. I slept in a trailer aboard ship and ate K-rations.

As we arrived off the coast of Okinawa, the Japanese kamikaze suicide planes attempted to destroy the American fleet. They were not very successful, but they did scare the hell out of us. Easter sunrise, April 1, 1945, signaled the commencement of

The "Turtle Back Tombs"

a heavy artillery barrage against the island from U.S. battleships and cruisers, along with shore bombardment from carrier-based airplanes. The invasion force made its way ashore at 0837 April 1, 1945, against almost no resistance. It appeared that the Japanese had elected to move inland to solidify their defenses rather than to resist the invasion on the beaches. Yontan airfield and Kadena air base were quickly taken, and our Marines moved north, through mountainous terrain and heavy vegetation, to secure the city of Nago and the Motobu Peninsula. After our lightly opposed landing, I spent the first night ashore sleeping in a weird turtle-shell-shaped cement bunker filled with large jars. The turtle structures dot the landscape of Okinawa. I learned later that this was an Okinawan family tomb, and the jars contained the ashes of their ancestors.

As our marines moved into battle, guns were firing from both sides, and it was often hard to decide what was friendly fire and what was enemy fire. Because the Okinawan refugee civilians tended to migrate from their villages and homes at night and could not answer the code word challenges of the Americans, many were shot as possible Japanese soldier intruders. Passwords were changed daily, to identify friendly patrols or movement of troops anywhere. We always tried to use passwords with a lot of "Ls" in the word, because the Japanese pronounced these as "Rs" and, therefore, any attempt to sneak into secure areas or camps by the Japanese could be thwarted. This trick also helped identify snipers, who tried to lure the Marines into the open with friendly phrases so that they could be shot.

Japanese mortars were landing close to our position and much too close to gasoline drums that we had stored in the area. This drove us to seek refuge in tunnels and caves in the mountainous hillside as we moved north to secure that part of the island. Some of the tunnels were filled with lice, and some of my unwary Marine buddies came out itching. After heavy fighting, the entire northern half of this sixty-mile-long island was secured on May 1, 1945, by Marines of the Sixth Division. We were then ordered south to join the battle around the capitol city of Naha. We reached Chibana outside Naha on May 6, 1945. For the next seven days, the weather became atrocious; it rained heavily, turning everything to mud. The average rainfall on Okinawa is over 120 inches per year.

The Japanese enemy was heavily concentrated around the Old Imperial Castle at Shuri Heights. General Mitsuru Ushijima's main concentration of troops and artillery at Shuri were protected by a valley with three defensive high-ground-forward positions meant to block any advance toward Shuri. Each of these three positions was like a protective arrow. Sugar Loaf Hill was the point of the arrow, flanked

Marine Major General Lemuel C. Sheperd Jr. visits the front lines at Sugar Loaf Hill. (From the collection of Gardner N. Soule, Shelburne, Vermont.)

Bombed-out sugar factory, Naha, Okinawa. Note the total devastation after the battle. (From the collection of Gardner N. Soule, Shelburne, Vermont.)

by Half Moon and Horseshoe Ridge. These positions were each heavily fortified, heavily manned, thoroughly tunneled, and armored.

On May 12, 1945, the assault by the Twenty-ninth Marines on Sugar Loaf Hill began. The battle was as brutal as any conflict anywhere during World War II. Our Marine infantry was repelled numerous times, and sometimes several times per day, from their attempts to take Sugar Loaf. For the next ten days, it was to be a battle of attack and counterattack along a nine hundred-yard front. Casualties were enormous on both sides. Marine units attacking with fifty to one hundred men often returned with only a handful alive and a large number of wounded. Our marines fought gallantly to the last grenade, the last bullet, and their last ounce of energy during these charges against Sugar Loaf. It was a foregone conclusion that the chance of survival was small. Courage was commonplace and heroic bravery, unselfish leadership, and unwavering dedication were the norm.

Fortunately for me, the artillery positions were in the rear of the frontal attacks, but this did not stop the Japanese from firing mortars, artillery, and small arms at us. One night I was sleeping directly above my foxhole in a mosquito-protective hammock tied at both ends to disabled machinery when incoming fire led to a quick attempt to unzip the hammock and drop into the foxhole, only to find that the zipper was stuck. Any man will understand this frustration. I slit the hammock with a knife and safely entered the muddy foxhole, half filled with water.

I contracted malaria on Okinawa and for the next twenty years suffered from attacks of fever and shaking chills. I refused to go to the field hospital and, therefore, this was never entered into my service record and I received no disability from this serious illness. I avoided the hospital primarily because the walking wounded and the walking ill were expected to be stretcher bearers for the severely wounded. The thought of constantly being this close to the dead, dying, and severely wounded was not to my liking. I saw enough of this on the battlefield without going to where the casualties were all concentrated.

After the battle, the only thing left standing in the city of Naha, was one wall of a sugar factory. There were no trees and no buildings. The battlefield was a rain-soaked, muddy, barren terrain devoid of life.

The final American flag-raising of the final battle of World War II was celebrated at Ara-Saki, Okinawa, Ryukyu Islands, on June 22, 1945.

After the Battle of Okinawa, the Sixth Marines were sent to Guam, and I had high hopes of returning home. It was not to be. Following the dropping of the atomic bombs on Hiroshima and Nagasaki, the war ended and the Sixth Marine Division was sent to Tsingtao, China, to assist with the Japanese surrender and the stabilization of the area. At Tsingtao, ten thousand Japanese surrendered to our twelve thousand Marines.

I was shipped home on a transport ship, and it was truly a "slow boat *from* China" as it took thirty days to reach the United States. I had not had a furlough throughout my military career, from the fall of 1943 until the spring of 1946. I had spent three Christmases and two Easters away from home and had witnessed some of the worst carnage known to man, all of this before I was twenty-five years old.

One year after I had marched ashore on Okinawa on Easter Sunday 1945, I finally returned home. On Easter Eve 1946, while still in my Marine dress uniform, I was leaning against a jukebox at the Windmill Bar near Waupaca, Wisconsin, trying to find some songs that I recognized. There were none. A young lady, with a kind alto-toned voice and a pleasant smile, offered this skinny, shy kid assistance. (I had survived on two slim meals a day for three years and a lot of K-rations.) Jane Leach, that young lady, became Mrs. Raymond Moe shortly thereafter, and we have spent more than fifty-six happy years together. I worked for the Waupaca County Highway Department as a bridge and road builder and built many of the bridges throughout the county. I became the Waupaca County Highway Commissioner, a position I held for several years prior to retiring, with thirty-eight years of service to the community and the county.

The Sixth Marine Division was assembled and activated at Guadalcanal on September 7, 1944, for the express purpose of preparing for the invasion of Okinawa. It was the only Marine Corps division that was never active in the continental United States. Battle hard-

ened veterans, who had fought at Tulagi, Guadalcanal, Saipan, Guam, and all over Micronesia and Melanesia, were melded together with new replacement regiments arriving from the United States to form the Sixth Division, U.S.M.C. They were placed under the command of Major General Lemuel C. Shepherd Jr.

Between September 1944 and March 1945, the division trained together in vigorous battlefield exercises typical of the Marines, fine-tuning their skills, tactics, maneuvers, and coordination of regimental units in preparation for embarkation to Okinawa. On March 15, 1945, the twelve hundred ship Battle Flotilla sailed for Okinawa. It was the largest war fleet ever assembled. Following a several-thousand-mile journey, they arrived off the shores of Okinawa on Easter eve, March 31, 1945.

The Battle of Okinawa resulted in the Sixth Marine Division receiving the Presidential Unit Citation. Four Marines were awarded the Medal of Honor. An additional 27 received the Navy Cross and 134 received the Silver Star. Hundreds received the bronze star, and way too many received a purple heart. A total of 1,592 military awards were presented to the men of the Sixth Marine Division, in addition to the purple hearts.

The Sixth Marine Division was decommissioned on April 1, 1946, in Tsingtao, China, and reduced to brigade strength and redesignated the Third Marine Brigade. It had been commissioned and trained for a specific purpose. It dispatched its duty with honor.

THIS IS TO CERTIFY THAT

CORPORAL RAYMOND M. MOE, USMCR

PARTICIPATED IN THE CEREMONY AT THE SURRENDER OF JAPANESE MILITARY FORCES IN THE AREA OF TSINGTAO, CHINA, 25 OCTOBER 1945

Lemuel C. Shepherd Jr.
MAJOR GENERAL USMC
COMMANDING 6th MARINE DIVISION

THE SUN ROSE CLEAR

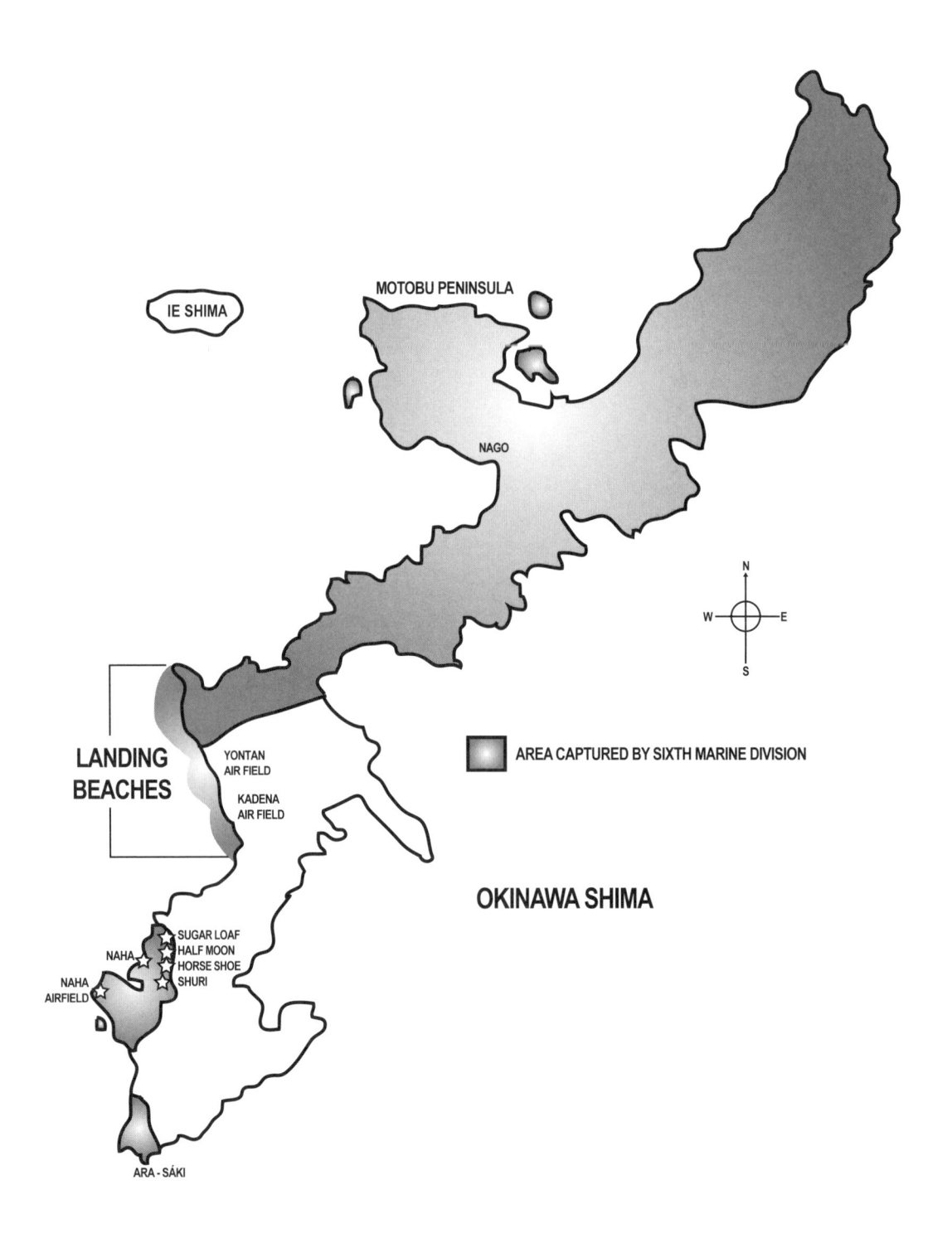

THE AIR APACHES
As told by
Albert W. Gruer Jr.

It is almost incomprehensible to imagine that young men age twenty to twenty-two years old were put in charge of aircrews and four-engine bombers, and had the maturity and discipline to command respect and get the job done. It did not happen once or twice, but hundreds of times during World War II, day in and day out, in Europe and in Asia. The feeling of invincibility of these young men was tested over and over again. They certainly had "the right stuff".

I left Dartmouth College at the age of nineteen, volunteered for the Army Air Corps in 1942, and was called up for service in March 1943. My decision to volunteer for the Air Corps instead of the Army Infantry was influenced, in no small part, by the fact that my father had become a paraplegic during World War I, from German machine-gun fire while serving in the infantry in France. I completed my pilot training, receiving my pilot Wings as a second lieutenant in May 1944. I was assigned to the 345th Bomb Group and was soon on my way to New Guinea to join the war effort.

In 1944 and 1945, my crew and I flew three missions out of New Guinea, twenty-four missions out of San Marcelino in the Philippines, and several missions out of Okinawa. Our average combat missions lasted eight hours. We flew at very low altitude, under sixty feet from the surface of land or sea. After returning from one mission, my crew chief found a chicken head in an engine, presumably from a low level pass over trees where the chicken was roosting. Our airplane received some combat damage during these missions and, on one occasion, the entire nose section was blown off. Fortunately, however, my crew of six that I embarked with made it through the war with the entire crew still intact. We were one of the few who made it "all the way".

THE SUN ROSE CLEAR

Search-and-Destroy Mission – 3/10/45

Our search-and-destroy missions were scouting flights looking for Japanese shipping. If we found no shipping targets, we would bomb and strafe a secondary or tertiary target on land, such as railroad marshaling yards, truck convoys, airfields, etc. On March 10, six planes of the 498th Squadron were on patrol along the east coast of French Indochina. Our search identified a huge Japanese oil tanker loaded with fuel and riding very low in the water near the Port of Qui Nhon. Several hits were made on the tanker, and it exploded. As the tanker was consumed by fire, smoke rose to eight thousand feet.

Lieutenant B. F. Chambers, pilot of one of the planes, made a direct hit on the tanker, but the five hundred pound bomb exploded immediately instead of being activated four or five seconds after impact. The bombs had delayed-action fuses to allow the plane to clear the area before detonation. At an altitude of only twenty to thirty feet above the water, a released bomb remains directly under the plane on impact. The bomb that Lieutenant Chambers dropped had a malfunction of its fuse. After the bomb exploded, Chambers checked his engine instruments, which showed no apparent damage, even though the plane had holes punctured throughout the fuselage from shrapnel.

Lieutenant Chambers and his crew were about halfway home when the left engine started vibrating and smoking. Apparently the bomb explosion had caused an oil leak, and the oil had slowly drained away. The propellers need oil to "feather" and, therefore, Chambers was unable to stop the windmilling of the propeller. His airplane progressively lost air speed, forcing him to make a decision to ditch. Ditching in a B-25 is like hitting a brick wall at one hundred miles per hour. I, along with the other four planes of our squadron, circled and watched the ditching. It appeared that none of the four crew members in the front compartment escaped. From the rear of the plane, Sergeant Lane, the tail gunner, and Sergeant Grier made their way out through an escape hatch. Lane could not swim, and even though he had his lifejacket on, he failed to reach a one-man life raft thrown to him by Grier.

Grier managed to swim to the main life raft designed for five men, which had released and inflated just before the plane sank. He took the oars that come with the raft and began paddling toward Lane, who was no longer visible due to the twelve foot swells on the ocean. After ten minutes or so, he gave up the effort. We stayed in the area watching, but low fuel necessitated returning to our home base. I had radioed details and location of the ditching and an extensive rescue effort was launched. This went on for the next several days, but the search missions produced no results.

Sergeant Grier drifted in his life raft for twenty-three days. The fact that he was alone in the five-man raft contributed to his survival, as the provisions of food and water aboard this size raft helped him to sustain himself. On April 2, 1945, the submarine USS *Sealion*, was on patrol looking for Japanese vessels and for air-sea rescue of downed airmen. The *Sealion* was on its way to rendezvous with another submarine when it spotted Sergeant Grier and took him aboard. Grier's body was sunburned and blistered, and he had a half-inch growth of beard. His weight was 125 pounds, down a third of his normal weight. He had drifted 550 miles from the spot where he ditched. He was taken to Subic Bay in the Philippines and, after a short stay in the hospital there, was sent home.

The Demise of Toofie's Taxi

In early April of 1945, at San Marcelino Air Base in the Philippines, a new, shiny aluminum B-25 J-22 #44-29655 was delivered to the 498th Bomb Squadron of the 345th Bomb Group. It was the latest model. It had a nose section with eight, .50 caliber machine guns, and on each side of the pilot's cockpit, were two more packages of two .50 caliber machine guns, which gave the pilot twelve forward-firing .50s. In addition, there were two .50 caliber machine guns in a top turret, two more .50s at the waist station, and two more for the tail section

Al Gruer Jr. (center) with crew members in front of his B-25, Toofie's Taxi. (Al Gruer collection.)

THE SUN ROSE CLEAR

(eighteen .50 caliber machine guns in all). This was a *real* strafing machine!

The plane was assigned to me, even though other crews would use it when I was not assigned to a mission. With this honor, I named the airplane "Toofie's Taxi," after my girlfriend of several years. The name in black letters with red shadowing was painted on the nose section with a background of black-and-white squares. It really did turn out to be attractive and an attention getter! I was proud of my efforts.

I recommended to my squadron commander that my co-pilot, Second Lieutenant John Holdener, become a "first pilot", and that he should be assigned his own crew. I had spent many hours working with John so that he would be ready for this promotion. On April 18, he took a test ride with Captain Elmo Cranford, which turned out to be a disaster. There was a beached Japanese ship not far from San Marcelino that we used as a practice bombing target for our air crews. When making a pass over this ship at very low level simulating combat, the bomb that dropped from Toofie's Taxi exploded prematurely upon impact. A very large piece of shrapnel came up through the bottom of the plane and crushed Cranford to the ceiling of the cockpit. Holdener managed to fly the plane back to base and landed it safely. Cranford died about twelve hours later. As a result of his exceptional handling of the crippled plane, Lieutenant Holdener became a first pilot. Toofie's Taxi had a number of holes through the fuselage, including a hole through the main spar in one of the wings. What parts could be salvaged were collected, including the engines, instruments, armament, etc. The eight-gun nose cone was removed intact, placed on another airplane, and painted over with Army olive drab to match the color of the fuselage.

Later, while we were stationed at Ie Shima on Okinawa, one of our B-25s crashed on takeoff at the end of the runway, burning and killing all on board. The burning caused the paint of the airplane to peel, and one could detect under the burned olive drab paint the name, Toofie's Taxi.

Typhoon - Island of Ie Shima, off Okinawa – 8/1/45 through 8/4/45

I was on a sweep of the southeastern coastal waters of Korea on a search and destroy mission looking for Japanese shipping, with orders not to proceed into Korean waters without fighter escort. Our fighters did not show up at the rendezvous point, so we turned our attention to a secondary target on the southernmost island of Japan, Kyushu, at the town of Makurazaki. We attacked in trailing flights of three ships each. At the completion of runs over the target, we received orders from base to hurry home, as a major storm was bearing down on the Okinawa area. We arrived in time to tie down the airplanes and head for cover. The storm lasted four days. At the height of the storm, the anemometer blew away as the wind reached 120 miles per hour. All of our tents were leveled. I shared an ambulance (with twelve others) held in place with chains through the wheels anchored with machine gun barrels driven into the coral. We existed on C and K rations during this time, only venturing out when we had to. The rain wasn't falling; it was going parallel to the ground. Our airplanes were also tied down by spikes into the coral bed of the sand-bagged protective revetments where they were parked. In the harbors, all small craft went ashore on the beach and buried their anchors in the coral. Large Navy ships were ordered out to sea to endure the storm's fury in an open area, to avoid smashing into each other in the harbors. U.S. forces on Okinawa at that time were building up an arsenal preparing for the invasion of Japan. At the end of the typhoon, the troops and arsenal were in disarray, but reassembly and recovery began immediately.

Mission: Search the Sea of Japan and the Tsushima Straights for Japanese Ships – 8/9/45

I flew my last combat mission of the war as a leader of twelve planes that embarked from Ie Shima at 2:00 a.m. on August 9, 1945, with strange orders to fly one-hundred and fifty miles west of Nagasaki, instead of by a direct route to the target area. The reason, unknown to us at the time: An atomic bomb was to be dropped on Nagasaki on August 9.

I was assigned to lead the flight. The Island of Tsushima is about halfway between Japan and Korea. The Japanese, shipping supplies from Korea to Japan at night, would anchor at Tsushima during the day and continue the next night to Japan, or vice versa. By taking off this early, it was likely we could engage more shipping in the open sea, because we would be in the target area about 0630, before the ships made it to the island. We took off at one-minute intervals and rendezvoused at daybreak at a designated spot off the east coast of Tsushima. It was a very dark night, and over the ocean there was no visible horizon, so we had to fly by instruments. About an hour out of Okinawa, my tail gunner, Staff Sergeant George Givens, reported he had seen a flare come up from the ocean, and I asked Lieutenant Cohen, our navigator, to put an "X" on the map where he thought we were. We were navigating by "dead reckoning", utilizing compass direction, speed, wind, and drift.

I, as flight leader, arrived at our designated area first and began circling with my wheels and flaps down awaiting the arrival of the others. One by one, they joined up in formation. We located one freighter trying to make it to Tsushima and the safety of antiaircraft protection. The ship was eventually identified as the Chichibu Maru. Passes were made with two planes at a time strafing the deck with .50 caliber machine guns and then dropping five-hundred-pound bombs.

THE SUN ROSE CLEAR

The bow of the three-thousand-ton freighter was blown off from six direct bomb hits, and the ship became a burning inferno. Lieutenant Treadwell and Lieutenant Trohmovich were given credit for the sinking.

On our return to Ie Shima, we were flying at three hundred feet above the ocean when a flash of light appeared in the cockpit. This came from a signal mirror flashed by a person in a single man life raft. I dispatched the squadron on to Ie Shima and began to circle the life raft radioing our base at Ie Shima to send out rescue sea planes. This probably was the person who had shot the flare earlier that morning, as reported by my tail gunner. The swells of the ocean were quite large, perhaps eight to ten feet, which made keeping the raft in sight quite difficult. We did sprinkle some dye marker out the back hatch and also dropped some smoke flares. We throttled back to conserve fuel, as we had already been in the air for eight hours. After about an hour, we directed two flying boats to the spot of the man in the raft. These were a PBY and a PBM and, since the seas were rather rough, the PBM made the rescue. We figured this was probably a fighter pilot who had engine trouble or ran out of gas, but we never did find out who it was that we helped save.

Seven days later, with the rank of Captain at the age of twenty-two, I was chosen to fly over Hiroshima and Nagasaki, with Army photographers in my airplane, to film the devastation that had launched the nuclear age. I also transported a military general and other VIPs to the Korean mainland to supervise the liberation of prisoner of war camps and finalize the surrender of the Japanese Armed Forces in Korea.

Trip to Nagasaki and Hiroshima – 8/25/45

Aircraft #43-28115. My crew: Captain Al Gruer, pilot; Second Lieutenant C. E. Street, copilot; First Lieutenant R. C. Farris, navigator; Staff Sergeant F. Holz, engineer and top turret gunner; Technical Sergeant B. W. Renaud, radioman and tail gunner; and photographers and headquarters staff, Major W. M. Schuck, Captain C. J. Russhon, and First Lieutenant B. F. Reyes.

The purpose of this flight was to take pictures of Nagasaki and Hiroshima. The Plexiglas windows were removed from the waist gun area on each side of the plane, so movies and still pictures could be taken. We took off from Okinawa at 0800 and proceeded to Nagasaki on the west coast of Kyushu. Our flight altitude was three hundred feet above sea level. We were armed, but there was no occasion to use ammunition, as the Japanese had already been to General MacArthur's headquarters in the Philippines to arrange surrender ceremonies scheduled to be held on the USS *Missouri* in Tokyo Bay on September 3. We made three passes over Nagasaki at low level, then we proceeded further inland on Kyushu and turned north toward Hiroshima on the Island of Honshu. Our instructions were to try and spot any prisoner of war camps, which the Japanese had been told to identify with big P-W letters on the roofs. En route, we spotted four or five camps marked with P-W and noted their locations on our maps. Food and clothing would then be dropped to these camps by Air Force cargo planes.

At Hiroshima we made three low-level, picture-taking passes and then went on to Kure Harbor on the Inland Sea. The Japanese, on their trip to the Philippines, had been told to dock their ships in this and other harbors as soon as possible. Our pictures were again taken at low level, to confirm for our intelligence operations how many and what kind of ships were there. We returned to Okinawa after a total of nine hours flying time. I had been one of the first people to view the devastation caused by the first two atomic bombs that effectively ended WWII. It is not a sight I will ever forget. The entire city of Hiroshima, two miles in every direction from the epicenter of the blast, had been totally destroyed. There were no houses, no stores, no trees, no people. It was a wasteland of devastation. It was hard to believe that less than three weeks earlier, this had been home to more than one hundred thousand human beings.

Al Gruer Jr. at controls of his B-25. (Al Gruer collection.)

THE SUN ROSE CLEAR

7 September 1945

Dear Mom and Dad,

As I sit here writing this to you, I can look out and see the whole town of Keijo, the capitol of Korea. The Koreans call this city "Kyongsong" (now called Seoul).

Yesterday about noon, we took off from Okinawa and flew a group of passengers up here. The general I carried with me was a wonderful passenger. In spite of the serious official business that he was about to conduct, he was calm, conversive, appreciative of our service to him, and anything but "officious." The weather was still rather bad, but we managed to get through without too much trouble. I circled the field once, found the direction of the wind, and landed.

Japanese met us at the end of the runway and parked us. There were six of our airplanes, and we were five in each plane, not counting the passengers. This would have made the odds rather bad for us if the Japanese had wanted to start something.

The U.S. Army general we transported was met by a Japanese general, and the surrender ceremony took place then and there. It was rather a historic occasion with the Japanese relinquishing total control of Korea to the occupation forces of the United States.

The Japanese had a convoy of automobiles waiting, but there wasn't enough room for everyone, so a few of us stayed at the airfield until the cars returned. While we were there, the commanding general of the airfield invited us in for something to eat. We were suspicious at first, but had some rather good food—chicken, pork, potatoes, carrots, salad and beer. The beer was much weaker and sweeter than American beer. The Japanese servants were very courteous, as each time they entered or left the room, they came to a halt and bowed.

Whenever I encountered any Koreans or Japanese, everyone would stop me. I imagine we were the first Americans they had ever seen. Most of the civilians we passed on the way into town had that surprised or indifferent look about them. And, as always, kids will be kids wherever you go, waving their hands as we passed by.

The town is rather large and has the appearance of Western

civilization. Many of the buildings are somewhat modern and mostly of brick, and the town has paved streets, gutters, sidewalks, telephone poles, street cars, automobiles, and many of the things our cities have, but on a smaller scale. I was surprised to see this. As I look out now from the Hanto Hotel, I can see many people in the streets rushing hither and yon, crowding into streetcars. Across the street is an office building with desks, like any office in the states.

My lodgings, by the way, are in the best hotel in town. It's an eight-story building with all the modern conveniences of running water, tiled baths, innerspring mattresses, rugs, etc. There is only one man to each room, and it is out of this world compared to the tents we are used to living in.

There aren't more than fifty of us Americans in the town at the present time. The convoy with the American occupation troops has not arrived as yet. We are confined to the hotel and have Japanese soldiers guarding us. We can't move without an escort. All the Japanese soldiers have their guns, and they are still patrolling the streets, but I suppose that will change when the American troops arrive. We are under guard for our own protection. The Japanese general in charge is responsible for our lives and safety and, if any of us are hurt, it would mean his life. Yes, it's all like a big dream—one day we kill, the next day we don't—it's hard to figure out just what attitude to take, so I take an indifferent one.

Give my love to all the family. I'm in the best of health and praying each day that our reunion may be soon.

Your loving son,
Junior

9 October 1945

Dear Mom and Dad,
The next day, after I wrote the letter from Korea, we watched the Japanese soldiers march out of the city. All day long, columns of Japanese were on the move. Packs on their backs, some pulling carts, horses with bundles, they all left town. We watched them from our hotel. It was quite an event.

On the same day, the Koreans put on a parade for our benefit, with a band playing American marches. They cheered us as we stood out on the veranda in front of the hotel. During all of this time, there were only fifty of us Americans in the city. The occupation forces were still forty or fifty miles away. It was quite inspiring to be cheered that way. The Koreans carried banners saying "WELCOME AMERICANS." Yes, I actually saw history being made.

That night, as the night before, we talked a long time with some British soldiers who had been prisoners of war for three and a half years. They had been taken prisoner at Singapore in February 1942. They sure were happy to see us. Two American pilots, who were shot down several days before the end of the war in their P-47 fighter planes, were there also.

As we pulled out of the city the next day in a bus powered by charcoal gas, we saw Americans entering the city by train and truck. We cheered them, but told them we had "taken" the city several days previous and that we'd let them have it now. They sure got a laugh out of that.

As you know, the airplane is always the center of attention. After takeoff, we came back over the airstrip and buzzed it with a low-level pass just to give the infantry boys a thrill.

Now that I'm back at Ie Shima, there's plenty of work in preparing to join the occupation. Upon landing, I was notified that I was now a captain. What do you think of your son now? My pay should now be nearly $350, in addition to $60 per month for housing, which I never use. The prestige of the rank has its benefits, more than the pay.

Another good thing about returning was that there were four letters from you waiting for me. Nothing like mail to help the morale.

This morning, I was presented my second Air Medal at a formal ceremony. General Crabb made the presentation, and the ceremony and his remarks were impressive.

Guess I've just about run out of news. Give my love to all the family. No news as to when I come home, but don't count on anything too soon.

Your loving son,
Junior

THE AIR APACHES

I returned to the states in December 1945. After the war, I completed my education in 1948, receiving bachelor's and master's degrees in business from Washington University, in St. Louis, Missouri. I worked for several Corporations before moving to Waupaca, Wisconsin, in 1978. I retired from the Waupaca Foundry in 1989, after serving for eleven years as Manager of Sales. I'm a member of the Riverside Hospital Health Foundation Board and an active promoter of my community. I faithfully continue to attend reunions of the 345th Bomb Group.

I would describe my experiences from age nineteen to twenty-two, as a lesson in maturity, work ethic, teamwork, duty, honor, patriotism, love, fear, courage, and respect for flag and country. It brought me a whole lot closer to God.

The 345th Bomb Group was known as the Air Apaches. Today, this name would probably be considered ethnically insensitive, but in the early 1940s, it designated a group of fierce warriors blazing a warpath across the Pacific, pitted against a fanatical enemy. These skilled young men of America joined together during World War II in fighting units like the Apaches of legend.

Warpath Across the Pacific, by Lawrence J. Hickey, describes the experience of the 345th Bombardment Group in great detail, as noted by the following information.

In a thirty-month period, from 1942 to 1945, more than 4,300 men served with the Apaches in the Pacific Theater. They flew 58,562 combat hours in 9,000 sorties and dropped over 58,000 bombs. They fired over 12,500,000 rounds of ammunition, sank 260 enemy ships, and damaged 275 others. Three hundred sixty-seven Japanese planes were destroyed by the Apaches, either on the ground or in aerial combat. Targets assigned to these warriors were bridges, tunnels, trains, marshaling yards, trucks, and industrial sites, but the primary Apache objective was to destroy the Japanese merchant fleet. This superb performance, unfortunately, cost the Air Apaches 712 men dead of all causes, 580 of these killed on missions and the loss of 177 aircraft during combat.

Colonel Jarred V. Crabb was the first commanding officer and activated the 345th Bomb Group on September 6, 1942, at Columbia Army Air Base, South Carolina. He later was to become a Major General with the Fifth Bomber Command. The 345th Group flew to Australia in May 1943, and then moved to Port Moresby, New Guinea, in June 1943. As the war progressed, the 345th moved on to Leyte Island and Luzon in the Philippines and later to Ie Shima, off the coast of Okinawa. The Apaches flew the Mitchell Bomber, a B-25, powered by twin 1,700 hp Wright-Cyclone engines.

In August 1943, Colonel Crabb and the 345th Bomb Group modified the B-25 from a medium-altitude bomber to a low-level strafer, with eight forward .50 caliber machine guns in the nose, two similar guns in the top turret, two at each waist gun position, and two in the tail. The B-25 could also carry fuse-delayed, 250-pound bombs and 207 parachute fragmentation (Parafrag) bombs, which would burst on contact into 1,600 fragments each. The Mitchell bomber was truly a heavily armored flying tank. When maneuvering and making final approach to the target at low level, the plane needed to clear the area before the bomb explosions occurred, necessitating the delayed fuses and parachute-delivered bombs.

Operations Officer of the 498th Bomb Squad, Albert Gruer, received the following decorations:

- Asiatic-Pacific Theatre Campaign Ribbon with five Bronze Stars.
- Victory Medal.
- Philippine Liberation Ribbon with one Bronze Star.
- Air Medal with one Oak Leaf Cluster.
- American Theatre Campaign Ribbon.

Symbols indicate Japanese airplanes destroyed and ships sunk or damaged by the 498th Squadron. (Al Gruer collection.)

THE SUN ROSE CLEAR
345th Escorts Japanese Emissaries to Ie-Shima
19 Aug. 1945

MAJOR McCLURE PICKS UP JAPANESE PLANES BELOW KYUSHU

OVER STRIP, FLANKED BY "APACHES" McCLURE AND DECKER

PLANES LAND AND TAXI TO WAITING C-54s.

Japanese bombers painted white with a red cross, on their way to General MacArthur's headquarters in the Philippines. Emissaries transfer to American C-54s at Ie Shima. (Al Gruer collection.)

THE AIR APACHES

EMISSARIES LEAVE BETTY BOMBER TO GO TO C-54

INSTRUCTIONS FROM GENERAL THOMAS.

THEN IT'S ON THEIR WAY TO MANILA AND MACARTHUR'S HEADQUARTERS.

Japanese emissaries on their way to the Philippines to arrange the unconditional surrender of Japan to the allies. (Al Gruer collection.)

253

THE GHOST OF ERNIE PYLE
As told by
Lowell Peterson

Ernie Pyle was born in 1900 and grew up on a farm in Dana, Indiana. When World War II began, Ernie Pyle was well beyond the draft age, at forty years old. However, he felt compelled by fate and desire to be a part of the war. He pleaded, and was able to convince his employers, the Scripps-Howard newspapers and the Washington Daily News, to allow him to become a war correspondent. His "sixth sense" convinced him that he had been predestined to be at the warfront.

Ernie Pyle, without question, became the quintessential journalist of World War II. Only the insightful radio reports from London of Edward R. Murrow and the haunting cartoons of "Willie and Joe" by Sergeant Bill Mauldin, came close to describing the war as well. Pyle's reports about soldiers, in combat at the front line, would subsequently earn him a Pulitzer Prize for journalistic excellence.

Ernie Pyle's style carried a dateline, and a plain, down-home, midwestern, honest description of the events he observed and experienced, day in and day out. His thoughtful, in-depth, interviews with real troops, giving their name, rank, and hometown, gave the news-hungry folks at home, information about the war that they could relate to.

I recently read an account of Ernie Pyle's wartime experiences, and my mind began to wander back to a day in 1965, when I visited the Ernie Pyle Memorial on the island of Ie Shima, off the shore of Okinawa. I had first heard about Ernie Pyle and his battlefront newspaper stories from my parents in the early 1940s.

I began to daydream and reminisce. I wondered how the ghost of Ernie Pyle might write an epilogue to World War II, based on the reports of correspondent Ernie Pyle. I think it might go something like this:

EPILOGUE
April 18, 1945-Ie Shima, Okinawa, Japan

I met a nice common fella the other day, and we have been at the front together night and day since. His name is Ernie Pyle, and he is from a small town in Indiana. We have been in combat since the invasion of Okinawa on

THE GHOST OF ERNIE PYLE

April 1, 1945. The battle of Okinawa should be the last great battle and island conquest, before the invasion of the mainland of Japan itself. While we were dug in along the sea, in foxholes last night, things were pretty quiet except for the slapping of the waves on the shore, the buzz of mosquitoes, and the constant pitter-pat of the rain on our helmets. It rains constantly here and the terrain turns to mud.

Ernie told me he was looking forward to the end of the war and going home. He was tired. The constant presence of death and destruction had worn him down. He feared what civilian life would be like. War was all he had known for four-and-a-half years. He guessed that somehow human sensibility and kindness would return to mankind, and he and his fellow soldiers would be able to adjust. He knew that he would never be mentally or emotionally the same again—none of us would.

I asked him to relate what he had seen and how it had affected him. He seemed relieved to be able to talk and get it off his chest, a ventilation of sorts, to clear the mind and soul. We did not sleep the whole night, just sat there in our foxholes, in the rain, as we had done countless times before, but this time not in expectation of danger and death, but in fraternal camaraderie. This is how Ernie related it. I'm paraphrasing what he said.

> I first viewed the war in December of 1940 from a hotel balcony in London overlooking the Thames River. The Battle of Britain was on. The droning of the German Luftwaffe bombers overhead and the whistling sound of the bombs was eerie. The blasts made the ground shake, and the city lit up with fire. Sirens of firetrucks and ambulances were constantly wailing. Fires were being fought all over the embattled city. I soon learned to go to the shelters when the air raid sirens began their ominous, high-pitched scream. What I found in the shelters were not only people like me escaping to a safer place, but displaced people who had been bombed out of their homes, and had taken up living like moles underground.
>
> I was pleased to get a combat zone assignment to join the front-line troops in the North African desert in 1942. For the first time, I experienced sleeping on the ground, shaving out of my helmet, and bathing, as well as washing my clothes, with water from five-gallon gas cans. The days were hot; the nights were cold. I viewed, in ominous anticipation, the warehouses full of medical supplies.
>
> I accompanied the troops as we began moving out to meet the

enemy in battle. Trucks were groaning and tanks were clanking across the sandy countryside. I would not have another bath for a month. Casualties started coming in. Hate started to build. Ever-present danger was overwhelmed only by physical discomfort. Fatigue and tiredness numbed the suffering of the wounded. They fell asleep, sometimes for good.

By 1943, I was a hardened veteran, but no one ever becomes hard enough to accept the daily tragedies that you observe. On February 14, 1943, the German Afrika Corps, under Field Marshal Erwin Rommel, attacked the American forces at the Kasserine Pass in Tunisia. It was an ambush. Twenty-three hundred Americans were taken prisoner. We were quickly forced into retreat. The battle was intense, and no one expected to live through the night. The shrill sound of the shells overhead and the noise of the clanking tanks was unending. Soldiers, unconscious on their feet, were marching in total exhaustion. Dirt, exhaustion, and fatigue made everybody look the same. Soldiers died alone. No one had time to grieve their loss. Fortunately, our Army was able to retreat, regroup, and defeat the Germans in North Africa, but the costs had been high, very high.

The Allies swept through Sicily to Messina and Palermo in July and August of 1943. I even took a bath in the Mediterranean Sea before the invasion on the mainland of Italy. In the fall of 1943, U.S. troops landed at Salerno and Anzio. In Italy, it rained daily, and fog and clouds obscured enemy positions, preventing supportive air cover by our bombers.

The hardship was inconceivable. As winter approached, there was rain, snow, cold, and mud. We were not dry for weeks. The Germans held the high ground on the mountains and travel through the valleys put our troops at a hazardous disadvantage. The battle for one hill was just replaced by another. We lived on cold K rations and often had no blankets. We packed supplies to the top of the mountains with mules and horses, and brought the dead back down the mountains, strapped across the mule's back. I wrote at that time, "You feel small in the presence of a dead man, ashamed at being alive." The only epitaph was often, "I'm sorry," or "God damn it to hell!" We had learned to hate. War was our existence. Duty was our comfort.

There were few places to hide as we traversed through the hillsides and valleys of Southern Italy. All you had was your foxhole, and it was often half-filled with water. Soldiers returning from combat at the front lines could not comprehend that they were still alive. They stared, but did not see! The hopeless gaze of the starving Italian refugee children was often more compelling than the war itself. We shared what we could.

After a furlough to the United States, I returned to London, joining the expeditionary forces preparing for D-day. This greatest of all invasions in the history of mankind took place on June 6, 1944. Journalists were allowed to go ashore at Omaha Beach on June 7, 1944. The scene that greeted us was gut-wrenching. Men lay motionless on the sand, or gently cradled on the surf, as if in their mother's arms. Some were partially buried by the sand, with only a bloody leg or elbow visible. Body parts lay everywhere. Destroyed tanks, ships, and landing craft were partially visible, covered by sea and sand.

The first wave of soldiers had been able to break out from the beaches and, by July, we were moving through the hedgerow country of Normandy. The going was tough, and opposition by the German defenders was strong. Front-line troops averaged about four hours sleep in a three-day period. In the fields, and along the roads, bullet punctured helmets lay alongside bodies resting in perpetual sleep. Bloated cows, victims of the shelling, lay dead in the pastures.

The advance was slow, oftentimes only a few hundred yards per day. Some of the soldiers traded with French farmers offering candy and cigarettes in exchange for milk, bread, wine, and even puppies. It gave them a feeling of home. Life was simple. Clothes, food, and cigarettes were our only needs. By August 28, 1944, the American forces liberated Paris. What a celebration! It was too bad that reality would again have to spoil the party. I enjoyed it while I could.

There were many more battles to go in Europe, but I had been overseas almost two-and-a-half years, and more than one year on the front lines. I was mentally exhausted and unable to view the war or write about it any longer. General Omar Bradley ordered me home.

I went back to the United States, and for the first time, I realized that our front-line troops were living an ugly, unreal existence. I recalled what I had witnessed at the front. Officers, on field telephones, conducted the war oblivious to the noise and death that surrounded them. I remembered the bombs, the artillery shells, the earth shaking, the sniper fire, the machine-gun fire, and the airplanes screaming overhead. I remembered the monotonous sight of the dead in the ditches and the fields, day-in and day-out. I remembered fear, fatigue, sleeplessness, and unbearable hardship.

I became a little fed up with all of the honors, receptions, and adulation back home and the constant questions of "What's it like over there?" The home front was doing a wonderful job of supporting the war effort and felt very much a part of it, but there was no way that they could ever possibly comprehend the misery of war at the front.

The people out in the Pacific War wanted me to come and join them, so I could report to the home folks what they were doing, so here I am. It sure is a different kind of war out here. There is a monotony which was never present in Europe. The islands of the Pacific are thousands of miles apart and we patiently await the word to move out to attack a new beachhead which may be many days away. We do have our misery out here, with the heat, the humidity, the jungles, malaria, and the rain. The fraternalism and camaraderie of my fellow soldiers is as strong here as any place I have been, but I miss Europe. Combat fatigue here is partially due to boredom, loneliness, homesickness, and having no place to go for a change of scenery. Just endless water, day after day.

I landed on the island of Okinawa on Easter Sunday, April 4, 1945. In the early morning hours, we obtained our supplies and rations, received holy communion, and a last hot meal before boarding our landing craft. We landed on a beach like none I had ever seen and certainly not like Normandy. The landing was unopposed by the Japanese! They had withdrawn inland. The dead were not on the beaches to greet us. I stayed with the Marines for several days, moving inland, cleaning up snipers. Some Japanese soldiers who were hiding in caves were flushed out and taken prisoner. They were extremely frightened, as they had been indoctrinated to believe that the Americans were devils. The Marines, after securing the northern half of the island, are continuing their drive on to the south, toward a hill called Sugar Loaf, and on to Naha City, and the Shuri Castle, where the heaviest concentration of Japanese is waiting to make a stand.

It was suggested that I might join you fellows out here on the island of Ie Shima to observe a mopping-up operation, which might convey to the folks back home that the end of the war is near, and we are getting closer, and closer, to the mainland of Japan.

Well, I guess I've probably rambled on long enough, boring you with my experiences in this horrible, worldwide conflict. It's starting to get light out and I expect we'll get the order to move out shortly. I'm sorry. I guess I didn't even get your name. I like to put the names and hometowns of the soldiers whom I interview in my articles. "What is your name?"

The ghost in the foxhole next to Ernie Pyle answered, "Just call me Ernie. I'm from Indiana."

On the morning of April 18, 1945, Ernie Pyle was killed on the island of Ie Shima, off the coast of Okinawa, by a Japanese sniper's bullet through the brain.

The author at the Ernie Pyle memorial - 1965.

THE SUN ROSE CLEAR

He was buried by his fellow soldiers in a simple wooden box. A monument stands at that site to this day. It states simply,

"At this spot,
the 77th Infantry Division
lost a Buddy."
Ernie Pyle,
April 18, 1945

Ernie Pyle was mourned by the entire nation.

Based on the book *Ernie's War - the Best of Ernie Pyle's WWII Dispatches*, by David Nichols.
Printed with permission of the Scripps Howard Foundation.

A MOTHER'S LOVE
As told by
Lowell Peterson

If the United States had been forced to invade the mainland of Japan, it has been conservatively estimated that one million American casualties would have occurred, and there was no assurance of victory. The attack would also have brought Russia into the Pacific War, leading most likely to a divided and dually occupied Japan, similar to Cold War Europe and Korea. The atomic age changed the course of history and the lives of friend and foe alike.

Ruins of Agriculture Promotion Hall, Hiroshima, Japan. "Ground Zero" for the first atomic bomb.

THE SUN ROSE CLEAR

"Oh, Tori, it has been so wonderful to have you home, even if it was only for a few days," Mama said, as she cleared the supper dishes from the table.

"Yes, I treasure the time I have had with you and Papa during this furlough," Tori answered. "The glory of wearing the uniform and fighting for our country has given way to the reality of daily death and destruction. Suffering and pain is always visible. I am glad my younger brothers don't have to see what I see."

"Tori, haven't you done your share of fighting? It has been more than three years since you were inducted into the army. I think it is time for you to come home with us and try to resume a normal life."

"I can't, Mama. I'm an officer and a platoon leader. My men depend on me. To leave now would be cowardly. Even if my troops didn't think of me as a coward, I would feel that I had let them down. I must go back. The battle of Okinawa is almost over, and the next big push will be an all out attack on the mainland of Japan. I have survived thus far; I will survive that also."

Papa said, "Tori, where have you been in the past three years? Can you tell me, or is that classified?"

"No, Papa, most of it is common knowledge. I started out in New Guinea and island-hopped to the Philippines and most recently to Okinawa. The South Pacific was the worst: malaria, heat, humidity, snakes, jungle rot, monsoon rains, trench foot, leeches, diarrhea, and dehydration. The only satisfaction was in knowing that the enemy had it just as bad as we did. The food was scarce, and we often had to live off the land or scavenge from the natives. Fish from the ocean was a real treat, but it was usually too dangerous on the beaches or in small boats.

"Okinawa was a fire fight from the beginning. Aerial bombardment, mortars, flamethrowers, naval gunfire, grenades, and rifle fire were constant. Suicide in the face of failure and defeat was common among Japanese generals and also among the troops who threw themselves off cliffs into the ocean. I was fortunate to get withdrawn from the battle early in anticipation of the mainland invasion."

"Tori, you better get to bed; it's getting late," Mama said. "Papa has to go to work at 5:00 a.m. He has been working sixteen hour days, seven days a week at the munitions factory down by the fork in the river south of downtown. The stress and strain is making him look very old. He figures if you have to suffer because of the war, that he must suffer also."

"Okay, Mama. My train leaves early. Come on kids, let's get to bed."

"Yes, we have to go to school," Tori's brother said. "With the shortage of teachers because of the war, we only go a half-day. School is being held in the Industry and Agriculture Promotion Hall down by the river near Papa's factory."

Mama said, "I'm afraid I'll have to miss your departure on the train, Tori. I must be at work at the clothing factory making uniforms for the troops by 9:00

a.m. The factory is in the old department store, not far from the Industry Promotion Hall."

August 5, 1945

The next morning, Mama said, "You better hurry and get cleaned up and dressed in your best dress uniform. I want my number one son to look sharp. I am so proud of you, as proud as any mother anywhere in the world can be, and so thankful you are alive, safe, and healthy. I don't want you to see me cry. I pray for you daily and cry myself to sleep at night hoping you are safe."

"Okay, Mama. I am ready to leave. Thanks for washing all my clothes and packing my bag. Come on, I will walk with you part way to your job."

"Okay, let me get my shawl. Papa and the kids have already left."

"Mama, it's almost 8:15 a.m. and time to say goodbye. I love you, Mama. Don't cry. Have hope. I will return soon and then we can be a family again."

"Hiroshima Central Railroad Station is at the end of the street," said Mama.

"I must hurry! What's that noise?"

"Oh, Tori, it's just another airplane. We hear a lot of them these days. Goodbye my son."

At 8:15 a.m. on August 5, 1945, the first atomic bomb was dropped by a B-29, the Enola Gay, on Hiroshima City in the southwest region of the main Japanese island of Honshu. The Promotion Hall was at "Ground Zero". Everything within eight thousand feet in every direction was destroyed. Seventy-one thousand people died instantly, and countless thousands suffered from severe burns, blast injuries, and radiation sickness. Two-hundred thousand civilians died of the injuries and radiation in the next five years. The atomic attack on the cities of Hiroshima and Nagasaki led to the unconditional surrender of Japan on September 2, 1945. The tangled steel dome of the Promotion Hall in Hiroshima stands to this day as a monument to the inhumanity of war, while across the river a cenotaph with an eternal flame stands as a monument to lasting peace.

THE SUN ROSE CLEAR

THE THRESHER MAN
As told by
Lowell Peterson

The end of World War II was an emotional event. The clouds of uncertainty, fear, anxiety, and concern for country, ideals, and military personnel were lifted from a nation. People began to smile again. Each in his own way expressed or nurtured his thoughts as once again, "the sun rose clear".

Martin Holtebeck, Harvey Floistad, Andrew Holtebeck, Oscar Peterson, and Jim Peterson, the thresher man, by the old Reeves steam engine.

THE SUN ROSE CLEAR

The amber fields of grain yielded the bounty of the harvest to the sickle each July and August, as the McCormick harvester, pulled behind the Farmall "B" tractor, cut the straw, tied the bundles with twine, and spit the sheaves out onto the ground, one after another. Hired men skillfully placed the grain bundles into "shocks", north-to-south, lined up like houses along a city street, to dry like fish on a rack, as the warmth of the sun moved daily, east to west.

It's time for the thresher man!

In 1945, this man again assembled his trusty threshing crew, as he had done each August for the previous twenty years, and as his father before him had done dating back into the late 1800s.

Why would these trusty men leave their regular jobs as farmers, truckers, and mill-sawyers for the month of August each year to perform this six-day-per-week, twelve-to-fourteen hour per-day job? It was because they couldn't imagine themselves anywhere else. It was a privilege.

The Reeves steam engine that would run the threshing machine had been fired up and driven off a flatbed railroad car at the Waupaca depot, in 1920, by the thresher man when he was a teenager. He maneuvered it across dirt roads and rickety railroad trellises to the home farm under the eyes of an admiring father. He had passed a test of succession. Unfortunately, and unforeseen, only six years later the thresher man, along with his brother, would assume the entire responsibility, forced upon them by the untimely death of their father. Through the next twenty years, the late summer harvest ritual was repeated annually, moving from farm-to-farm, to thresh the neighbors' grain with power generated by this mammoth machine.

By 1945 the engine was getting old. The flu pipes running the length of the water jacket periodically needed replacing to keep the rusted areas from leaking water into the firebox, decreasing the heat, and thereby decreasing steam-driven power. A privileged few, brothers Oscar and Kermit, as well as friends Pat, Harvey, and Walter, made up a lineage of engineers hired to fire and run the engine. In 1945, Walter Grove returned for what had become his fifth annual "vacation" from being chief sawmaster at the Strebe sawmill to run the engine. He enjoyed threshing, but he did not enjoy the thought of having to replace flu pipes from inside the cooled-down firebox in the middle of July in preparation for the upcoming threshing season. He confided to me years later that the old Reeves had "bad lungs".

The preparatory work having been completed, it was show time!

The Reeves steam engine was fired up until the steam pressure reached adequate power levels, and then the engine was attached to the Huber grain separator. The engine steamed its way out of the farm driveway, obediently followed by the separator, and made its way down the road toward Clarence Peterson's farm under the diligent control of Walter. Excitement and anticipation began to mount.

THE THRESHER MAN

The sight of the steam engine pulling the separator down the road at three miles per hour was a spectacle that drew the attention of the entire neighborhood.

As the puffs of white smoke from the smoke stack cleared the crest of the hill, and the chuga-chuga-chuga sound broke the air with powerful ease, a black monster slowly came into view. The thought of this sight brings tears to my eyes and chills to my spine to this day.

The barefoot kids, with their bib overalls rolled up to the knees, ran to meet the engine, waiting to be scared off by a couple of shrieking blasts from Walter's steam whistle. The aproned housewives waved white dishtowels in greeting, and the weathered farmers, leaning on their pitch forks, watched motionless in awe.

The engine and separator passed the one-room schoolhouse, crossed the river bridge, and entered Clarence's hillside farmyard. The powerful separator was moved into place, positioned, and leveled with a slight pitch to the rear toward the straw blower to aid delivery of the grain through the machine. The separator was an intricate conglomeration of belts, pulleys, shafts, cams, knives, shakers, elevators, and blowers, enclosed in and attached to a galvanized steel container majestically set on heavy steel wheels.

The separator's grain blower eliminated the need to bag and carry the oats to the granary. Every half bushel of grain, cleaned of weed seed and debris by this efficient machine, would be weighed, counted automatically, dumped into the blower, and wind blown through eight-inch pipes by a 2,000 rpm fan hundreds of feet into the waiting bins of the granary, passing the dust on straight through a screen and out the rear window into the air. The straw, now separated from the grain, would likewise be blown by a high-speed fan out the blower pipe to indoor barn storage or mushroom-shaped stacks outside.

Walter would fire the engine, the thresher man would man the separator, a blower man would stack the straw, and a "water monkey" would hand pump water out of the streams and ponds into a tank on a wagon and transport it to the thirsty engine with the wagon pulled by horses. The sixty-foot separator drive belt was crossed in its middle, placed on the steam engine's large fly wheel, drawn tense, and prepared for its energizing destiny. The escaping steam from the safety release valve was audible evidence of the pent up power awaiting the signal to be released. The one hundred forty pounds of steam pressure, rivaling a railroad locomotive, generating 40 to 60 hp on the drive belt, would power the separator and grain blowers effortlessly. The grease and oil lubricating the gears and pistons, warmed by the heat of the engine, created a characteristic sweet smell that surrounded the powerful beast.

Each day thereafter began when the stealthy fog lifted and the damp morning dew evaporated into the intensifying heat of the day. The day would not end until

THE SUN ROSE CLEAR

Walter Grove, engineer, and Harlan Stoltenberg, "water monkey".

the red harvest sun began to set in the west and the condensing moisture again descended out of the quiet air.

The neighboring farmers and their hired men all came to help. Harvest at their farms was coming soon as well. That's the way it was done. No one complained. Harvesting forty acres at one farm was not any more or any less important than ten acres at another farm. No arguments or finger pointing. Get the job done and move on. Brotherhood such as this has never been practiced any better, at any time, anywhere else.

The wooden wagons drawn by a team of sturdy work horses departed to the fields to be loaded with the shocks of grain, one bundle at a time. The horses walked slowly between the rows, as the men pitched the dried grain bundles onto the wagon. Full, the wagon and its hired hand driver departed for the farmyard to await a turn to pitch the bundles into the continuously moving, razor-sharp, shark-like jaws of the separator. Two wagons would unload simultaneously, the bundles of grain entering the machine side-by-side, separated by a vertical board.

The easy chuga-chuga-chuga of the engine was unending as field after field emptied its contents to the insatiable mouth of this hungry machine. The engine continued to suck up the water from the water wagon and the blocks of wood in the firebox continued to make steam to drive the cylinders and create the power.

The call to dinner each day was sounded by a short whistle, and the machinery became eerily quiet for thirty to forty-five minutes. Perspiration and dust were splashed off by clean, cold, well water before the workers entered the welcoming farmhouse kitchen and dining room. Potatoes, beef gravy, beef roast, vegetables, and homemade bread filled plates to overflowing. Twenty to thirty people were, amazingly being fed at a single setting by the industrious housewives. Homemade pies of multiple varieties and strong Norwegian coffee gave the meal an exclamation point.

Then it was back to work. Grease the pulleys, start the belt power, release the kinetic energy, hear the musical whir of the belts, and unleash the workers' muscle and sweat.

In late afternoon, Kool-Aid, lemonade, cookies, and cake were brought out from the house to be consumed under a spreading elm, with only a short break in the work action.

The scene was repeated day-after-day. The march from farm-to-farm continued, clearing the fields of grain. The sweat poured from the bodies of the field workers as their skin bronzed deeper and deeper.

When the last bundle had been threshed at each farm, and the spilled grain was all shoveled from the ground-covering canvas into the trough of the separator, the belts would whir away for a pregnant period at full speed, flaunting their power. From the top of the separator, the thresher man after this pause, would then give the signal that the job was done. This was the sign for Walter to blow the steam whistle three very long blasts. The shrill, high-pitched, two-hundred decibel sound echoed from the hills and through the valleys, audible for miles. It was a sound of pride, of success, and of accomplishment. It reflected, in a lighthearted way, the fun that went with the job.

An old 1928 Whippet Coupe with an "ooga" horn and a Swiss cheese muffler took the thresher man home after dark each day. The dopplered sound of the muffler getting closer and closer gave comfort and anticipation to his waiting family.

The thresher man's birthday, on August 12th, was celebrated after his evening arrival each year, on that date, with ice cream and cake. The accomplishment of the day by his beloved machines was birthday present enough for him.

The days of August defined the life of the thresher man. It was the

Don Terlson (author's cousin) and author get the grain "shocks" ready for threshing. Note the patriotic sailor cap! 1945.

271

THE SUN ROSE CLEAR

time when he had felt closest to his dad and subsequently his sons to him. These were days of sweat and toil, dust and sun, fun and camaraderie.

One of the hired men remembered recently that on the 14th of August in the year of 1945, he had been pitching bundles of grain into the threshing machine at Pete Jensen's farm, when Jim, the thresher man, surprisingly gave the signal to Walter to blow the whistle in the middle of the afternoon. The action stopped. The puzzled workers laid down their forks. What was the reason for the pause? As the belts hummed to a slow halt, followed by an eerie silence, Jim walked slowly to the top of the separator and announced to one and all, in his characteristic few words, "The war is over! I think we should take the rest of the day off."

Straw hats flew in the air, "yahoos" echoed in the valleys, and the steam engine's whistle blasted out a steady two-hundred-decibel shriek, joining the chiming of church bells across America, seeming never to end.

Walter smiled, his red cheeks glowing, his mischievous eyes twinkling, as he closed down the steam engine for the day, spit out his chaw of tobacco, laughed his characteristic laugh, and slowly drove off down Highway Q to Rohde's Tavern, followed by several others.

The thresher man went home quietly in his trusty Whippet, with the "ooga" horn and the Swiss cheese muffler, a long-awaited, thankful satisfaction, in his heart.

Jim, the thresher man, was my dad. This had been one of his finest hours.

THE BENEFICIAL EFFECTS OF WORLD WAR II

As told by
Earl Spangler, Ph. D. and Lowell Peterson

"…even a cataclysm…is not a downfall only. Mountains crumble, but others are thrust up. Lands vanish, but others rise from the sea. So it is with the social cataclysms of our time."

R. R. Palmer
A History of the Modern World

The United States is a nation born of war, reunited by war, and made a superpower by war. The quest for representative governance compelled the colonial patriots to wage the American Revolution, and the American Civil War was necessary to preserve and perpetuate the nation so conceived. The need to oppose and defeat ideologies of tyranny, despotism, and exploitation of people's minds and bodies, plus the morality of a just cause, led the United States into World War II. Wars deal with the nature and purpose of government, the rule of law, and a recognition that humanity, despite differences of color, religion, national philosophy, and living standards, deserves better than to be destroyed in a holocaust of brutality and tyranny.

Those who experienced war up close remember the whoosh and whine of artillery, the resounding explosions, the screams of the wounded, the stillness of death, the rows of those awaiting burial, and the uncomfortable feeling of contributing to another human being's death. These soldiers universally hated war, yearned for peace, and hoped that their sons and daughters would

The military I.D. card of Earl Spangler.

never have to endure such experiences.

It is very easy to focus, as well we should, on the tragedy of World War II, its great economic burden, its inherent loss of life, its destruction of the infrastructure of nations, and the sacrifices that were necessary to preserve freedom for our nation and the world. In contrast, the beneficial effects of World War II are often overlooked and we need to examine this aspect of the war as well.

World War II, by providing full employment, helped end the Great Depression of the 1930s. Families lost self-respect during the Depression, and often unwillingly took relief or charitable offerings just to stay alive, keep their family together, or put food on the table. It is difficult to envisage a time in our history when at least twenty-five percent of the workforce was unemployed, when boxcars were filled with transients (hobos) criss-crossing the land in despair, and when families gave their children away because they could no longer clothe or feed them. As the 1930s merged into the 1940s, families that had been on government relief and in "charity soup lines" to survive could finally shed the onus of diminished self-respect and make a living by their own efforts. During World War II, rationing and shortages of food items, gasoline, tires, and luxuries created a common element of sacrifice and a deep feeling that civilians somehow shared in the sacrifices of those in the military. Having overcome the devastating adversity of the Depression, the men and women who entered the war in the 1940s never doubted that they could also overcome this challenge.

World War II emancipated hundreds of thousands of women, increasing their feeling of self-importance and esteem, as they moved out of the home to work on farms, in defense industries, and in the military. "Rosie the Riveter" became, and remains to this day, the symbol of women in the workforce. Thousands of civilian women, replacing men going off to war, worked on assembly lines, did clerical work, test drove vehicles on proving grounds, worked in hospitals, filled government jobs, and drove trolleys, buses, and even locomotives. Thousands more joined the uniformed service and learned to live under extreme conditions; some also became casualties. They did their jobs, took pride in their accomplishments, and developed confidence that they had a stake in this country and could contribute much. They would never again be denied.

As millions of men went into barracks, drilled, ate, slept, and fought in mutually challenging situations, a slow but progressive breakdown of prejudice, parochialism, stereotypes, and regional antagonism began. When sixteen million people from all walks of life, all parts of the country, and all races, colors, and religions are brought together in a common cause, things happen. In combat, living, fighting, dying, working, worshipping, being afraid, and supporting a common cause together distinguished the World War II soldiers. Exposure to another culture, civilization, climate, history, and language allowed the soldier to absorb some of what that society experiences. For millions, it would be the only foreign culture experience they would ever have. Although problems of race, ethnicity, religion, education, and economic status continue to plague our nation sixty years later, a milestone on a long road began during WWII that would have otherwise been delayed for decades.

World War II also loosened the bonds of colonialism and imperialism, resulting in the formation of more than one hundred new nations. Almost without exception, these new nations structured themselves with constitutions and declarations that were patterned after the European parliamentary system or the United States constitutional government. In most cases, this new nationalism advanced the cause of human rights. Vast invulnerable oceans yielded to increasingly rapid transit, opening introspective nations to a world economy rather than a regional economic system. In the post-war period, the imperialistic, militaristic nations of WWII, Germany and Japan became democratic, constitutional nations to the benefit of the whole world.

World War II exponentially advanced technology, nuclear power, rocketry, jet power, radar, and mass production. Developments in sanitation, medicine, and the care of trauma, wounds, burns, and stress were no less than miraculous. The Space Age and the Computer Age were a natural outgrowth of the technology developed during World War II. A new, energized America emerged in the postwar period. Perhaps not so tangible was the knowledge that Americans could do anything they had to do, when put to the test. On the downside, the Cold War, higher taxes, McCarthyism paranoia, pollution, anti-establishmentism, increased bureaucracy, and more wars emerged.

At the end of World War II in 1945, a vast demobilization occurred. Twenty-five thousand veterans were being discharged each day and by the fall of 1946, nine million had been discharged. (David Gosoroski, *VFW Magazine*, October 1997, page 38). A program was needed to reestablish the veteran's place in a peacetime society.

After World War II, veterans received higher education or vocational trade training through the U.S. Government-sponsored and funded Servicemen's Readjustment Act of 1944, "GI Bill of Rights" raised the educational level of the United States to unprecedented heights. The self-satisfaction and social and economic benefits forthcoming to these veterans as they were exposed to literature, languages, sciences, economics, social studies, and professional studies is immeasurable.

In a report prepared by the Veteran's Administration and entered in the Congressional Record, June 22, 1954, the following information was made public. Seven million eight hundred thousand World War II veterans, half of all those who served during the war, studied under the GI Bill. Of that total, two million, two hundred thousand attended colleges and universities. Six million veterans used the GI Bill to train in vocational, trade, and agricultural areas, providing the country with an enormous well-trained labor force. One hundred fifty thousand were given the opportunity to learn to read and write for the first time. Four hundred eighty thousand engineers, 180,000 doctors and nurses, 113,000 scientists, 243,000 accountants, 107,000 lawyers, 36,000 ministers, 17,000 writers and journalists, 438,000 television and radio repairmen, 711,000 mechanics, 383,000 construction workers, and 188,000 metal workers were products of the GI Bill.

In addition, two million veterans used the home purchase provisions of the GI Bill. Prior to the war, two-thirds of Americans were renters; after the war, two-thirds were homeowners—a remarkable reversal. Those trained by the GI Bill paid one billion dollars more each year in income taxes because of their education and employment level, which reimbursed the entire GI Bill program in just fifteen years.

World War II produced a healthier, better educated, more confident, and more determined generation than the United States had ever seen. The educational level of the population, literacy in general, and the introduction to literature, history, ideas, philosophy, cultural differences, and campus life made this a better nation. Did these changes for society justify the war? Of course not! Could they have occurred without the war? Probably not, or certainly at a much more painfully slow pace.

The war unleashed the United States as a sleeping giant, not only in industry, but on farms, in small businesses, and in natural resource exploration and production. The United States and Russia moved from agrarian isolationist countries to the status of world superpowers. The United States, ranked eighteenth in military power in 1940, rose to one of two superpowers after the war, and in time would become the only one.

Never in the history of humankind had change occurred so rapidly and with such magnitude, as it did during World War II. The nation continued its postwar industrial growth, advanced by technological innovation that was created in large part by the ambition, skills, and training of those who had served in World War II. When the Berlin wall came down and the Soviet Union collapsed in 1989-91, the World War II veterans had won the greatest victory of all. To the generation of Americans that fought World War II, it meant that their victory on the battlefield had been consummated by victory in the ideological battle against tyranny as well. What better legacy for posterity could there be for the "Greatest Generation"?

Earl Spangler, 1944.

THE FINAL REVEILLE
As told by
Lowell Peterson

Here lie officers and men, negroes and whites, rich and poor—together. Here are Protestants, Catholics and Jews—together. Here no man prefers another because of his faith or despises him because of his color. Here there are no quotas of how many from each group are admitted or allowed. Among these men, there is no discrimination. No prejudices. No hatred. Theirs is the highest and purest democracy.

Navy Lieutenant Roland B. Gittlesohn, Jewish Chaplain,
delivered at the dedication of the Marine Cemetery,
Iwo Jima, 1945
Iwo Jima, Legacy of Valor
By Bill D. Ross, Vintage Books, 1986, page 223.

From the personal collection of Gardner N. Soule, Shelburne, Vermont.

THE SUN ROSE CLEAR

"Rise and shine! Reveille! Pack your duffel bags and look sharp! Parade dress uniforms are the order of the day. Line up for inspection in one hour." Moans and groans met this rude awakening from the first sergeant, but a sense of anticipation moved the troops to a quick response. A hurried shower and shave preceded the donning of the dress uniform, spit shine of the GI shoes, and a last minute mirror check of the results.

A short while later, the troops stood at attention in perfect alignment on the parade ground. "Attention! Gentlemen, we leave these hallowed grounds at Henri-Chapelle today for the last time. The soil that we shared with our comrades will be left behind. In respect to the monuments we leave behind, please, on command, do an about face, view our field of honor and offer your respect." Sergeant Goodfellow commanded: "About face! Salute!" A faint image of a bugler, erect in the morning fog, was visible, as "Taps" was played and the American flag was lowered for the last time. "Parade Rest! Silence!" (There wasn't a dry eye in the ranks anywhere.)

"About face! All right men, we have a plane to catch. Pick up your packs. We will march to the train station and board the Gare du Nord for Paris. We will be joined at the airport by all of our colleagues from St. James, St. Laurent-sur-Mer, Margraten, Neupré, St. Avold, Epinal, Draguignan, and other locations. Right Face! Forward March!"

"Bonjour, Monsieurs, this is your captain speaking. Be patient, s'il vous plaît. We will depart shortly. This is Charter Flight 1945 departing Charles de Gaulle Airport in the 'City of Light,' Paris, France. We expect a very smooth flight. You will be served a gourmet meal and select wines of Bordeaux and the Coté de Rhone of France en route, which I am quite sure will be a significant change from what you consider standard fare. The stewards and stewardesses are aboard for the purpose of serving your every need. Their angelic kindness is provided to you as a courtesy by this airline. Now, settle back, relax and enjoy the flight; I will talk with you again, once we are at our cruising altitude. Bon voyage!"

"It is so good to finally be leaving France. It's been such a long time since I left my home in the States. I wonder what changes have occurred since I left."

"Well, John, you won't believe it," said Paul, who was seated in the next seat. "I have read where there are cars everywhere, people everywhere, money everywhere, not the hardship we suffered for so many years."

"I wonder what has happened to my friends. They were all so young, just like me. We had such great fun together. We only thought of proms, cars, girls, music, burgers, and Cokes. Our biggest problems were pimples and rejection for dates. We laughed together and had our entire life in front of us. The separation from friends and family has gone on for so very long."

Paul said, "Well, remember that you're not the only one who left. Your friends were also scattered. Their duties required them at a young age to assume responsibility, just like it did for you. I am sure that some were lucky enough to return to the neighborhood and get jobs, get married, raise families, and become school board and church members. In other words, because of the job we did, some people were given the privilege of leading normal lives."

John answered, "Well, good for them. I probably wouldn't even know them now and they probably wouldn't know me. The whole world has changed and I'm going to have to learn to accept it. I guess it's time to move on, but I'm afraid, Paul; I'm really afraid."

"Monsieurs, we have received our final clearance; please prepare for takeoff. We are number 6/6 for departure in this flight group. The other charter flight groups will follow in groups of six also. We shall arrive at our destination on time."

The takeoff of the huge Air France Boeing 747 was smooth as silk. "It's good to be finally airborne and on our way. I hope everybody else got off on time also. The charter flight groups need to stay together, so that we can reconvene at our destination. It feels strange to be flying in an airplane without a parachute—and so fast—wow!"

"Yes, John, you're right, but don't worry, after all these years, it is unlikely—no, impossible—that we will be late. It is comforting to know that we are traveling with all of our buddies on this special charter," Paul said.

"Yes, it is a consoling thought that we are flying together as a unit, just as we functioned when we were performing our ground duties. These troops are the salt of the earth and represent the reincarnation of everything that is good in the world."

Paul responded, "Thirty thousand of our colleagues will join us at our destination every ensuing month until all, in diminishing numbers, have been accounted for."

"Monsieurs, we have now reached our cruising altitude. The other charter flight groups have also reached cruising altitude. We will keep in contact throughout the flight. Enjoy the bread and the wine, sil vous plait!"

"John, your trip to this point has been a long and tiring one. Why don't you get some sleep?"

"Paul, I feel like I've been sleeping for more than fifty years; I want to stay awake and share the sense of excitement that I detect in all our companions on this flight. When do we arrive?"

"Sergeant John, I'm pleased to tell you that our charter flight group, and all the other charter flight groups that accompanied us, will fly on forever, as the "Ghost Warriors in the Sky". We will arrive at our destination and be resurrected on the final Easter Sunday or day of judgment. Do not be afraid! You have served your fellow man above and beyond the call of duty. I can only say, well done, young man! Well done, oh humble servant! You have died so men may live. What greater sacrifice is there? Bon Voyage!"

> THINK NOT ONLY UPON THEIR PASSING
> REMEMBER THE GLORY OF THEIR SPIRIT

Quotations from the chapel wall, American World War II Cemetary, Omaha Beach, Normandy.

> THROUGH THE GATE OF DEATH MAY THEY PASS
> TO THEIR JOYFUL RESURRECTION

SOURCES

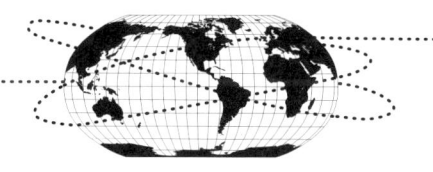

Ambrose, Stephen E. *Citizen Soldiers*. New York, NY: Simon & Schuster, 1998.

Ambrose, Stephen E. *The Wild Blue*. New York, NY: Simon & Schuster, 1998.

Ambrose, Stephen E. *The Victors*. New York, NY: Simon and Schuster, 1998.

Arthur, First Lieutenant Robert A., and First Lieutenant Kenneth Cohlmia, USMCR. *The Third Marine Division*. Vance, Lieutenant Colonel Robert T., USMC, ed. Washington, DC: Washington Infantry Journal Press, 1948.

Barker, Lieutenant Colonel A. J. *Okinawa*. London, England: Bison Books Ltd., 1981.

Bauer, Eddy. *Histoire Controversee de la Deuxieme Guerre Mondiale*. Monaco: Rombaldi, 1966.

Benford, Timothy B. *The World War II Quiz and Fact Book*. New York, NY: Gramercy Books, 1984.

Brooks, Thomas R. *10th Mountain Division*. Paducah, KY: Turner Publishing Co., 1998.

Cartier, Raymond. *La Seconde Guerre Mondiale*. Paris, France: Larousse, 1965.

Cass, Bevan G. *History of the Sixth Marine Division*. Washington, DC: Washington Infantry Journal Press, 1948.

Childers, Thomas. *World War II: A Military and Social History*. Chantilly, VA: The Teaching Company, 1996.

Connor, Howard M. "The Fall of Suribachi." *The Spearhead: The World War II History of the 5th Marine Division*. Washington, DC: Infantry Journal Press.

Feifer, George. *The Battle of Okinawa*. Guilford, CT: The Lyons Press, 2001.

Frank, Richard B. *Guadalcanal*. New York, NY: Penguin Books, 1990.

Groh, Richard. *The Dynamite Gang: The 367th Fighter Group in World War II*. Woburn, MA: Charm Publishing, 1983.

Hickey, Lawrence J. *Warpath Across the Pacific: The Illustrated History of the 345th Bombardment Group During WWII*. Boulder, CO: International Research and Publishing Corp., 1984.

Jablonski, Edward. *Wings of Fire*. New York, NY: Doubleday and Company, 1972.

"Japan Invasion: Gone With the Wind." Winchester, OH: *The Strafer: Quarterly Publication of the 345th Bomb Group Reunion Association*, December 1997.

Katz, Phillip P. *World War II in the Philippines: A Pictorial Review*. Makati, Philippines: Eugene G. Adams, Publisher, 1993.

Keegan, John. *The Second World War*. New York, NY: Penguin Books, 1990.

SOURCES

Keegan, John. *The Time's Atlas of the Second World War*. New York, NY: Harper and Row, 1989.

Koepp, Stephen. "Heroes and Icons." *Time*, 14 June, 1999.

Lloyd, Charles A. "The Liberty Ships of World War Two." *U.S. Navy Armed Guard World War II Veterans*, 1998.

Meltesen, Clarence R. *Roads to Liberation from Oflag 64*. San Francisco, CA: Oflag 64 Press, 1990.

Manchester, William. *The Last Lion: Winston Spencer Churchill, Alone 1932-1940*. Boston, MA: Little, Brown & Co., 1988.

Meinke, Albert H. Jr. M.D. *Mountain Troops and Medics*. Kewadin, MI: Rucksack Publishing Company, 1993.

Molesworth, Carl. *Sharks Over China*. Edison, NJ: Castle Books, 1999.

National Centennial Commission. *Philippines: Archipelago of Smiles*. Manila, Philippines: S.O.S. Incorporated, 1998.

Nichols, David. *Ernie's War: The Best of Ernie Pyle's World War II Dispatches*. New York, NY: Simon and Schuster, 1986.

O'Neill, William J. "The Battle for Japan—What Might Have Been." Merrifield, VA: *Marine Corps League*, Summer 1995, pp. 29-39.

O'Neill, William J. "World War II's Last Bloody Battle, Okinawa." Merrifield, VA: *Marine Corps League*, Spring 1995, vol. 51, 1, pp. 14-27.

Ota, Masahide. *The Battle of Okinawa: The Typhoon of Steel and Bombs*. Tokyo, Japan: Kume Publishing Co., 1984.

Oxford Essential Dictionary of the U.S. Military, The. New York, NY: Berkley Books, 2001.

Palmer, R. R. *A History of the Modern World*. New York, NY: Alfred A. Knopf, 1950.

Parrent, Erik. *China Marine Association*. Herbert Banks, ed. Paducah, KY: Turner Publishing Co., 1995.

Pu Yi, Aisin-Gioro. *From Emperor to Citizen: The Autobiography of Aisin-Gioro Pu Yi*. Beijing, China: Foreign Language Press, 1989.

Ridge, Captain William T., USNR. *The Pearl Harbor Story*. Honolulu, Hawaii: Tongg Publishing, 1991.

Rosholt, Malcolm. *Days of the Ching Pao*. Appleton, WI: Graphic Communications, 1978.

Rosholt, Malcolm. *The Press Corps of Old Shanghai*. Rosholt, WI: Rosholt House, 1944.

Ross, Bill D. *Iwo Jima, Legacy of Valor*. New York, NY: Random House, 1985.

Russell, Michael. *Iwo Jima*. New York, NY: Random House, 1974.

Schlesinger, Arthur Jr. "The Rediscovery of WWII." *345th Bombardment Group* newsletter, vol. 17, 4, pp. 8-9, 1999.

Schnepf, Ed. "Sea Classics." *U.S. Naval Armed Guard of World War II*, vol. 34, 11 November, 2001.

Sears, Stephen W. *World War II: The Best of American Heritage*. New York, NY: Houghton Mifflin Company, 1991.

Spiller, Roger J., etal. "World War II Chronicles." New York, NY: *Supplement to American Heritage*, 1996.

Standring, William. "Everyone Knew Ernie." Merrifield, VA: *Marine Corps League*, Spring 1995, vol. 51, 1, pp. 28-32.

Stern, Donald E. *483rd Bomb Group (H)*. Paducah, Kentucky: Turner Publishing, 1994.

Steury, Donald P. *The Intelligence War*. New York, NY: Metro Books, 2000.

Sullivan, Robert. "Pearl Harbor: Americas Call to Arms." *Time Special* 2001.

Sulzberger, C. L. *The American Heritage Picture History of World War II*. New York, NY: Crown Publishing, Inc., 1966.

Time. 10, 17, 31 July; 28 August; 18, 25 September, 1944.

Whitlock, Flint, and Bishop, Bob. *Soldiers on Skis*. Boulder, CO: Paladin Press, 1992.

World Book, The. encyclopedia, vol. 21, pp. 470-500. Chicago, IL: World Book, Inc., 1988.

Yahara, Colonel Hiromichi. *The Battle for Okinawa*. New York, NY: John Wiley & Sons, Inc., 1995.

"…from these honored dead, we take increased devotion to that cause for which they gave the last full measure of devotion—that we here highly resolve that these dead shall not have died in vain…"

—Abraham Lincoln, *Gettysburg Address*

THE SUN ROSE CLEAR

STORIES OF WWII
EDITED AND TOLD BY
LOWELL PETERSON

WITH A SPECIAL FOREIGN CONTRIBUTION BY PIERRE DEHAY

For more information (or to order) write to or e-mail:

PETERSON HOUSE
2627 Beechwood Court
Appleton, WI 54911
SRoseClear@aol.com

6/22

7/11
9/12
7/18
5/20